THE BEGINNING

Greenwich Counc
Library & Information Service

SYSTEMS

THE BEGINNINGS OF
ENGLISH PROTESTANTISM

EDITED BY

PETER MARSHALL

AND

ALEC RYRIE

CAMBRIDGE
UNIVERSITY PRESS

PUBLISHED BY THE PRESS SYNDICATE OF THE UNIVERSITY OF CAMBRIDGE
The Pitt Building, Trumpington Street, Cambridge, United Kingdom

CAMBRIDGE UNIVERSITY PRESS
The Edinburgh Building, Cambridge CB2 2RU, UK
40 West 20th Street, New York, NY 10011-4211, USA
477 Williamstown Road, Port Melbourne, VIC 3207, Australia
Ruiz de Alarcón 13, 28014 Madrid, Spain
Dock House, The Waterfront, Cape Town 8001, South Africa

http://www.cambridge.org

First published 2002

Printed in the United Kingdom at the University Press, Cambridge

Typeface Baskerville Monotype 11 / 12.5 pt.   *System* LaTeX 2ε   [TB]

A catalogue record for this book is available from the British Library

ISBN 0 521 80274 1 hardback
ISBN 0 521 00324 5 paperback

For Susan Brigden and Diarmaid MacCulloch

Contents

List of illustrations   *page* ix
Notes on contributors   x
List of abbreviations   xi

Introduction: Protestantisms and their beginnings   1
Peter Marshall and Alec Ryrie

1   Evangelical conversion in the reign of Henry VIII   14
Peter Marshall

2   The friars in the English Reformation   38
Richard Rex

3   Clement Armstrong and the godly commonwealth:
radical religion in early Tudor England   60
Ethan H. Shagan

4   Counting sheep, counting shepherds: the problem
of allegiance in the English Reformation   84
Alec Ryrie

5   Sanctified by the believing spouse: women, men and
the marital yoke in the early Reformation   111
Susan Wabuda

6   Dissenters from a dissenting Church: the challenge of
the Freewillers 1550–1558   129
Thomas Freeman

7   Printing and the Reformation: the English exception   157
Andrew Pettegree

8   John Day: master printer of the English Reformation   180
    John N. King

9   Night schools, conventicles and churches: continuities
    and discontinuities in early Protestant ecclesiology   209
    Patrick Collinson

    Index   236

Illustrations

1 Coat of arms of Catherine Brandon, duchess of Suffolk.
From Hermann von Wied, *A Simple and Religious Consultation
by What Mean a Christian Reformation May Be Begun* (1548). By
courtesy of the Rare Book and Manuscript Library, The
Ohio State University Libraries, Columbus, OH.   *page* 187

2 The execution of Anne Askew. From John Foxe, *Actes
and Monuments of These Latter and Perilous Days* (1563).
By courtesy of the Bodleian Library, Oxford University.   194

3 Initial E: Edmund Becke giving his revision to Edward VI.
From John Day's 1551 Folio Bible, edited by Edmund
Becke. By courtesy of the Bodleian Library, Oxford
University.   201

4 The Royal arms. From John Foxe, *Actes and Monuments
of These Latter and Perilous Days* (1570). By courtesy of the
Rare Book and Manuscript Library, The Ohio State
University Libraries, Columbus, OH.   202

5 'ARISE, FOR IT IS DAY.' Title-page border from
John Day's *Whole Works of William Tyndale, John Frith and
Doctor Barnes*, edited by John Foxe (1573). By courtesy
of the Rare Book and Manuscript Library, The Ohio
State University Libraries, Columbus, OH.   203

6 Portrait device of John Day. From *The Works of Thomas
Becon*, vol. 1 (1564). By courtesy of the Rare Book and
Manuscript Library, The Ohio State University
Libraries, Columbus, OH.   207

Notes on contributors

PATRICK COLLINSON is Regius Professor of Modern History Emeritus in the University of Cambridge and a Fellow of Trinity College.

THOMAS FREEMAN is Research Editor of the British Academy John Foxe Project at the University of Sheffield.

JOHN N. KING is Professor of English at Ohio State University.

PETER MARSHALL is Senior Lecturer in History at the University of Warwick.

ANDREW PETTEGREE is Professor of Modern History at the University of St Andrews and Director of the St Andrews Reformation Studies Institute.

RICHARD REX is University Lecturer in Church History at the University of Cambridge, and Director of Studies in History at Queens' College.

ALEC RYRIE is Lecturer in Modern History at the University of Birmingham.

ETHAN H. SHAGAN is Assistant Professor of History at Northwestern University, Illinois.

SUSAN WABUDA is Assistant Professor of History at Fordham University, New York.

List of abbreviations

AM	John Foxe, *Actes and Monuments* (1563–83; 1583 edition used unless noted otherwise)
APC	*Acts of the Privy Council of England*
BL	British Library
BRUO	A. B. Emden, *A Biographical Register of the University of Oxford, AD 1501 to 1540* (Oxford, 1974)
CCCC	Corpus Christi College, Cambridge
ECL	Emmanuel College Library, Cambridge
EHR	*English Historical Review*
FOR	*Faculty Office Registers, 1534–1549,* ed. D. S. Chambers (Oxford, 1966)
EETS	Early English Text Society
JBS	*Journal of British Studies*
JEH	*Journal of Ecclesiastical History*
LM	*Certain Most Godly, Fruitfull and Comfortable Letters of Such True Saintes and Holy Martyres . . . ,* ed. Henry Bull (1564)
LP	*Letters & Papers, Foreign & Domestic, of the Reign of Henry VIII,* ed. James Gairdner and R. H. Brodie (1862–1932)
Reformation Narratives	*Narratives of the Days of the Reformation,* ed. John G. Nichols (Camden Society o.s. 77, 1859)
PRO	Public Record Office, Kew
PS	Parker Society
SCH	*Studies in Church History*
STC	*A Short-Title Catalogue of Books Printed . . . 1475–1640 . . . revised,* ed. W. A. Jackson, J. F. Ferguson and K. F. Pantzer (1986)

The place of publication for all books is London unless otherwise noted.

Protestantisms and their beginnings

Peter Marshall and Alec Ryrie

Once, the English Reformation made sense. The story went like this. In late medieval England, as elsewhere in Europe, the people were groaning under the tyranny of the Roman Catholic Church. It oppressed the people through its grievous taxation and its brutal persecution of dissent; at the same time, it neglected the faithful, failing to use its immense wealth to bring the parish clergy up to the educational and disciplinary standards that an increasingly assertive laity demanded. It was obscurantist, suspicious of new scholarship and jealous to keep theological knowledge (and vernacular scripture) out of the hands of the laity, who were reared instead on a diet of mummery and superstition. Enter stage left Martin Luther and his English disciple William Tyndale, with a newly translated English Bible; enter stage right the awesome and monstrous figure of Henry VIII. In the 1520s the Protestant message began to win converts among English people eager to throw off the Romish yoke. Then, at the end of the decade, the king, anxious to be released from a marriage to his now-barren Spanish wife, set himself on a collision course with the pope. Casting around for allies, he fell in with the early Protestants (notably Thomas Cranmer and Thomas Cromwell). They persuaded him that Rome was not merely the source of his matrimonial problems, but had usurped a part of the sovereignty that was rightfully his as king. In 1534 he declared himself Supreme Head over the English Church, and with a few romantic exceptions, most English people were ready to follow his lead. While not embracing Protestantism as such, Henry laid the groundwork for the future Reformation by abolishing monasticism and legalising the English Bible. Moreover, by having his young son educated by Protestants, Henry ensured the inevitability of an eventual Protestant settlement. The short reign of the boy king Edward VI (1547–53) saw England become decisively Protestant; but the achievement was marred by political instability and an alarming lurch towards radical, Continental forms of Protestantism. After his

premature death Edward was succeeded by his half-sister Mary, barren daughter of a barren mother, a figure by turns brutal and tragic.
Her quixotic attempt to restore Catholicism was doomed; her only
lasting achievement the creation of a pantheon of Protestant martyrs.
Finally, in 1558, the last of Henry VIII's children, Elizabeth, ascended the
throne, and presided over a popular and truly English settlement: clearly
Protestant, yet shorn of the excesses and instabilities of Edward VI's
reign.[1]

From the 1970s onwards, however, this narrative was challenged by
another, interpreting the same set of events in a radically different way.
The late medieval church was an impressive and humane institution,
largely staffed by conscientious priests, and loved and respected by the
people. If there was a desire for reform, there was certainly no thirst
for religious revolution. When Henry VIII embarked on his battle with
the papacy, his main allies were political trimmers and lawyers trying
to extend their jurisdictions, not Protestants, who were an insignificant
minority. Henry's assaults on traditional religion were immensely unpopular, and in 1536 provoked an astonishingly large mass rebellion, the
Pilgrimage of Grace. Henry loathed Protestantism as much as popery,
but in the last months of his life an extraordinary series of events left his
court dominated by a faction of Protestants and their fellow-travellers.
This clique seized power in 1547, and proceeded to ram a fully-fledged
Protestant programme down the throats of a bewildered and hostile nation. However, when the young king died, and the same clique attempted
to cling on to power by the dubious expedient of declaring Jane Grey
queen, Mary Tudor was swept to power in the name of the old religion. Her restoration of Catholicism made remarkable progress in the
face of formidable practical difficulties, and was cut short only by her
untimely death. The return to Protestantism under Elizabeth was met
with exhaustion and sullen acceptance. That her 'settlement' eventually
had some measure of success was due to her longevity, and to the many
echoes of traditional religion which she wisely allowed to persist in her

---

[1] Allowing for an element of caricature, this is the interpretation of the Reformation which informed
influential nineteenth-century Protestant accounts such as J. A. Froude's *History of England from the
Fall of Wolsey to the Defeat of the Spanish Armada* (12 vols., 1856–70). More recent variants, notably
A. G. Dickens's modern classic, *The English Reformation* (1964; 2nd edition, 1989), have added an
emphasis on popular support for religious change to a narrative that had previously been focused
on high politics. Ultimately, this tradition takes many of its bearings from the greatest contemporary history of sixteenth-century Protestantism, John Foxe's *Actes and Monuments* (4 editions,
1563–83).

Church. Even so, it was only in the second half of her reign that Protestant England became anything more than preachers' wishful thinking.[2]

This rereading of England's sixteenth-century religious history has proved a salutary corrective to the progressivism and partisanship of earlier accounts. The heart of the 'revisionist' case looks broadly convincing, especially its rehabilitation of the late medieval church. The majority of scholars currently working in the field would accept Professor Scarisbrick's observation that 'on the whole, English men and women did not want the Reformation and most of them were slow to accept it when it came'.[3] Yet revisionism has brought its own partisanship, and some aspects of its programme are as open to question as the 'Whig-Protestant' grand narrative it aspires to replace.[4]

As the revisionist narrative acquires the status of an orthodoxy, a few gaps in its interpretation have become evident. In particular, it has little direct to say to the problem of how the English Reformation eventually came to be, in Diarmaid MacCulloch's phrase, a 'howling success'. Much recent scholarship on this question – including some outstanding work – has followed the logic of revisionism by focusing on the gradual 'inculturation' of Protestant ideas over the late sixteenth and early seventeenth centuries. This has left us with a greatly improved understanding of the games of Chinese whispers through which the Protestantism of the preachers was adapted to become a religion of the masses.[5] As a

---

[2] The most significant works here are Christopher Haigh, *Reformation and Resistance in Tudor Lancashire* (Cambridge, 1975); Christopher Haigh, *English Reformations: Religion, Politics and Society under the Tudors* (Oxford, 1993); J. J. Scarisbrick, *The Reformation and the English People* (Oxford, 1984); Eamon Duffy, *The Stripping of the Altars: Traditional Religion in England 1400–1580* (New Haven and London, 1992). Though often regarded as a revisionist troika, it should be noted that Haigh, Scarisbrick and Duffy have rather different views concerning the pace of change and the potential for popular resistance. Note, too, that 'revisionism' itself has discernible scholarly antecedents, most obviously perhaps in Catholic and Anglo-Catholic histories of the late nineteenth and early twentieth centuries. See for example F. A. Gasquet, *The Eve of the Reformation* (1890); H. Maynard Smith, *Pre-Reformation England* (1938).

[3] Scarisbrick, *Reformation and the English People*, 1.

[4] That partisanship of various stripes has not been banished from the debate is suggested by the tendency of reviewers to comment on the Catholicism of Scarisbrick and Duffy, and in another way, by Haigh's determination publicly to dissociate himself from Roman Catholic affiliation. See *English Reformations*, vii–viii.

[5] Diarmaid MacCulloch, 'The impact of the English Reformation', *Historical Journal* 38 (1995), 152. The most important 'post-revisionist' works on the later period include David Cressy, *Bonfires and Bells: National Memory and the Protestant Calendar in Elizabethan and Stuart England* (1989); Tessa Watt, *Cheap Print and Popular Piety 1560–1640* (Cambridge, 1991); Judith Maltby, *Prayer Book and People in Elizabethan and Early Stuart England* (Cambridge, 1998); Alexandra Walsham, *Providence in Early Modern England* (Oxford, 1999). Surveys of the recent historiography are provided in Peter Marshall, 'Introduction', *The Impact of the English Reformation 1500–1640*, ed. Marshall

result, it has become fashionable, almost *de rigueur*, to think of the English Reformation as 'the long Reformation'. This approach, however, can leave important parts of the story untold. Patrick Collinson has observed that many recent studies of the 'long Reformation' concern themselves 'not at all with where it came from but only with where it was going, and how long the journey took'.[6] Renewed interest in the vitality of traditional religion, and in orthodox resistance to religious change, has been matched by a neglect of early Protestant reformers and reform movements in the first half of the sixteenth century.[7] There has, astonishingly, been no general modern scholarly study of sixteenth-century English Protestantism. The theologians, preachers and authors who were once given excessive importance as the central players in the Reformation drama have now been reduced to walk-on parts. There is a danger that this neglect will leave us with an essentially one-dimensional conception of the early Reformation as chiefly an 'act of state', an unexpected calamity passively experienced by a reluctant but ultimately obedient nation.

This collection of essays represents an attempt to redress the balance in recent historical writing by directing attention back to those critical early years of the Reformation under Henry VIII, Edward VI and Mary I, and to the establishment and growth of the movement that was to become English Protestantism. There is no agreed interpretative programme here, and the contributors have in no sense consented to sally forth under a single historiographical banner, 'post-revisionist' or otherwise. Nonetheless, what unites these essays is the conviction that the process which Christopher Haigh has called 'the making of a minority' remains vitally important.[8] It is fairly clear that evangelicals and proto-Protestants were indeed a minority, probably a small one, throughout this early period; but (as argued in Alec Ryrie's essay) they certainly cannot be written off as marginal or unimportant. The stark choice sometimes offered of Reformation 'from above' or 'from below' is a false one.[9]

(1997); Patrick Collinson, 'The English Reformation, 1945–1995', *Companion to Historiography*, ed. M. Bentley (1997).

[6] Patrick Collinson, 'Comment on Eamon Duffy's Neale Lecture and the Colloquium', *England's Long Reformation 1500–1800*, ed. Nicholas Tyacke (1998), 72–3.

[7] Notable exceptions to this trend include Susan Brigden, *London and the Reformation* (Oxford, 1989); Diarmaid MacCulloch, *Thomas Cranmer: a Life* (New Haven and London, 1996); Diarmaid MacCulloch, *Tudor Church Militant: Edward VI and the Protestant Reformation* (1999); Andrew Pettegree, *Marian Protestantism: Six Studies* (Aldershot, 1996).

[8] Haigh, *English Reformations*, ch. 11.

[9] Cf. Christopher Haigh, 'The Recent Historiography of the English Reformation', *Historical Journal*, 15 (1982).

The small portion of the nation which was actively involved in religious politics helped to shape the implementation of reform policies at local, regional and national level in the reigns of Henry and his two successors. It was, moreover, in this period that the religious cultures and religious battlelines which were to shape the lives of later generations were substantially, if uncertainly, formed.

The title of this collection is 'the beginnings of English Protestantism'; yet none of the contributors would wish to describe the range of movements for religious reform in early sixteenth-century England as 'Protestant' in an unproblematic or anachronistic way, and some prefer to avoid the term altogether. At the risk of seeming pedantic, it is worth paying some attention to the etymology of the word itself. It was coined in Germany in 1529 to refer to those princes who issued a 'protestatio' against the revocation of religious privileges at the Diet of Speyer, and for twenty years following, its use in English was almost exclusively to refer to the military alliance of German Lutheran states against Charles V.[10] Thus, for most of the period covered by this volume, a 'Protestant' was by definition a German. In the late 1540s we begin to find English reformers described as 'Protestant', and the term is fully current by the middle of Mary Tudor's reign; yet even then its meanings are not unambiguous. In earlier decades there was no agreed terminology at all. Reformers spoke of themselves as brethren, as gospellers or evangelicals, or simply as true Christians. They were also unwilling to let go of the term 'Catholic', although this was a battle which they eventually lost, just as their opponents were unwilling to relinquish their right to be considered evangelicals or gospellers.[11] Those opponents instead labelled them as heretics; as new men; as Lollards; as Lutherans, Zwinglians, sacramentarians, Anabaptists or other, more exotic breeds of heretic, usually without any precision at all. In other words, both sides were still using a common vocabulary. Men and women of all religious shades shared many of the same terms of approbation and derogation. This is important in itself, as a reminder that a permanent fissure in English Christianity was not yet institutionalised or accepted. As a result, there was no commonly agreed terminology for the religious divides which were plainly opening up. Archbishop Cranmer apparently once tried to characterise religious reformers and conservatives as the parties of

[10] See for example PRO SP 1/202, 193r; *LP* XIX (i) 302, 558; XX (i) 1226.
[11] On this theme, see Peter Marshall, 'Is the Pope a Catholic? Henry VIII and the Semantics of Schism', *Catholics and the Protestant Nation: English Catholicism in Context, 1534–1640*, ed. M. Sena and Ethan Shagan (Manchester, forthcoming).

Cambridge and of Oxford respectively.[12] Even the terms used in this paragraph, 'reformer' and 'conservative', are beset with problems, and carry with them possibly misleading modern resonances. The Catholic martyr Thomas More was nothing if not an advocate of reform; and the sometimes aggressive conservatism of so-called reformers is evident in Susan Wabuda's and Thomas Freeman's essays in this volume. The religious antagonists of mid-sixteenth century England positively resist rigid categorisation and definition. Every solution introduces its own problems; for this volume, the editors have made no effort to impose a uniform consistency of terminology on the contributors.

These terminological difficulties are an inconvenience. Yet this is neither a minor nor a merely technical point. If historians' terminology is becoming increasingly fluid and indeterminate, this is because we increasingly recognise that in the first decades of the Reformation the religious situation itself was fluid and indeterminate. Boundaries were unclear, where they existed at all, and identities were nascent and contested. Confessional histories of the Reformation over many generations have served to obscure this point. For all their mutual antagonism, Catholic and Protestant historians have long agreed that the divide between Catholic and Protestant was from the outset absolute and unbridgeable, and that fully-formed Catholic and Protestant identities can therefore legitimately be projected back to the earliest years of religious upheaval. It is true, of course, that the divide was not bridged in any significant sense until well into the twentieth century, and it is also clear that by the 1560s or thereabouts the religious protagonists in Europe were sorting themselves into several clear, entrenched and mutually antagonistic camps. However, this backdating of later confessional divisions has meant that the religious leaders of the 1520s and 1530s have been posthumously shoehorned into anachronistic and falsely rigid categories. Indeed, one of the most troubling conundrums in English Reformation historiography has been the stubborn refusal of one key figure, Henry VIII, to fit into any neat Protestant or Catholic pigeonhole.[13] It is becoming clearer, moreover, that Henry was not alone in this. The papalist, 'Roman' tradition

---

[12] CCCC MS 128 p. 133 (*LP* XVIIII (ii) 546 p. 323).

[13] See the contrasting interpretations of the king's religious morphology in Diarmaid MacCulloch, 'Henry VIII and the Reform of the Church', *The Reign of Henry VIII: Politics, Policy and Piety*, ed. MacCulloch (Basingstoke, 1995); G. W. Bernard, 'The Making of Religious Policy, 1533–1546: Henry VIII and the Search for the Middle Way', *Historical Journal* 41 (1998); Peter Marshall, 'Mumpsimus and Sumpsimus: The Intellectual Origins of a Henrician *Bon Mot*', *JEH* (2001); Alec Ryrie, 'English evangelical reformers in the last years of Henry VIII', D.Phil thesis, University of Oxford (2000), 56–82.

which came to dominate Catholicism after the Council of Trent certainly existed before the Reformation, but neither as the only nor, arguably, as the dominant form of Catholic belief. It is considerably harder to find confessional Lutheranism, Calvinism or – most perversely of all – 'Anglicanism' in the early decades of the Reformation. While it has always been recognised that these traditions began to develop over the course of the sixteenth century, too often this recognition has implicitly or explicitly been underpinned by the teleological assumption that the confessions already existed in embryo in the 1520s. On this view, later synods and theologians were doing no more than systematising and clarifying traditions that already had a clear, if ill-defined, existence; and attempts to find compromises or common ground were flying in the face of history. All later Protestantisms become footnotes to Luther or some other patriarch, and the Tridentine Fathers were merely expounding a pre-existing set of doctrines. This also implies a Reformation which moved almost immediately from being a war of movement to a war of fortification, in which the theological battles were fought and refought on the same terms and on the same ground.

Many contemporaries did indeed see the world around them in terms of a polarised conflict between Christ and Antichrist, between God's will and the presumptuous teachings of men; but they could not often agree on where the crucial dividing line fell. One of the themes of this volume, then, is that the divides which did eventually emerge were contingent, not preordained – the result of a complex interplay of social, political and religious forces, rather than of theological destiny. As Patrick Collinson's essay reminds us, it was purely the accident of Mary's death that ensured that the long-term future of English Protestantism would be played out in a national 'Church', rather than in separatist congregations on the French Huguenot model. Furthermore, the people whom we tend to corral into a 'Protestant' or 'reformist' category were themselves a highly diverse lot. Ethan Shagan's essay discusses one individual from the 1530s, Clement Armstrong, whose writings reveal a highly original (not to say eccentric) approach to religious and social reform. Armstrong's wildly radical theories, tinged with Lollardy and Anabaptism, are a reminder of the breadth of 'reformist' ideas which were in circulation during the early Reformation. They are also a hint that many other apparently straightforward 'early Protestants' may have harboured beliefs which, because they did not become established, would later seem bizarre and eclectic. Indeed, Alec Ryrie's essay suggests that those who saw themselves as evangelicals in these early years included

many whose moral libertinism or social radicalism horrified more respectable reformers. Thomas Freeman describes how, by the 1550s, these
crosscurrents had spawned open conflict, and how one of the strongest
dissident groups, the 'Freewillers', was stamped out with considerable
determination by the strain which we have come to recognise as orthodox Protestantism. Yet as Collinson's essay argues, the religious dividing
lines were never as clear as the partisans would have wished. The questions of where the boundary of the true church should be drawn, what
that boundary meant, and indeed whether there was a single boundary, all remained unresolved throughout this period. Religious reform
was a many-headed monster. 'Orthodox' Protestantism was not the
only contender for the reformist identity, nor was its orthodoxy defini-
tively established during the first generation. Subsequent confessional
clarity should not be allowed to obscure the kaleidoscopic diversity of the
early years of the Reformation, or the messy complexity of the processes
by which those possibilities were resolved into the Protestantism which we
know.

As well as asserting the complexity and contingency of the beginnings
of English Protestantism, several of the essays in this volume are concerned to emphasise the roots of religious reform in the medieval past.
For centuries it seemed axiomatic that Protestantism represents a total
discontinuity from Catholicism, and, until very recently, adherents of
both confessions have been keen to minimise their common inheritance.
Catholics disclaimed any responsibility for Luther's heresies, except perhaps in the sense that their predecessors' inability to live up to their own
established standards of discipline may have made the Catholic faithful vulnerable to the seductive teachings of heretics. Conversely, later
Protestants wished to see their true religion as having sprung full-grown
into life in the 1520s, and to deny common attributes with the 'papists'.
They had, they insisted, merely revived ancient apostolic truth; if they
drew on any mediate human influences, it was those of the faithful few
who had continued to reject Romish corruption throughout the centuries of darkness, such as (in England) the followers of John Wyclif,
the so-called Lollards.[14] Interestingly, a notable exception to the relative
dearth of recent work on unorthodoxy in early Reformation England has
been an interest in the flowering of later Lollardy, and its crosspollina-
tion with the new strains of reformist thought imported from Germany

---

[14] Alec Ryrie, 'The problem of legitimacy and precedent in English Protestantism, 1539–47',
Protestant History and Identity in Reformation Europe: The Medieval Inheritance, ed. Bruce Gordon
(Aldershot, 1996).

and Switzerland.[15] The theme is picked up in this volume by Ethan Shagan, who detects Wycliffite fingerprints on the theological motifs of Clement Armstrong; and in Patrick Collinson's adducing of the personal and geographical links between old and new dissent. But Collinson also suggests that the differing mentality of Lollards and evangelicals over whether their society constituted a 'Church' (in either the sociological or the theological sense) represents a 'critical discontinuity'. Lollardy was a tributary stream of English Protestant development, but hardly its main headwater.

Other essays in this volume direct attention away from the putative Lollard-Protestant continuum and towards the 'Catholic' context within which early reformers were formed and from which they emerged. Conversion, the subject of Peter Marshall's essay, has typically been seen as an absolute break between the old religion and the new, a bare fact which almost defies analysis. Yet the ideal of conversion itself was cultural common ground between antagonistic religious traditions. Moreover, evangelical converts were often not the marginalised and the discontent, but the most committed and pious Catholics, drawing on cultural and intellectual resources from their own past histories. These organic connections between late medieval Catholicism and the new movements for reform are explored in a more specific context by Richard Rex, whose essay traces the critical role played in early English evangelicalism by converts from the ranks of those most aggressive upholders of Catholic orthodoxy, the friars. Susan Wabuda's essay on the shifting evangelical attitudes towards the role of women raises many of the same issues, showing how an unmistakably evangelical approach was nevertheless grounded in the work of 'good Catholics' such as Juan Luis Vives. Protestantism – as the very word suggests – did not happen in isolation. It drew on Catholic piety and Catholic priorities, defined its doctrine in Catholic terms and, in the end, formed its identity against its Catholic opposition. Protestants insisted in their creeds that they represented the true Catholic Church; we can see that this was true in a sense which they might have resisted.

English Reformation historiography has been plagued not only by the barriers between Catholic and Protestant, but also by those between England and its European neighbours. Protestantism was a European

---

[15] Anne Hudson, *The Premature Reformation: Wycliffite Texts and Lollard History* (Oxford, 1988); Andrew Hope, 'Lollardy: the Stone which the Builders Rejected?', *Protestantism and the National Church in Sixteenth-Century England*, ed. Peter Lake and Maria Dowling (1987); *The World of Rural Dissenters* 1520–1725, ed. Margaret Spufford (Cambridge, 1995); *Lollardy and the Gentry in the Later Middle Ages*, ed. Margaret Aston and Colin Richmond (Stroud, 1997).

phenomenon with local manifestations. Its English variant did have, in Lollardy, a distinctively indigenous grandparent; yet both the generic similarities and the direct points of contact between the European movement and its English counterpart have been too readily sidelined in most traditional histories. 'English exceptionalism' has tended to be assumed rather than established or analysed.[16] Fortunately, some recent scholarship has moved towards a more nuanced view of the Reformation's international aspect. Diarmaid MacCulloch has emphasised the extent to which English Protestantism's intellectual roots lay in Europe; Andrew Pettegree and others have reminded us of the importance of the religious exiles in maintaining Protestant internationalism, as English reformers became by turns refugees and hosts for Continental exiles; and Anthony Milton's work is reminding us that well into the seventeenth century, England was a leading player in the intellectual world of European Calvinism.[17]

Part of this process is a growing realisation that there is no normative Reformation against which the English experience can be labelled as deviant or substandard. The English experience was certainly unique. Yet so, in their own ways, were those of France, the Netherlands and the Scandinavian kingdoms. The German Reformation, which inevitably can seem like a reference point, was perhaps the most exceptional of all.[18] English Protestantism's international context is a subject which awaits its modern historian. Nevertheless, several of the contributors to this volume explore how English Protestantism can be considered in its international context: not seeking to impose a false uniformity on a complex European scene, but recognising that theology is no respecter of frontiers. Peter Marshall's essay understands Protestant conversion to be a European phenomenon, and gives due prominence to Martin Luther's experience. Luther was also the most prominent example of the appeal of evangelical theology to the mendicant orders, and the friars' membership of actively international orders is central to Richard Rex's exploration of their role in England. Ethan Shagan's essay shows us a

---

[16] A fault shared by both sides of the historiographical divide. See Basil Hall, 'The Early Rise and Gradual Decline of Lutheranism in England (1520–1660)', *Reform and Reformation: England and the Continent c. 1500–1750*, ed. Derek Baker (*SCH* Subsidia 2, 1979), 110; Christopher Haigh, 'Introduction', *The English Reformation Revised*, ed. Haigh (Cambridge, 1987), 6–7; Haigh, *English Reformations*, 12–13.

[17] MacCulloch, *Cranmer*, especially 173–92; Pettegree, *Marian Protestantism*; Andrew Pettegree, *Foreign Protestant Communities in Sixteenth-Century London* (Oxford, 1986); Ole Peter Grell, *Calvinist Exiles in Elizabethan and Stuart England* (Aldershot, 1996). Anthony Milton's work on the English contribution to the Synod of Dort is forthcoming with the Church of England Record Society.

[18] *The Early Reformation in Europe*, ed. Andrew Pettegree (Cambridge, 1992), 1–23.

more exceptional Englishman: Clement Armstrong's startling beliefs, with their dizzyingly high concept of royal supremacy, could hardly have been conceived in any other country. Yet Shagan also demonstrates how Armstrong drew on a rich mixture of themes from Continental Protestant and Anabaptist thought. Susan Wabuda, likewise, shows how English Protestant concepts of gender roles drew heavily on (rather more respectable) European sources. Andrew Pettegree's essay is less concerned with English Protestantism's intellectual debt to the Continent than with its industrial dependence. He emphasises the critical role of French and, especially, Dutch expertise in providing the early English Protestants with their printed books. It was not only in a theological sense that Protestantism was a Europe-wide phenomenon. Such direct connections aside, however, the range of Protestant experiences within Europe provides a consistently instructive set of contrasts and comparisons for the English experience. In particular, the suggestive parallels between the course of the Reformations in England and France are touched on by Alec Ryrie, Thomas Freeman and Patrick Collinson. For a time in the 1550s, the evangelical movements in the two countries look startlingly similar; the very different outcomes may reflect the turbulent dynastic politics of both countries as much as any English, or indeed French, exceptionalism.[19]

A final unhealthy set of 'barriers' inherited from the older confessional historiography are those between the 'religious' and 'social' histories of the Reformation. Theologically minded historians have long been suspicious of 'reductionist' social analyses of events, preferring to see the conception of theological ideas as being immaculately spiritual and intellectual, and insisting that those ideas are the driving force of change. By contrast, and partly in reaction, many social historians (particularly Marxist social historians) have been reluctant to take religion on its own terms or to ascribe real causal power to ideas, theological or otherwise. The new emphasis on cultural history is awakening us to what we should always have known: namely, that religion and society interact, and do so in complex, unpredictable and at times perverse ways.[20]

A number of chapters in this volume are concerned to continue breaking down unhelpful demarcations in approaches to religious and social

---

[19] Aspects of this theme are explored more fully in R. J. Knecht, 'The early Reformation in England and France: a comparison', *History* 57 (1972).

[20] There are models for English historians to follow here in recent work on other European Reformations, particularly that of Natalie Davis on France and Robert Scribner on Germany, exemplified in their collections *Society and Culture in Early Modern France* (Oxford, 1987) and *Popular Culture and Popular Movements in Reformation Germany* (1987).

change. The essays by Peter Marshall and Alec Ryrie, examining the manner and scale of evangelical conversion, both consider this question as one of the interaction of theological ideas with social conditions through the medium of religious culture, and present it as a two-way process. Likewise, Susan Wabuda's essay looks at how the theology of gender relations and the social reality of women's lives both shifted in reaction to one another, in step with changes in the broader religious culture. Yet perhaps the most important meeting place for the intellectual world of theology and the material world of society was printing, the 'sacrament' by which abstract religious ideas were given physical and commodified form. While historical interest in sixteenth-century printed books has tended to focus on their texts, Andrew Pettegree's essay emphasises their material nature, as artefacts produced through distinct technical processes which could have a significant impact on their capacity to inform and persuade. Many of the same points are explored in John King's more detailed study of one key printer-publisher, John Day. The road from the author's pen to the book market at St Paul's Cathedral was a tortuous one, and the practicalities of the book industry materially affected the contents and reception of its products. Yet it was not always a case of theology being at the mercy of industrial practicalities. The trade was vulnerable to shifts in religious politics, as when Dutch printers flocked to England in the reign of Edward VI. Nor was printing immune to the shifting particularities of theology. Reformer and conservative both made use of printing, yet England's primitive industry was far better placed to provide the simple, text-heavy publications for which evangelicals looked than the complex devotional works which bolstered traditional piety. Moreover, the industry operated in a social context, and thus in a religious one. The personal commitment of central figures such as Day to the reformist cause was as important as the economics of the book trade. Indeed, in a culture whose approach to 'social' issues was determined in 'religious' terms, and whose 'religion' reflected the shape and pace of 'social' change, it could scarcely have been otherwise.

Collectively and individually, the essays in this volume do not seek to propose a fresh 'grand narrative' of the English Reformation, or even of its Protestant half, in the decades prior to the accession of Elizabeth and the (as it turned out, permanent) Protestant political ascendancy which that event inaugurated. If there is an overall thesis, it is that, while acknowledging the strength and vitality of traditional piety, we should also pay close attention to the highly complex and multifaceted processes through which an English Protestant movement was formed and sustained, and a distinctive Protestant identity created, in these crucial years. That we can speak with some confidence about the characteristics of English 'Protestantism' of 1558, as we cannot for 1528, reflects the developmental significance of the themes addressed in these essays: experience of, and reflection on, conversion and martyrdom; political and polemical engagement and activism; rethinking of social and gender roles; identification and elimination of dissent. Pre-Elizabethan 'Protestantism' was a loose and fractious movement, a cacophany of voices advocating personal and corporate reform through appeals to 'the Gospel'. But out of it dominant political and theological refrains were able to emerge. It can (and perhaps should) appear to be a deeply medieval movement, rooted in its own time; yet through its formative crises it reinterpreted that heritage in ways which seem, with hindsight, to be distinctly modern. Elizabethan and later English Protestantisms, in both their solidarities and their tensions, were the children of this earlier movement; but reading the story forwards rather than backwards allows us to appreciate that there was no prescribed 'English way' in matters of religion. English Protestantism was a movement which failed to transform society as it hoped – indeed, a movement whose ambitions were probably beyond realisation in this world – yet whose interaction with English religious culture undoubtedly engendered profound social change. It was subversive, combative, intellectual and individualistic, drawing on the printshop and the pulpit; and at the same time hierarchical, universalist and eager to ally with the magistrate. It is perhaps in these tensions, and certainly in this period, that we can find the roots of English Protestantism's ultimately Pyrrhic victory. It could not convert the nation; but it could, and did, permanently divide it.

CHAPTER I

Evangelical conversion in the reign of Henry VIII

Peter Marshall

I

If the early Reformation in England was more than merely an 'act of state', then integral to the process was a pattern of individual religious conversions. Beginning in the reign of Henry VIII, significant numbers of men and women who had been brought up with the old faith turned their backs on aspects of traditional devotion, and embraced a new set of understandings about what was essential in the exercise of Christian belief. Naturally enough, this is a theme which has been touched on in many individual biographies, national surveys and regional studies. Yet it is remarkable that to date there has been little or no attempt to explore the phenomenon of evangelical conversion in the early Tudor period in any systematic or broadly thematic way.[1]

In any age religious conversion is a particularly intangible and elusive historical topic, which involves complex definitional and evidential problems. What do we mean when we say people 'convert' or 'are converted'? Does this signify an intellectual process, the substitution of new ideas and doctrinal propositions for repudiated old ones? An institutional or social one, the crossing from one ecclesiastical body or network of believers to another? Or a more intimate and psychological kind of transformation, involving moral renewal and reordered personal priorities? None of these is, of course, mutually exclusive. The sources for studying conversion are particularly problematic. Only the convert's own account, a so-called 'conversion narrative', is likely to bring us close to the inner meanings and logic of the event, but these by definition are written

---

[1] There are some suggestive general remarks in Susan Brigden, *London and the Reformation* (Oxford, 1989), 119–21; Christopher Haigh, *English Reformations: Religion, Politics and Society under the Tudors* (Oxford, 1993), 189–90; Alec Ryrie, 'English evangelical reformers in the last years of Henry VIII', D.Phil thesis, University of Oxford (2000), 156–60, 187–8. F. W. Bullock, *Evangelical Conversion in Great Britain 1516–1695* (St Leonards on Sea, 1966) is a rather sketchy account intended to provide 'a notable testimony to the manifold workings of the spirit of God' (viii).

after the occurrences they describe, and are likely to involve to varying extents the reordering and reshaping of experience in the light of subsequent understanding and intention. Autobiography is always a form of fiction, and historians of the sixteenth century have now enjoyed sufficient acquaintance with the subtleties of 'rhetorics of life-writing' and 'renaissance self-fashioning' not to take at face value their subjects' own versions of their personal history.[2] These difficulties are exacerbated in studying conversion in the early sixteenth century. Later studies of early modern conversion, 'puritan' and Catholic, can draw on the burgeoning evidence of spiritual diaries, personal correspondence and printed apologia.[3] But hardly any full-blooded conversion narratives survive for the pre-Elizabethan period in England, leaving only scraps of biography and (frequently stylised) autobiography tucked away in a range of printed and manuscript sources. It is striking that modern biographers of many of the leading English reformers of the first generation have found considerable difficulty in attempting to date with any precision at all when it was that their subjects converted from traditional Catholicism.[4] In making the focus of this essay the origins of the evangelical movement in the reign of Henry VIII, the problems are intensified further, for the people identified in a classic study as 'England's earliest Protestants' were not Protestants at all.[5] That is, they would not have applied to themselves a term which was not recognised in a domestic context before the reign of Edward VI, and not universally employed until later even than that.[6] The subject of this discussion is therefore not 'conversion to Protestantism', a phrase which connotes a much greater clarity of confessional categorisation than is appropriate for the period. Following the lead of recent scholarship, 'evangelical' will be employed as the least-worst label for bringing together a variety of forms of early sixteenth-century heterodoxy.[7] Nonetheless, I will contend that it is

[2] *The Rhetoric of Life Writing*, ed. T. F. Mayer and D. R. Woolf (Ann Arbor, 1995); S. Greenblatt, *Renaissance Self-Fashioning* (Chicago and London, 1980).

[3] M. Questier, *Conversion, Politics and Religion in England, 1580–1625* (Cambridge, 1996); N. Petit, *The Heart Prepared: Grace and Conversion in Puritan Spiritual Life* (New Haven, 1966); P. Delany, *British Autobiography in the Seventeenth Century* (1969); P. Caldwell, *The Puritan Conversion Narrative: the Beginning of American Expression* (Cambridge, 1983).

[4] J. Ridley, *Nicholas Ridley* (1957), 48; A. G. Chester, *Hugh Latimer: Apostle to the English* (Philadelpha, 1954), ch. 3; L. P. Fairfield, *John Bale: Mythmaker for the English Reformation* (West Lafayette, IN, 1976), 33–5; David Daniell, *William Tyndale* (New Haven and London, 1994), 38–40; Diarmaid MacCulloch, *Thomas Cranmer: a Life* (New Haven and London, 1996), chs. 2–3.

[5] W. A. Clebsch, *England's Earliest Protestants 1520–1535* (New Haven and London, 1964).

[6] Diarmaid MacCulloch, *Tudor Church Militant: Edward VI and the Protestant Reformation* (1999), 2.

[7] G. Walker, *Persuasive Fictions: Faction, Faith and Political Culture in the Reign of Henry VIII* (Aldershot, 1996), 136–7; M. Dowling, *Humanism in the Age of Henry VIII* (1986), 'Note and Acknowledgements'.

legitimate to identify in Henry's reign a meaningful phenomenon we can call 'evangelical conversion', with generic features and patterns which contemporaries were able to recognise, and which proved in the end more significant than the discrepancies. The intention is not so much to attempt to explain why English men and women, individually or collectively, became evangelicals, but rather to suggest a set of approaches to the concept of conversion itself, as its protagonists appear to have understood it.

There is an irony, albeit a highly appropriate one, in the fact that the early evangelical conversion experience historians think they know most about is that of Martin Luther himself. Luther's conversion may or may not be the key causal element in the development of the European Reformation, but it is worth considering briefly at the outset here for the light it sheds on the problems and potential of studying the phenomenon in its English context. Luther described his conversion in a preface to the first volume of his complete Latin works (1545), a passage generally referred to as 'the autobiographical fragment'. An Augustinian friar of the strict observance, Luther found himself weighed down with a sense of sin, and an inability to believe that God could or would be content with the works of satisfaction he had long undertaken. But studying in the tower room of the Augustinian house in Wittenberg he underwent a moment of breakthrough and illumination, the so-called 'tower experience' (*Turmerlebnis*). After repeated reflection on the writings of St Paul, he at last felt he understood the importance of a sentence in Romans 1: 17, 'the righteous shall live by faith'. Men's own 'good works' were worthless in the sight of God, who accepted them as 'justified' on account of their faith alone: 'At this I felt myself straightway born afresh and to have entered through the open gates into paradise itself.'[8]

Here we seem to have the template for explaining both why and how sixteenth-century people came to turn their backs on the faith of their parents, and indeed there are English cases which appear to present close similarities to the Luther model. The Cambridge scholar Thomas Bilney, burned as a relapsed heretic in 1531, wrote to Bishop Tunstall in the course of his trial recounting how he had found no peace of mind in repeated recourse to fasting, pardons and masses. But in Erasmus's New

---

[8] *Martin Luther*, ed. E. G. Rupp and B. Drewery (1970), 5–6. Among the plethora of English-language Luther scholarship, I have found the following most effective in crystallising the issues and controversies: H. Oberman, *Luther: Man between God and the Devil*, trans. E. Walliser-Schwarzbart (1993), 151–74; S. Ozment, *The Age of Reform 1250–1550* (New Haven and London, 1980), 229–30; A. McGrath, *Reformation Thought: An Introduction* (Oxford, 1988), 73–5.

Testament he had chanced upon a passage in 1 Timothy 1: 15, 'Christ Jesus came into the world to save sinners; of whom I am chief':

> this one sentence, through God's instruction and inward working, which I did not then perceive, did so exhilarate my heart, being before wounded with the guilt of my sins, and being almost in despair, that immediately I felt a marvellous comfort and quietness.

Thereafter he also understood that it was necessary to condemn dependence upon 'works of man's righteousness'.[9] An apparently similar case of excessive 'scrupulosity' resolved by accepting justification by faith is that of Thomas More's son-in-law, William Roper, as recounted in Nicholas Harpsfield's life of More. Roper's fall into heresy 'did grow of a scruple of his own conscience'; he 'daily did use immoderate fasting and many prayers . . . thinking God therewith never to be pleased'. With such exercises he reportedly 'did weary himself even *usque ad taedium* [even to exhaustion]' until through his contacts with the German merchants of the Steelyard he became acquainted with Luther's works, and became convinced 'that faith only did justify, that the works of man did nothing profit'.[10]

Fascinating as these accounts are, they should not be taken absolutely at face value, still less as self-evidently normative for the motives and processes of evangelical conversion.[11] It has been argued that Bilney's apparently frank autobiographical narrative was in fact a carefully constructed exculpatory strategy, designed to appeal to the humanist sympathies of Tunstall.[12] Though Harpsfield's account most likely drew directly on Roper's own reminiscences, its pivotal figure is Thomas More, rescuer of his son-in-law from erroneous ways.[13] The narrative is shaped around this happy conclusion, and one suspects that the prominence in it of Luther's works is to underscore the achievements of More as Luther's principal English opponent.

Luther's own 'autobiographical fragment' is problematic in all sorts of ways. In common with other conversion acounts of this period, it is thin on circumstantial detail; no year is provided for the tower experience, which has been variously dated by historians. Further, scholars have

---

[9] *AM*, 1005.

[10] Nicholas Harpsfield, *The life and death of Sir Thomas More*, ed. E. V. Hitchcock and R. W. Chambers, EETS 186 (1932), 84–6.

[11] See here the remark of E. G. Rupp in his *Studies in the Making of the English Protestant Tradition* (Cambridge, 1947), 160, that Luther's 'discovery' was 'not like some scientific invention, a theological spinning jenny to be passed round, adapted, improved and finally patented by others'.

[12] Walker, *Persuasive Fictions*, 160–2.   [13] R. Marius, *Thomas More* (1984), xvi–xvii.

been sceptical about what Luther himself represents as a single dramatic moment of discovery, finding in his sermons over the period 1513–18 a number of distinct theological advances and 'breakthroughs'.[14] Whether we should see Luther's moment of catharsis as primarily an intellectual or an emotional one is another point at issue. A. G. Dickens has argued that Luther's *Turmerlebnis* was not a 'religious experience' as we might apply the term to either medieval mystics or modern Protestant revivalists; rather it 'claimed to be a "moment of truth" in a more literal and obvious sense. Luther was not concerned to achieve a revelation from within his own emotional resources.'[15] Alister McGrath by contrast insists that Luther's concern with salvation and righteousness 'shows a strongly existential dimension' and was no mere theological problem.[16] 'Conversion narratives' bring out more strongly than almost any other biographical source a temptation on the part of some historians to psychologise their subjects.[17] In his famous study of 'young man Luther', the psychoanalyst Erik Erikson remarked on the significance of Luther's conversion experience taking place when the reformer was in his early thirties, 'an important age for gifted people with a delayed identity crisis'.[18] More recently, the historian Richard Marius has related Luther's experience to 'the psychological self-examination that made so many in the later Middle Ages scrutinise their own hearts, test their own emotions, crawl dismally on all fours through the dark sewers of their hidden selves'.[19]

Enough has been said, I think, to establish that the language and structure of conversion narratives is complex, and lends itself to deconstruction of various kinds. But there may be limited utility here in attempting to strip back the rhetoric and tropes to uncover a putative 'real' motivation on the part of converts. Excessively reductionist approaches to a phenomenon like religious conversion run the risk of turning it into a mere reflection of the concerns of our own society,

---

[14] Oberman, *Luther*, 151–74.

[15] A. G. Dickens, *Martin Luther and the Reformation* (1967), 30.

[16] McGrath, *Reformation Thought*, 73.

[17] Seminal in this respect are the two lectures on conversion by the nineteenth-century American philosopher William James in his *The Varieties of Religious Experience*, ed. F. H. Burkhardt (Cambridge, MA, 1985), 157 ff. James interpreted conversion in psychoanalytical terms as the process 'by which a self hitherto divided, and consciously wrong, inferior and unhappy, becomes unified and consciously right, superior and happy, in consequence of its firmer hold upon religious realities'. For a survey of the literature on the pyschological/psychoanalytical approach to writing about conversion (and some caveats), see L. R. Rambo, 'Current Research on Religious Conversion', *Religious Studies Review* 8 (1982), 146–59.

[18] E. H. Erikson, *Young Man Luther: A Study in Psychoanalysis and History* (paperback edition, 1962), 201.

[19] Marius, *More*, 320.

and conversion demands to be understood on its own terms, rather than rationalised or explained away.[20] In what follows the emphasis will be on the construction of a concept or idea of conversion among early English evangelicals; on seeking to understand how it was patterned and represented, to the self and to others; on the sources of its language, imagery and internal structure; and on what such an investigation may have to tell us about 'the beginnings of English Protestantism'.

II

A final glance at the case of Martin Luther should remind us of an important fact about conversion in the early Tudor period: neither the word nor the range of meanings it might signify originated with the evangelical protest against Rome. At the time of the tower experience, Luther had already undergone one dramatic religious conversion: his decision to become a monk.[21] 'Conversion' was a term widely used in later medieval England to evoke that 'death to the world' involved in the transformation from the secular to the religious life. The Yorkshire hermit Richard Rolle, for example, described a demonic temptation that had come to him 'in the beginning of my conversion'; and the revelation of purgatory and paradise to an anonymous monk of Evesham (printed 1482) came to him after a sickness suffered 'about the beginning of his conversion'.[22] More prosaically, the first English translation of Thomas à Kempis's *The Imitation of Christ* admonished new religious, 'in the beginning of thy conversion thou keep thy cell and dwell well therin'.[23] Conversion was thus hardly a new concept to the many English evangelicals who, as Richard Rex shows elsewhere in this volume, emerged from the ranks of the regular clergy.

[20] The most convincing attempt to ascribe a general underlying pattern to early evangelical conversion is Susan Brigden's suggestive exploration of the links between support for the Reformation and youthful protest against authority: 'Youth and the English Reformation', *Past and Present* 95 (1982), 37–67. I have not attempted to pursue this theme further, largely because it does not appear prominently in the accounts of evangelicals themselves, who believed that 'men are called to repentaunce, some in youth, some in myddle age, and some in olde age'. See N. Wyse, *A consolacyon for chrysten people to repayre agayn the lordes temple* (1538), E1 r.

[21] In later years he ascribed this decision to a vow made to St Anna when praying for protection during a thunderstorm: Rupp and Drewery, *Martin Luther*, 2.

[22] Richard Rolle, *English Prose Treatises*, ed. G. G. Perry, EETS 20 (1866), 5; *The Revelation to the Monk of Evesham*, ed. E. Arber (1901), 19.

[23] Thomas à Kempis, *The Imitation of Christ*, ed. B. J. H. Biggs, EETS 309 (1997), 26.

'Conversion' was also used with reference to Jews and pagans. Late medieval pious texts looked forward to the time when 'jews shall convert', and back to the age when heathens were by holy men 'converted . . . to Christian faith'.[24] The travel narrative of Sir John Mandeville, which appeared in at least four editions in the reign of Henry VII, included the intriguing snippet that the court of the Great Chan contained many Christians, 'converted to good faith by the preaching of religious Christian men'.[25] But the words 'convert/conversion' seem to have been most commonly employed in late medieval sources to indicate not so much an outwardly measurable category change (layman to monk, heathen to Christian) as a turning away from sinfulness to a greater love and service of God. Perhaps the most famous example of this type of convert in fifteenth-century England was the laywoman Margery Kempe, formerly 'a sinful woman' whose confessor could refer to how things stood 'after your conversion'.[26] In a text printed by Caxton in 1484, the devil boasts of his success in acquiring the soul of a dead woman, telling a priest that he had feared he might have 'take[n] her away from me, and converted her with thine long preaching and good examples'.[27] In Stephen Hawes's verse treatise *The Conversyon of Swerers* (1509), swearers are represented as rending the body of Christ, and Christ addresses them: 'Be by me converted/Tear me now no more'.[28] Conversion to and by Jesus is a recurrent theme of *The Imitation of Christ*. The reader is advised to 'learn to despise outward things and to convert thee to inward things'; 'Convert us, Lord, to thee, that we may be meek, kind, and devout.' Like an iron in the fire losing its rust, 'so a man converting himself wholly to God is . . . changed into a new man'.[29]

This understanding of conversion even had its distinct and regular celebration in the Church's calendar, with the institution on 25 January of the festival of the Conversion of St Paul. The homily provided for this feast in the popular sermon collection *The Golden Legend* asked rhetorically, 'Why is Paul's conversion celebrated, while that of other saints is not?' The answer given was that 'no sinner, no matter how grievous his sin,

[24] *Cursor Mundi*, ed. R. Morris, EETS 57–109 (7 vols., 1874–93), iii. 1096, iv. 1279; J. Mirk, *Festial*, ed. T. Erbe, EETS 96 (1905), 217.

[25] *Mandeville's Travels*, ed. M. C. Seymour (Oxford, 1967), xiii, 172.

[26] *The Book of Margery Kempe*, ed. S. B. Meech, EETS 212 (1940), 44.

[27] *The Book of the Knight of La Tour-Landry*, ed. T. Wright, EETS 33 (1868), 140. See also the reference to Christ's converting common whores and turning them to goodness in Book 16 of Langland's *Piers Ploughman*, ed. J. F. Goodridge (Harmondsworth, 1959), 201.

[28] Stephen Hawes, *The Conversyon of Swerers*, ed. D. Laing (Edinburgh, 1865), A3v.

[29] *The Imitation of Christ*, 40, 45, 77, 115.

can despair of pardon when he sees that Paul, whose fault was so great, afterwards became so much greater in grace'.[30] This was a sentiment with which evangelicals, not noted for their admiration of *The Golden Legend*, could scarcely have found fault.

In fact, if we turn to look for examples of usage of the phrase 'to convert' in evangelical writings of the 1520s and 1530s it is this sense of a penitential reorientation that comes most clearly to the fore. In 1534 Robert Barnes explained that the attack on litigiousness in his famous Cambridge sermon of Christmas Eve 1525 (which marked the start of his public career as a reformer) had been prompted by the behaviour of a grasping churchwarden suing a poverty-stricken executor in pursuit of a small legacy to the church. Barnes had reasoned with him in private to no avail, and spoke in public 'because I had not clearly converted him'.[31] This was not a question of recruitment into an evangelical brotherhood, but of calling him to repentance. The same quality of hardheartedness, though with clearer doctrinal overtones, is alluded to in George Joye's 1531 call to the clergy to allow the scripture in English, and 'to repent you therefore and be converted to God'.[32] In a letter of around 1539, the future archbishop Matthew Parker declared that there was nothing more acceptable to God 'than to convert the hearts of his reasonable creatures in true faith and knowledge unto him'.[33]

In many ways, conversion and repentance were more than linked concepts; they were virtual synonyms which together connoted that 'turning to God' which early Tudor evangelicals thought they were about. In his translation of Luther's *Prologue to the Epistle of Paul to the Romans*, William Tyndale spoke of the status of a man that 'hath forsaken sin and is converted to put his trust in Christ'.[34] In his own preface, 'W. T. unto the Reader', in the New Testament of 1534, Tyndale explained at some length the philological and theological connections between repentance and conversion, in the process justifying the attack on traditional sacramental practice implicit in his decision to translate the Greek verb *metanoeo* as 'repent' rather than 'do penance':

[30] J. de Voragine, *The Golden Legend*, trans. W. Ryan (2 vols., Princeton, NJ, 1993), i. 119. See also J. Mirk, *Festial*, 52–6.
[31] Robert Barnes, *A supplicacion unto the most gracyous prynce H. the .viii* (1534), F3r. See J. P. Lusardi, 'The Career of Robert Barnes', in Thomas More, *The Confutation of Tyndale's Answer*, ed. L. A. Schuster et al. (New Haven, 1973), 1367–1415.
[32] George Joye, *The letters whyche Iohan Ashwell Priour of Newnham Abbey besydes Bedforde sente secretly to the Byshope of Lyncolne* (Strassburg, 1531), Biv.
[33] Matthew Parker, *Correspondence*, ed. J. Bruce (PS, 1853), 10.
[34] *Tyndale's New Testament*, ed. D. Daniell (New Haven and London, 1989), 211.

Concerning this word repentance or (as they used) penance, the Hebrew hath in the Old Testament generally *Sob* [shub] turn or be converted. For which the translation that we take for Saint Jerome's hath most part *converti* to turn or be converted, and sometime yet *agere penitenciam*. And the Greek in the New Testament hath perpetually *metanoeo* to turn in the heart and mind, and to come to the right knowledge, and to a man's right wit again . . . And the very sense and signification both of the Hebrew and also of the Greek word, is, to be converted and to turn to God with all the heart, to know his will and to live according to his laws.[35]

Tyndale went on to argue that this 'conversion or turning if it be un-feigned' would be accompanied by four elements: confession of sinful-ness, not to a priest but before God and the congregation; contrition or sorrowfulness; faith; and satisfaction or the making of amends, not to God but to those we have offended.[36]

What most clearly differentiates Tyndale's sense of conversion/repentance from that of Thomas à Kempis is, of course, the new *theological* framework through which the concept is mediated. Here it is significant that the context of the discussion is St Paul's Letter to the Romans, for Tyndale, following Luther, was convinced that 'the sum and whole cause of the writings of this epistle, is, to prove that a man is justified by faith only'.[37] Throughout the reign of Henry VIII, English evangelicals dis-agreed about a great deal, from eucharistic theology to the possibilities of compromise with the regime, but the one clear common denomi-nator, if not the defining element of evangelicalism, was the belief that men were saved only through their faith in Christ, and not through their own works. In order to ask what was distinctive about *evangelical* con-version in the reign of Henry VIII, we need to consider more closely the symbiotic relationship between an existential or emotional experi-ence, and the internalisation of a profoundly theological and intellectual proposition.[38]

Mature Protestant theology of the sixteenth century, particularly in its Lutheran manifestation, preserved a fairly clear distinction between two modes of divine action upon the Christian believer: justification and sanctification. The former was, in forensic terms, an unmerited verdict of acquittal, which did not in and of itself effect an inward transformation of

---

[35] Ibid., 9–10.   [36] Ibid., 10.   [37] Ibid., 223.

[38] That English Christians other than evangelicals underwent conversion experiences in this pe-riod is a point worth bearing in mind: in the early 1530s, for example, the courtiers Sebastian Newdigate and Sir John Gage renounced wealth and office to enter the London Charterhouse. See Brigden, *London and the Reformation*, 227.

life. In theological jargon, justification was a matter of 'imputation' rather than 'impartation'. Sanctification was the subsequent, and complementary process whereby the Holy Spirit brought about the regeneration of the elect, and a visible and outward holiness which was the consequence not the cause of salvation. Reformers regarded it as a fundamental error of Catholic theologians, pre- and post-Reformation, that they understood by justification a process of 'making righteous', rather than simply 'declaring righteous'.[39]

Yet from the outset the dynamics of the conversion process functioned to blur the boundaries between external judgement and internal change in the subjectivity of the believer. Luther's influential concept of the 'Law/Gospel dichotomy' is a case in point. This was the mechanism through which God brought sinners to an understanding of their condition, and their total dependence on Christ. For English readers a clear account of the doctrine was set out by George Joye in his 1531 printed apologia. The Word of God contains both Law and Gospel, and the function of the former is to instil despair: unable to meet the demands of God's Law, 'a sinful conscience feeleth herself bounden and holden under the power of sin and carried towards damnation'. But hearing and believing the glad tidings of forgiveness through the death of Christ, the sinner 'feeleth his heart eased, comforted & loosed'.[40] The justifying faith which Joye proclaimed here was surely not just a theological principle, but an experimental one, encompassing an *experience* of conversion. Joye fell out spectacularly with William Tyndale over some points of theology, but on this they spoke with one voice.[41] Tyndale urged readers of his *Prologue to Romans* to behold their just damnation in the Law of God, and then to turn their eyes to Christ to see the exceeding mercy of the Father. Further, they were to remember that Christ did not die for their sins so that they could live in them still, 'but that thou shouldest be a new creature and live a new life after the will of God'.[42] Indeed, it seems to have been broadly characteristic of the theology of Tyndale and other early English reformers to emphasise the element of moral transformation

---

[39] On these points, see McGrath, *Reformation Thought*, 82–4; B. Reardon, *Religious Thought in the Reformation* (2nd edition, 1995), 117–18, 126–7; Rupp, *English Protestant Tradition*, 165–70; C. Trueman, *Luther's Legacy: Salvation and English Reformers 1525–1556* (Oxford, 1994), 56–67. The elaboration of the doctrine of sanctification is particularly associated with Philip Melanchthon.

[40] Joye, *Letters*, A6v-7r.

[41] Specifically, the fate of souls prior to the Last Judgement, Joye charging Tyndale with teaching the error of 'soul sleeping'. See N. T. Burns, *Christian Mortalism from Tyndale to Milton* (Cambridge, MA, 1972), 102–11.

[42] *Tyndale's New Testament*, 224.

inherent in justification by faith.[43] In the so-called *Cologne Fragment* of
1525, Tyndale wrote that the hearts of the elect 'begin to wax soft and
to melt at the bounteous mercy of God' when salvation through Christ
is preached, and five years later in his prologue to the Pentateuch he described the process thus: 'the Spirit entereth the heart, and quickeneth
it, and giveth her life, and justifieth her'.[44]

III

The use of such language in the foundational texts of English reformed
theology should give pause for thought. There has been a tendency
to perceive the rise of Protestantism in terms of the triumph of intellect over emotion, of the controlled and printed Word over the affective, ritual and mimetic religion of the Middle Ages. It has recently
been argued that in the first generation of the English Reformation
'conversions to reforming ideas were on the whole described in intellectual terms', as a progression from ignorance to knowledge, from darkness to illumination.[45] It is undeniably the case that 'knowledge' was
regarded as a crucial element in the process of conversion. According to his secretary, Ralph Morice, Cranmer once defended himself
against a fellow evangelical's charges of overleniency to papists, re-
marking, 'What will ye have a man do to him that is not yet come
to the knowledge of the truth of the gospel?'[46] The London mer-
cer Henry Brinklow remembered in his will the men who 'laboured
in the vineyard of the Lord to bring the people...to the knowledge of Christ's gospel'.[47] In a letter accompanying the gift of a New
Testament to his mother in around 1536, the Yorkshire law student
Robert Plumpton sententiously advised her not to worry about her
understanding, 'for God will give knowledge to whom he will give
knowledge of the Scriptures, as soon to a shepherd as to a priest'. In
a subsequent letter he stressed that his admonitions were not designed
'to bring you into any heresies, but to teach you the clear light of God's
doctrine'.[48]

   This metaphor of enlightenment was a recurrent one in evangelical
sources – light from heaven had of course been central to the archetype

---

[43] Trueman, *Luther's Legacy*, 89–94. In this, Trueman argues, Tyndale was rather closer to Continental reformers with a humanist background (such as Martin Bucer) than to Luther.
[44] Ibid., 89, 99.   [45] Ryrie, 'English Evangelical Reformers', 187.
[46] *Reformation Narratives*, 246.   [47] Brigden, *London and the Reformation*, 418.
[48] *The Plumpton Correspondence*, ed. T. Stapleton (Camden Society o.s. 4, 1839), 231–2.

of Christian conversion narratives, Paul's experience on the Damascus road. At his trial in 1538, John Lambert acknowledged his debt to the works of Luther 'for by them hath God showed unto me, and also to a huge multitude of others, such light as the deceivable darkness of them . . . that name themselves, but amiss, to be the holy church, cannot abide', and in a treatise of the same year Nicholas Wyse addressed himself to 'ye that are the people of God and have received the light of his gospel'.[49] John Bale described George Joye's conversion in terms of 'the light of truth dawning upon him', and Joye himself called on his enemies to pray God 'that he would illumine your hearts and loose you with the keys of the knowledge of his holy word, and unlock your wits out of this blind ignorance and unbelief'.[50] Writing from exile in Mary's reign, John Olde described his 'first entry into the gospel' of ten or eleven years earlier as a calling out from 'the damnable darkness of Antichrist's iniquity into the true light of Christ's gospel's verity'.[51]

Knowledge and ignorance, light and darkness: these were the states separated by the 'turning to God' that gospellers had identified in themselves and looked for in others. But when they recounted a transformative encounter with the Word of God, evangelicals did not typically do so in terms which spoke only of an intellectual, credal type of conversion. When Henry VIII's last wife, Katherine Parr, wrote of how she had come to know Christ as her saviour, she regarded it as a knowledge 'infused by grace, into the hearts of the faithful, which can never be attempted by human doctrine'.[52] The language used to describe the experience of conversion was often sensual, somatic, sometimes even sexual in its emphasis. The courtier George Zouche was reported to be 'so ravished with the spirit of God' upon reading a copy of Tyndale's *Obedience of a Christian Man* filched from a lady-in-waiting to Anne Boleyn that he could scarcely be prevailed upon to return it.[53] Cranmer spoke of the need to 'allure men to embrace the doctrine of the gospel', an image that appealed also to Brinklow ('repent and believe the Gospel in embracing the same') and to William Turner, who later wrote to Foxe of how he had exhorted his friend Rowland Taylor 'zealously to embrace the

---

[49] *AM* 1102; Wyse, *Consolacyon for chrysten people*, G2r.

[50] C. C. Butterworth and A. G. Chester, *George Joye 1495?–1553* (Philadelphia, 1962), 24; Joye, *Letters*, B1v.

[51] John Olde, *A confession of the most auncient and true christen catholike olde belefe* (Emden, 1556), E7r, A2v.

[52] Katherine Parr, *The Lamentacion of a Sinner* (1547), B6r.

[53] *Reformation Narratives*, 52.

evangelical doctrine'.[54] The promise of the gospel absorbed the senses as well as the mind. Latimer recalled in 1552 how he had begun 'to smell the word of God' after an encounter with Bilney.[55] Bale said of Joye's conversion that 'from the purest fonts of the Gospels did he drink the spiritual and wholly undiluted philosophy of Christ, with which he bedewed the parched hearts of many'.[56] The imagery of physical nourishment permeated evangelical discourses on conversion to a remarkable degree. At his trial in 1538, John Lambert insisted that 'the Scripture is the spiritual food and sustenance of man's soul', and others, including Bilney, Tyndale, Joye, Cranmer and Coverdale vividly described the experience of 'tasting' God's holy word.[57] This habitual substitution of 'tasting' for reading/comprehending/believing persisted into the martyrological accounts of a subsequent generation. According to John Foxe the monk Richard Bayfield was one of those who, having spent time in Cambridge, 'tasted so well of good letters' that he could never return to his abbey. In his account of the early career of Martin Luther, Foxe noted that those hearing his sermons 'received good taste of this sweet doctrine' and began to understand the difference between the law and the gospel.[58]

That the experience of receiving the gospel could be one of 'sweetness' is an intriguing pointer. In a discussion of Shakespeare's Sonnet 73 with its 'bare ruined choirs where late the sweet birds sang', Eamon Duffy has recently argued that in terms of religious imagery 'sweet' was a quintessentially Catholic word. All-pervasive in the prayers, primers and homilies of the pre-Reformation period, references to the 'sweetness' of Christ and his passion were progressively expunged from Protestant devotional language because of their affective, sentimental associations, and their potential to be distractions from faith.[59] Yet in the reign of Henry VIII evangelicals seem to have had few qualms about this adjective. Years after the event Foxe's correspondent William Maldon

---

54 Ibid., 246; Henry Brinklow, *The Complaynt of Roderyck Mors . . . & the Lamentacyon of a Christen Agaynst the Cyte of London*, ed. J. M. Cowper, EETS extra series 22 (1874), 120; Nicholas Ridley, *Works*, ed. H. Christmas (PS, 1843), 494.

55 Hugh Latimer, *Sermons*, ed. G. E. Corrie (PS, 1844), 334.

56 Butterworth and Chester, *George Joye*, 24.

57 *AM*, 1005, 1116; Trueman, *Luther's Legacy*, 89; Joye, *Letters*, B6r; *Reformation Narratives*, 247; H. C. Porter, *Reformation and Reaction in Tudor Cambridge* (2nd edition, Hamden, CT, 1972), 46.

58 *AM*, 844, 1021.

59 Eamon Duffy, 'Remembering Catholicism in Shakespeare's England', a paper given at the conference on 'Catholic England', St Mary's College, Strawberry Hill, 27 April 2000. For the ubiquity of 'sweet' in pre-Reformation devotional discourse, see Duffy's magisterial *The Stripping of the Altars: Traditional Religion in England 1400–1580* (New Haven and London, 1992), *passim*.

recalled as a young man joining the throng gathered on Sundays in Chelmsford church in 1538 to hear men reading from the newly sanctioned vernacular bible, 'that glad and sweet tidings of the gospel'. Despite parental disapproval, the experience made him determined to learn to read English for himself.[60] At much the same time, a more socially elevated convert, the courtier Sir Nicholas Carew, was reportedly giving thanks to God 'that ever he came in the prison of the tower, where he first savoured the life & sweetness of God's most holy word, meaning the Bible in English'.[61] By withholding the Bible in English, charged Nicholas Wyse, the clergy denied people 'the sweet fruit that they should have had in his scripture', and Joye similarly accused opponents of vernacular scripture of pretending 'that which is sweet to be bitter'.[62] Tyndale urged hearers of the Word preached to consider 'how sweet a thing the bitter death of Christ is' and to 'feel the goodness or . . . sweetness' in God's law.[63] The Yorkshire reformer Francis Bigod contrasted the 'judicial captivity of that babylonical man of Rome' to 'the sweet and soft service' of the gospel.[64] Bilney reported how a sentence discovered by chance in Paul's First Letter to Timothy acted as a 'most sweet and comfortable sentence to my soul'. Thereafter 'the Scripture began to be more pleasant unto me than the honey or the honey-comb', with its message that good works done without trust in Christ were worthless.[65] Katherine Parr was another who found 'pleasant and sweet words' in the New Testament, as, according to a later acount, was the London grocer John Petyt: 'one of the first that with Mr. Frith, Bilney, and Tyndale caught a sweetness in God's word'.[66] Here the reformers might deploy exactly the same kind of imagery as their religious opponents, such as the conservative Kentish priest in the early 1540s who, disliking the Pater Noster in English, compared it to the hard shell of a nut, 'and the Pater Noster in Latin to the sweet kernel'.[67]

It should occasion no surprise to discover either that the evangelical concept of conversion borrowed from a range of ideas developed over the course of the middle ages, or that the language used to describe the experience drew on a contemporary repertoire of religious imagery. After

[60] *Reformation Narratives*, 348–9.
[61] Edward Hall, *The Union of the Two Noble and Illustre Famelies of Lancastre and Yorke* (1548), 234r.
[62] Wyse, *Consolacyon for chrysten people*, F6v; Joye, *Letters*, Biv.
[63] Trueman, *Luther's Legacy*, 89, 100.
[64] A. G. Dickens, *Lollards and Protestants in the Diocese of York 1509–1558* (Oxford, 1959), 70.
[65] *AM*, 1005.   [66] Parr, *Lamentacion*, B2v; *Reformation Narratives*, 25.
[67] Peter Marshall, *The Catholic Priesthood and the English Reformation* (Oxford, 1994), 102.

all, 'early evangelicals were late medieval Christians'.[68] The study of the early Reformation, in England and elsewhere, has undoubtedly suffered from ·an anachronistic obsession with the 'origins' of later confessional movements, and an insufficient interest in or understanding of the extent to which early evangelicals were shaped within, and emerged from, the complex religious culture of their own age. Nonetheless, in investigating the experience of evangelical conversion in the quarter-century follow- ing Luther's break with the papacy it would be strange to suggest that we are not somewhere near the 'beginnings of English Protestantism'. Though it is right to be wary of anachronism and premature confessional labelling, it is equally valid to suggest that those persecuted as heretics in the 1520s and 1530s for acting on the imperatives of a scripturally patterned experience of conversion were something more than slightly heterodox Catholics punished for indulging an ill-judged religious enthu- siasm. In the remaining part of this chapter, I want to sharpen the focus on the ways in which shared understanding of the meanings of conver- sion contributed towards the formation of subjective religious identities in sixteenth-century England, and towards the permanence of religious division.

IV

The evangelical representation of conversion was by no means all sweetness and light, and nor was the experience of being converted. Contemporary social scientists characterise conversion as 'a problematic discontinuity demarcated by distinctive continuous states either side of the conversion happening'.[69] Or as another modern authority more succinctly puts it, 'conversion is from and to'.[70] The 'from' of evangelical conversion narratives, the understanding of the preconversion self, is an issue that requires further examination if we are to place the phe- nomenon meaningfully in a context of emergent confessional identities.

If conversion was typically represented as repentance, a turning to God and away from sin, then, logically enough, the former life of the convert was likely to appear in unflattering terms. This is certainly the case with

---

68 B. Gregory, *Salvation at Stake: Christian Martyrdom in Early Modern Europe* (Cambridge, MA, 1999), 141. See also ibid., 158–160, for the argument (parallel to mine) that early Protestant martyrs continued a 'medieval monastic vocabulary', and that the terms they used about scripture 'do not reflect dispassionate encounter with a text'.

69 R. Ireland, 'Pentecostalism, Conversions and Politics in Brazil', *Religion* 25 (1995), 141.

70 *The Encyclopedia of Christianity*, ed. E. Fahlbusch et al. (Grand Rapids, MI, 1999), i. 683. See also A. J. Kreilsheimer, *Conversion* (1980), 157.

one of the earliest of English evangelical autobiographical fragments, 'the author's prologue' in *The myrrour or lokynge glasse of lyfe* (1532) by the London publisher John Gough. The mirror in question was 'the holy words of God, by the writing of the evangelists and of St Paul . . . and the more I looked in this most pure glass, the more knowledge I had of my foul spotted soul'. Gough described himself as 'one that hath lived many years in the enormity and ambition of vainglory'.[71] A more expansive treatment of the same theme was provided in Katherine Parr's *The Lamentacion of a Sinner*, composed probably in the winter of 1545–6, and published in the first year of Edward VI's reign.[72] Much of the treatise was taken up with reflection on an 'evil and wretched former life', Parr feeling 'forced and constrained with my heart and words, to confess and declare to the world, how ingrate, negligent, unkind, and stubborn, I have been to God my creator'.[73]

This postulation of an unregenerate former self, it should be said, was hardly an unfamiliar theme in the religious culture of the later Middle Ages. Among the saints, Paul and Mary Magdalene had long exemplified the possibility of sharp contrast between the 'before' and 'after' of conversion. It was also at the centre of that *locus classicus* of conversion narratives, *The Confessions* of St Augustine, and those not familiar with the original might hear a potted version preached from *The Golden Legend*, recounting how the saint had once been a 'wicked slave of evil desires'.[74] Medieval hagiography also served up the formerly wicked lives of a number of less eminent saints, including St Pelagia, St Brice, and St Thais, courtesan.[75] It is worth noting, too, that Katherine Parr's *Lamentacion* was firmly rooted in a late medieval genre, looking back past Marguerite of Navarre's *The Mirror of the Sinful Soul* to the late fifteenth-century *Mirror of Gold to the Sinful Soul* of the monk Dionysius Carthusianus, translated into English in 1507 by Henry VIII's grandmother, Lady Margaret Beaufort.[76] Yet in evangelical sources of the early-to-mid-sixteenth century, there was a distinctive and decisive shaping element at work in the process we might call the invention of an 'other' self. Increasingly, past 'wickedness' was understood in terms of doctrine rather than personal morality. Gough stated that he had lived a life of vainglory 'judging myself a good Christian man', and in railing against 'the great enormity of sin reigning in the common people' he had in mind their disdain

---

[71] J[ohn] G[ough], *Here begynneth a lytell treatyse called the myrrour or lokynge glasse of lyfe* (1532), A2v.
[72] S. E. James, *Kateryn Parr: The Making of a Queen* (Aldershot, 1999), 234–6.
[73] Parr, *Lamentacion*, A1r.   [74] *The Golden Legend*, ii. 117.   [75] Ibid., 230, 301, 234.
[76] James, *Kateryn Parr*, 235–7.

for God's Word 'and the pronouncer or speaker thereof'.[77] Katherine Parr was even more emphatic: 'I would have covered my sins with the pretence of holiness, I called superstition, godly meaning, and true holiness, error . . . the blood of Christ was not reputed by me sufficient for to wash me from the filth of my sins.'[78]

It has been customary to think of individual trajectories from 'Catholicism' to 'Protestantism' following an arc passing through such points as 'humanism', 'anticlericalism' and 'disenchantment'. In many cases it may indeed have been so.[79] But those reformers who left first-person narratives of their spiritual odysseys seem almost to have vied with each other in stressing the depth and extent of their commitment to the worst type of unreformed Catholicism.[80] John Bale, for example, claimed to have been 'a most obstinate papist' (*obstinatissimus papista*) before the break with Rome, while an early anonymous biographer of Cranmer laid great emphasis on how in his youth at Cambridge the archbishop had been 'nouselled in the grossest kind of sophistry, logic, philosophy moral and natural . . . chiefly in the dark riddles and quiddities of Duns and other subtle questionists'.[81] In a letter to Heinrich Bullinger of January 1546, the exiled John Hooper bitterly repented the time when 'like a brute beast . . . I have been a slave to my own lusts'. These wicked impulses seem to have been spiritual rather than sexual ones: 'I had begun to blaspheme God by impious worship and all manner of idolatry, following the evil ways of my forefathers, before I rightly understood what God was'.[82] Writing in Edward's reign, another Henrician evangelical, Thomas Becon, included himself in a collective confession of past guilt: 'How ran we from post to pillar, from stock to stone, from idol to idol, from place to place, to seek remission of our sins . . . How were we bewitched to believe, that in observing the pope's ceremonies there was everlasting salvation, and in neglecting them eternal damnation.'[83] The reformer who seems to have returned to the theme most insistently, however, was

---

[77] Gough, *Myrrour or lookynge glasse of lyfe*, A2v-4r. [78] Parr, *Lamentacion*, A2v, A4v.

[79] In his recantation of 1528, for example, the Augustinian friar Thomas Topley warned all Christians to 'beware of consenting to Erasmus's Fables [*The Colloquies*], for by consenting to them, they have caused me to shrink in my faith'. See *AM*, 1047.

[80] A point noted by J. J. Scarisbrick, who remarked how converts to Protestantism did not suggest their conversion had been preceded by slow disillusionment, but rather 'came as a sudden release from an elaborate way of life which, up to the moment when scales fell from eyes, had enjoyed wholehearted commitment'. See *The Reformation and the English People* (Oxford, 1984), 56.

[81] Cited in Richard Rex, 'John Bale, Geoffrey Downes and Jesus College', *JEH* 49 (1998), note 491; *Reformation Narratives*, 218–19.

[82] *Original Letters relative to the English Reformation*, ed. H. Robinson (2 vols., PS, 1846–7), i. 33–4.

[83] Thomas Becon, *The Catechism . . . with Other Pieces*, ed. J. Ayre (PS, 1844), 413–14.

Hugh Latimer. In a letter to Sir Edward Baynton in December 1531, Latimer confessed that:

I have thought in times past, that the pope, Christ's vicar, hath been Lord of all the world, as Christ is; so that if he should have deprived the king of his crown, or you of the lordship of Bromeham, it had been enough; for he could do no wrong ... that the pope's dispensations of pluralities of benefices, and absence from the same, had discharged consciences before God ... that the pope could have spoiled purgatory at his pleasure with a word of his mouth ... that if I had been a friar, and in a cowl, I could not have been damned, nor afraid of death; and by occasion of the same, I have been minded many times to have been a friar, namely when I was sore sick and diseased: now I abhor my superstitious foolishness ... I have thought in times past that divers images of saints could have holpen me, and done me much good, and delivered me of my diseases ... It were too long to tell you what blindness I have been in, and how long it were ere I could forsake such folly, it was so corporate in me.[84]

There was perhaps an element of calculation in Latimer's frank confession. He was under investigation by Bishop John Stokesley of London, and denied the bishop's right to search out the secrets of his conscience, slyly noting that 'men think that my lord himself hath thought in times past, that by God's law a man might marry his brother's wife'. But in a subsequent letter Latimer vehemently defended himself against the charge of some of Baynton's friends who 'think that I made a lie, when I said that I have thought in times past that the pope had been lord of the world'.[85] Years later, in a sermon of 1552, Latimer recalled that he had once been 'as obstinate a papist as any was in England, insomuch that when I should be made bachelor of divinity, my whole oration went against Philip Melanchthon and against his opinions'.[86]

Whether any of these fragments of personal history represent totally reliable accounts of an individual's lived experience is of course a distinctly moot point. They should probably be regarded as part of the construction or 'fictionalisation' of conversion experience, something which heightens rather than reduces their value and interest. Then, as now, religious 'conversion' acquires its name and meaning only through a process of subsequent reflection, and contemporary sociological studies identify distinct elements of stereotyping in the accounts provided by religious converts. The paradigm of sinfulness-conversion-regeneration seems particularly prominent among recruits to modern

[84] Hugh Latimer, *Sermons and Remains*, ed. G. E. Corrie (PS, 1845), 332–3.
[85] Ibid., 333, 348.   [86] Latimer, *Sermons*, 334.

Protestant sects.[87] Early sixteenth-century evangelicals were perhaps especially predisposed to (re)interpret their experience in this way. The search for validating biblical prototypes provided the epitome of instantaneous conversion in the experience of St Paul, and the widely recognised tendency among early moderns to construct their world-view in terms of binary oppositions may have served to sharpen an artificially antithetical juxtaposition of 'before' and 'after'. No doubt things were frequently less tidy in reality. We know that some converts to evangelical ideas in the 1520s and 1530s were not stout papists but long-standing Lollard sympathisers, and it is probable that many converts stumbled gradually rather than leaped suddenly to occupy new ground – needing, like the Winchester scholar William Ford, to be 'at length with much ado brought from the popish doctrine'.[88]

Yet there are few hints of caution, confusion, or gradualism in the accounts that have been bequeathed to us. A common thread was the sense of a profound ontological change. Evangelicals spoke of eyes being opened, of the 'veil of Moses' being lifted, of being clothed 'in a new garment'.[89] The idea of being 'born again', still prevalent in modern religious discourse, was used as well: one friar, a protégé of Latimer, was styling himself 'Two-Year-Old' in 1536.[90] There were sound theological reasons for representing things in this way. Being able to perceive the truth in religion was not the exercise of an active personal choice, but a receptiveness to the initiating action of the Holy Spirit: conversion was God's doing, not man's. The verb 'to convert' was itself sometimes used as a transitive rather than intransitive one, with God as the subject. Thus George Joye urged in 1544 that gospellers should pray to God for their persecutors 'that he would for Christ's sake have mercy upon them and convert them'.[91] There was clearly a fear in some quarters that to recognise the convert's own agency was to risk readmitting that 'works righteousness' against which the reformers had set their face so firmly. In a treatise on justification published in 1543, the Gloucestershire gentleman and lay reformer Richard Tracy denied that God gave justifying

[87] T. F. O'Dea, *The Sociology of Religion* (New Jersey, 1966), 61–3.

[88] Anne Hudson, *The Premature Reformation: Wycliffite Texts and Lollard History* (Oxford, 1988), ch. 10; *Reformation Narratives*, 29.

[89] Parr, *Lamentacion*, B4v, B5v; PRO SP 1 / 115, 31r (*LP* XII (i) 212); Brigden, *London and the Reformation*, 417.

[90] Susan Wabuda, ' "Fruitful Preaching" in the Diocese of Worcester: Bishop Hugh Latimer and his Influence 1535–1539', *Religion and the English People 1500–1640*, ed. Eric Carlson (Kirksville, MO, 1998), 68.

[91] George Joye, *A present consolacion for the sufferers of persecution for ryghtwyseness* (Antwerp, 1544), G4v.

faith to any man because of a virtuous disposition to repentance that he saw in him. Rather, he insisted (with St James) that 'every perfect gift is from above' and remarked on the absurdity of praising for its swift flying through the air a thrown stone 'whose nature is to lie still, if it be not removed'.[92] Joye emphasised that 'Paul as he was going to persecute Christ's Church was smitten down a murderer and rose again a justified man, which yet had done no good works'.[93] Katherine Parr claimed to have discovered that 'mine own power and strength could not help me, & that I was in the Lord's hand, even as the clay is in the potter's hand'.[94], In describing the conversion of a former conservative in 1545, John Bale laid all the emphasis on God's action: 'we laud that heavenly lord, which thus of mere pity and mercy hath found out his almost perished sheep, laid him upon his shoulders, and brought him again to his fold'.[95] The insistence in a modern reference work that 'conversion is a conscious act on the part of the subject, not an event passively experienced' would have seemed grossly presumptuous to all of these writers.[96]

Yet despite the emphasis on divine initiative in the conversion process, evangelical converts did not usually claim to resemble St Paul in being literally struck down by a blinding light from heaven as they went about their papist business. Conversion narratives featured a clear interest in instrumentality, in the mechanisms and means that God had employed to open the converts' hearts, and show them the error of their ways. Indeed, the characteristic fashioning of these narratives around the principle of fairly sudden transformation tended to accentuate the significance of stimuli, triggers and catalysts. Not surprisingly, a very common theme was the effect of exposure for the first time to vernacular scripture. For evangelicals the medium was the message here, the New Testament both imparting the doctrinal verity of justification by faith, and at the same time bringing about the possibility of experiential encounter with the risen Christ, the eternal 'Word' of God. Examples of subjects of Henry VIII supposedly converted by reading scripture could be multiplied without great difficulty, from the Essex Lollard John Tyball, confessing in 1528 how he fell into 'errors and heresies' by reading the evangelists and the Epistles of Peter and Paul in English, to the Lincolnshire gentlewoman Anne Askew, converted

---

[92] Richard Tracy, *The profe and declaration of thys proposition: fayth only iustifieth* (1543), A7r-v.
[93] Joye, *Letters*, B6r.   [94] Parr, *Lamentacion* D3r-v.
[95] John Bale, *A Mysterye of inyquyte contayned within the heretycall Genealogye of Ponce Pantolabus* (Antwerp, 1545), A3r-v.
[96] *The New International Dictionary of the Christian Church*, ed. J. D. Douglas (Exeter, 1974), 259.

'by oft reading of the sacred Bible'.[97] Books other than the text of scripture itself were sometimes credited with bringing about conversions (though presumably people taking the risk of reading forbidden heretical works must often have done so with some kind of predisposition to accept their arguments). John Foxe claimed that, in addition to the New Testament, it was Tyndale's works, *The Parable of the Wicked Mammon* and *The Obedience of a Christian Man*, that had persuaded Richard Bayfield; and the *Wicked Mammon* was also claimed to have converted the London leather seller John Tewkesbury.[98] Luther's works were identified by the temporarily apostate evangelical William Barlow in 1531 as the means whereby he had been 'enticed unto their faction'; and similar confessions, or boasts, were made by John Lambert and William Roper.[99] Another member of the More circle, Sir Thomas's brother-in-law, John Rastell, had engaged in a literary disputation with the young reformer John Frith over the question of purgatory, and was converted to the cause of radical reform in the last few years of his life by reading Frith's rejoinder.[100] Rowland Taylor was reportedly converted by the Lutheran tract *Unio Dissidentium*; and, without specifying titles, Nicholas Shaxton confessed during his recantation sermon of August 1546 that his sacramentarian views were the result of reading 'heretical books of English'.[101]

It was sometimes suggested that the suffering of persecuted evangelicals subverted the intention of the persecutors by inspiring others to find the truth. George Joye suggested in 1544 that 'our innocent blood shed for the gospel shall preach it with more fruit . . . then ever did our mouths and pens'.[102] There must have been an element of wishful thinking here, but John Bale claimed in 1545 to have met several persons in Colchester who were 'converted from your papism unto true repentance' by the steadfast demeanour at the stake of the Anabaptist Peter Franke.[103] He also claimed that a great number of those present were converted by the

---

97   John Strype, *Ecclesiastical Memorials* (3 vols., 1721), I (ii). 35; Anne Askew and John Bale, *The lattre examinacyon, of Anne Askew* (Wesel, 1547), 15r.

98   *AM*, 1021, 1024.

99   William Barlow, *A Dialogue Describing the Originall Ground of these Lutheran Faccions*, ed. J. R. Lunn (1897), 70; Harpsfield, *More*, 85; *AM*, 1102.

100 John Frith, 'A Disputation of Purgatory', *The Work of John Frith*, ed. N. T. Wright (Oxford, 1978), 211. See the introduction by A. J. Geritz to his edition of Rastell's *The Pastyme of People and a New Boke of Purgatory* (New York, 1985).

101 Ridley, *Works*, 494; Charles Wriothesley, *A Chronicle of England during the Reigns of the Tudors*, ed. W. Hamilton, vol. 1 (Camden Society n.s. 11, 1875), 170.

102 Joye, *Present consolation*, B4v.

103 Bale, *Mysterye of inyquyte*, 54v.

burning of Anne Askew and her companions in 1546, though his allusions in this context to the centurion acknowledging Christ's divinity at the crucifixion should alert us to the elements of narrative structuring and stock topoi so clearly present in Reformation martyrology.[104]

Alongside books and burnings, it was brethren who were most commonly recognised as the secondary causes in God's plan to bring about the conversion of an individual. The word 'converter' was even used by contemporaries in this sense, an evangelical in Northamptonshire being reported to the authorities in May 1546 as 'a common converter of the people from the laws and ordinances of the Church'.[105] Pedigrees and genealogies of conversion are recurrent features of the narratives in Foxe's *Actes and Monuments.* John Frith's road to martyrdom began when 'he fell into knowledge and acquaintance with William Tyndale, through whose instructions he first received into his heart the seed of the gospel'. Thomas Bilney is said to have 'converted Dr Barnes to the gospel of Jesus Christ our Saviour' along with a host of others.[106] But the theme was already well established by the time Foxe began his compilation. From the perspective of Edward VI's reign, John Bale attributed his conversion to the persuasions of Thomas Lord Wentworth; and Hugh Latimer was in no doubt that 'Master Bilney, or rather Saint Bilney . . . was the instrument whereby God called me to knowledge; for I may thank him, next to God, for that knowledge that I have in the word of God'. After Latimer had delivered an aggressive sermon against the teaching of Melancthon, Bilney had come to him requesting Latimer to hear his confession, by which 'I learned more than before in many years . . . and forsook the schooldoctors and such fooleries'.[107] This, almost certainly, is the context for the sentiment (unusual in an evangelical) that Latimer is reported to have voiced in a sermon of 1536: 'if ever I had amendment of my sinful life the occasion thereof came by auricular confession'.[108] In his turn Latimer became identified by others as the cause of their entry into the gospel. The conversions of John Cardmaker and John Tyrel were attributed to Latimer's preaching; and John Olde was another proud to acknowledge 'the reverend father of blessed memory Hugh Latimer' as the 'right worthy instrument' for opening to him the true Christian faith.[109] William

---

[104] John Bale, *Select Works*, ed. H. Christmas (PS, 1849), 143, 243. On this theme, see *John Foxe and the English Reformation*, ed. D. Loades (Aldershot, 1997).

[105] A. G. Dickens, *Late Monasticism and the Reformation* (1994), 142.

[106] *AM*, 1031; *AM* (1563), 479.   [107] Fairfield, *John Bale*, 33; Latimer, *Sermons*, 334–5.

[108] PRO SP 1/104, 202r (*LP* X 1201).

[109] J. H. Fines, *A Biographical Register of Early English Protestants*, Part 2 (2 unpaginated vols., unpublished typescript 1981–1985), no. T3; *AM*, 1043; Olde, *Confession of the . . . olde belefe*, A2v.

Turner dedicated his *Preservative, or triacle, agaynst the poyson of Pelagius* (1552) to this 'most steadfast, godly, and true preacher of God's word', adding that 'first in Cambridge about 20 years ago, ye took great pains to put men from their evil works' and that 'this foundation of God's word once laid, we that were your disciples had much to do in Cambridge, after your departing from us'.[110] Though it involved a repudiation of past beliefs, and sometimes of friendships and family ties, evangelical conversion was not typically represented as a solitary or atomising process. The construction of a conversion experience was frequently cemented and buttressed by perceived personal obligations and solidarities, an aspect strengthened further when, as so often, the facilitator of one's conversion later died a martyr's death.

V

The Swiss historian Peter Blickle has confessed that 'I do not know what motives drove people from the Roman Church and to the reformers, nor does anyone else know it. Why did people around 1515 want to see the Body of Christ in the Eucharist, but around 1525 demand to hear the Word of God? No one has produced a plausible answer to this question, much less an adequate one.'[111] This chapter makes no claims to have solved Blickle's conundrum. Questions of deep-rooted motivation in religious conversion are individually opaque, and collectively present a kaleidoscope of shifting interpretative patterns. What is asserted here, however, is that for those who did follow this path, the sense of undergoing a profound change, of experiencing a 'conversion', and of being able to rationalise and, to an extent, systematise that experience, was a profoundly important aspect of a new religious and social existence. It was perhaps the most significant factor giving shape to an emergent 'Protestantism', in the years before that phenomenon found either institutional structures or an agreed set of descriptive labels.

In a classic study of conversion in the classical and early Christian world, A. D. Nock wrote that 'even when the fact of conversion appears wholly sudden and not led up to by a gradual process of gaining conviction, even when the convert may in all good faith profess that the beliefs which have won his sudden assent are new to him, there is a

---

[110] W. R. D. Jones, *William Turner* (1988), 9.

[111] Cited by R. N. Swanson, 'The Pre-Reformation Church', *The Reformation World*, ed. Andrew Pettegree (2000), 9.

background of concepts to which a stimulus can give new life'.[112] This observation certainly applies to the patterns of evangelical conversion we have noted under Henry VIII. Early evangelicals were formed in a religious culture which esteemed and espoused conversion as an ideal of Christian life. Nock also observed, with respect to the conversion of Augustine, that it did not represent progression in a continuous line: 'it is like a chemical process in which the addition of a catalytic agent produces a reaction for which all the elements were already present'.[113] In early Tudor England that catalytic agent was the solifidian theology of the Continental reformers and their English followers. The characteristic evangelical conversion was the powerful synthesis of a profound yearning for personal religious renewal, with a plausible theological explanation of how that yearning could be made effectual within the subjective experience of conversion itself. Historians who work with the phenomenon of religion in early modern England seem sometimes to want to keep the theology and sociology of the topic apart, like white and noncolourfast garments in the wash-cycles of meaningful historical explanation. But in this case we should perhaps let the colours run together. The 'conversion experience' of early English evangelicals was a dye finely compounded of social, cultural *and* theological pigments, and it made an indelible mark on the appearance of a distinctive Protestant identity.

[112] A. D. Nock, *Conversion: The Old and the New in Religion from Alexander the Great to Augustine of Hippo* (Oxford, 1933), 8.
[113] Ibid., 266.

CHAPTER 2

The friars in the English Reformation

Richard Rex

On first being made aware of the furore arising from the novel ideas of Martin Luther, Pope Leo X is notoriously reputed to have dismissed the whole business as 'a quarrel among friars'. If he did, he should have known better. He had seen his native city thrown into turmoil for a decade by the preaching of a friar, Girolamo Savonarola. For all the depth of the rhetorical resources available to the 'antifraternal' tradition, the friars remained the dominant force in preaching, embedded in the social structures, especially the urban structures, of the later Middle Ages.[1] Indeed, the place of the friars in popular satire and ribaldry is sufficient testimony to their importance in popular culture. Chaucer and Masaccio had a sounder sense of the role of the friars in their world than many a modern historian who barely mentions them. Given their enormous influence in the late medieval Church, there was no reason to assume that their quarrels would remain confined to the cloister or the quadrangle.

The history of the friars in England on the eve of the Reformation has yet to be written. Although the suppression of the mendicant orders in 1538–9, and the consequent dispersal of their libraries and destruction of their archives (not to mention their art and architecture), have deprived us of much source material, there remains a great deal in episcopal registers, wills and elsewhere to help us form some estimate of their place in English society. The mendicant houses at Oxford and Cambridge were evidently flourishing. There was a steady stream of friars taking theology degrees in the first fifty years of Tudor rule, and the ordination lists of the nearby dioceses (Ely, Lincoln, London and Salisbury) show us an even larger number of friars who spent time studying in the university towns without proceeding to degrees. (Friars did not take arts degrees – a

---

[1] For some perceptive discussion of this point, and references to further reading, see Geoffrey Dipple, *Antifraternalism and Anticlericalism in the German Reformation: Johann Eberlin von Günzburg and the campaign against the friars* (Aldershot, 1996), especially 4–6, 18–36, 212.

provision designed to prevent them from competing with secular masters in basic university teaching – but a very high proportion of them were certainly educated to BA standard.) John Bale's *Catalogus* shows us that the friars remained intellectually productive, while the antiquarian and bibliographical collections of John Leland confirm that their libraries were still valuable.[2] By the 1520s the impact of humanist learning was being felt in mendicant education: Robert Barnes and John Bale were both accomplished humanists.

Nor was the impact of the friars restricted to the realm of higher education. A sample of wills from almost any town which boasted a house of friars will soon reveal that mendicants continued to enjoy the support of their local communities, while rare indeed is the will of a nobleman or knight which does not extend its generosity to a bevy of convents and priories in nearby and even in distant towns. Among the papers of Thomas Lord Darcy is a fascinating draft of a letter to a house of Observant Franciscans placing a contract for hundreds of masses for recently deceased noblemen.[3] Surviving lists of the tombs in the London Greyfriars show that, for the aristocracy, burial among the friars was still a mark of social status as well as of devotion.[4] Dame Maude Parr (mother of Katherine), who died in September 1532, was granted burial in the London Blackfriars, beside her late husband, as she had requested in her will.[5] The household accounts of the Lestrange family of Hunstanton show regular donations to friars.[6] Those episcopal registers which record the granting of licences to preach show that senior friars (often the priors or wardens of houses, who were usually theology graduates) were customarily licensed to preach throughout a diocese.[7] When Sir John Markham reported to Thomas Cromwell in the early 1530s on the slanderous preaching of an Observant Franciscan in Newark, he warned

---

[2] John Bale, *Scriptorum Illustrium Maioris Brytanniae Catalogus* (2 vols., Basle, 1557). For the relevant extracts from Leland, and other material on mendicant libraries, see *The Friars' Libraries*, ed. K. W. Humphreys (1990). I owe this reference to the kindness of James Carley.

[3] *LP* XII (ii) 186 (22).

[4] C. L. Kingsford, *The Grey Friars of London* (Aberdeen, 1915), 70–144 ('De monumentis').

[5] For her will, dated 20 May 1529, see *Wills from Doctors' Commons*, ed. J. G. Nichols and J. Bruce (Camden Society o.s. 83, 1853), 9–20. In addition, she left legacies to all of the houses of friars in both London and Northampton, and £100 to the English Observant Franciscans.

[6] D. Gurney, 'Extracts from the Household and Privy Purse Accounts of the Lestranges of Hunstanton, from A.D. 1519 to A.D. 1578', *Archaeologia* 25 (1834), 411–569, and especially 419 (1519), 474 (1526), 538 (1533).

[7] See for example the licence of 15 April 1520 allowing John Smith STP, of the Hereford Franciscans, to preach throughout the diocese of Hereford. See *The Register of Charles Bothe, Bishop of Hereford (1516–1535)*, ed. A. T. Bannister (Hereford, 1921), 76; also published as *Registrum Caroli Bothe, Episcopi Herefordensis* (Canterbury & York Society, vol. 28, 1921).

of the great credit which the friars still had with the common people.[8]
Many friars' churches housed popular images or relics: for example, Our
Lady of Grace in the Cambridge Blackfriars.[9] Letters of confraternity
(which gave donors a share in the spiritual blessings of a house) remained
a desirable commodity, and the friars were still kept busy with the hearing
of confessions. Recruitment was buoyant into the 1530s, especially in the
newest of the mendicant orders in England, the Observant Franciscans.
Their seven houses were the only new 'religious' foundations (in the technical sense of monastic or mendicant foundations) of any consequence
since the reign of Henry V. Henry VIII's reign saw the English houses
erected into an independent province, and they were buzzing with devotion and learning by the 1520s. In short, the friars remained a force in
English religious life.

The significant role of the friars in the Reformation has been acknowledged ever since Leo X made his laconic observation. Many of the
urban preachers who planted the seeds of Reformation in the cities of
Germany and Switzerland were friars who abandoned their vows under
the liberating inspiration of the new gospel.[10] And it was among the friars
that the evangelical message found some of its earliest followers in Italy,
France and the Netherlands. The protomartyrs of the Protestant Reformation were a pair of Austin Friars from Brussels.[11] In England, as was
noted some time ago by Geoffrey Baskerville, the friars were likewise
at the forefront of the Reformation.[12] Robert Barnes, the Cambridge
Augustinian, was among the very first to embrace its teachings. Barnes
was, famously, converted to some form of evangelical doctrine in 1524,
with the result that he preached a controversial sermon in Cambridge a
little before Christmas, was convened before an ecclesiastical tribunal in
the New Year, and was obliged to recant and perform a public penance in
February.[13] His local influence within his order seems in turn to have led
to a flurry of evangelical activism among the Austin Friars of Cambridge
(including Miles Coverdale and Thomas Cambridge) and of Stoke by

---

[8] *LP* VI 1664.

[9] R. C. Finucane, *Miracles and Pilgrims* (1977), 206, referring to *LP* XIII (ii) 224.

[10] Robert Scribner, *The German Reformation* (1986), 21. See also Dipple, *Antifraternalism*, 1, for apostate Franciscans.

[11] Brad Gregory, *Salvation at Stake: Christian Martyrdom in Early Modern Europe* (Cambridge, MA, 1999), 1, 139, 145.

[12] G. Baskerville, *English Monks and the Suppression of the Monasteries* (1937), 236: 'It was among the friars that the "new learning" spread fastest and furthest.'

[13] Richard Rex, 'The early impact of Reformation theology at Cambridge University, 1521–1547', *Reformation and Renaissance Review* 2 (1999), 43–50.

Clare in Suffolk.[14] Recalling his controversy with Barnes in 1540 (which led to the friar's execution), Stephen Gardiner, bishop of Winchester, an acute observer of the English political and ecclesiastical scene, was perhaps the first to point out the role of the friars in the English Reformation. Shrewdly striking first against Catholicism, Gardiner described how, in the bad old days, indulgences were peddled to the people in order to distract them from genuinely good works, and how, in this enterprise, 'the devil used friars for his ministers'. He then went on to argue that, since the suppression of both indulgences and friars, the devil had gone one better, offering heaven by faith alone with no good works at all – an enterprise now promoted chiefly by ministers affecting to call themselves 'brethren', 'amonges whom be some of those that were friars'.[15]

The religious order in which evangelical teachings made their most striking early impact, however, was the one we have already noted as being perhaps the most vigorous in England: the Observant Franciscans. This should not surprise us. Interest in the latest currents of religious opinion is likely to have been found not among those who were disenchanted with the Church but among those who were most zealous for reform within it. What made the Reformation successful was not the support (if any) it received from deviants and the marginalised, but the support it received from the established elites in Church and state. The Observant John Rix or Ryckes, for example, though advanced in years, was drawn to the light of the new gospel in the mid-1520s, and composed under its influence a mildly evangelical tract, *The Ymage of Loue* (1525) which rapidly earned ecclesiastical censure.[16] It is not known whether Cardinal Wolsey's controversial visitation of the London Observants earlier that year had anything to do with suspicions about their doctrinal purity.[17] But it was probably also around this time that two Observant friars, Jerome Barlow and William Roy, fled the country to join William Tyndale on the Continent. Roy was eventually burned in Portugal in 1531.[18] Ryckes subsequently dedicated to Thomas Cromwell a translation of a work by the German evangelical Otto Brunfels.[19] And Jerome Barlow may well be the William Barlow whom Thomas More induced to

[14] Baskerville, *English Monks*, 236, for Stoke by Clare. For Coverdale and Cambridge, *AM* (1563), 601.

[15] J. A. Muller, *Stephen Gardiner and the Tudor Reaction* (1926), 86, citing from the bishop's apologia, *A Declaration of suche true articles as George Joye hath gone about to confute as false* (1546).

[16] STC 21471.5. See also Bale, *Catalogus*, ii. 102–3.

[17] For the visitation, in January 1525, see Peter Gwyn, *The King's Cardinal: the rise and fall of Thomas Wolsey* (1990), 276.

[18] *AM* (1563), 491.   [19] STC 421.17.

recant and publish A *Dialogue Describing the Original Ground of these Lutheran Faccions*, but who became a leading evangelical later in the 1530s.[20]

Preaching was the main trade of the friars, or at least of the better educated among them. It is doubtful whether every friar was equipped to preach, but it is a fair guess that almost all the priors or wardens (heads) of houses were. Many of this class were university educated, with baccalaureates or doctorates in theology. Typical among them was Dr William Duffield, warden of the Shrewsbury Greyfriars, who was more than once paid by the Shrewsbury town council for preaching.[21] Robert Barnes and John Bale are simply the best known of those friars who, after adopting the new doctrines, put their talents and training to fresh use. Having fled abroad in the later 1520s, Barnes was welcomed back into the English fold after the break with Rome, and was a prominent evangelical preacher. Indeed, it was his pulpit controversy with Stephen Gardiner in Lent 1540 which propelled him to the stake.[22] When John Bale was sent to the north to preside over the Carmelite community in Doncaster, he began to preach against certain aspects of the cult of the saints (perhaps provoked by the popularity of the cult of the image of Our Lady in the town), and was promptly confronted from the Franciscan pulpit by the warden of the Doncaster Greyfriars, Dr Thomas Kirkham. Kirkham won the contest, in that Bale was summoned before Archbishop Edward Lee and soon departed the diocese, while Kirkham was still there at the closure of his house in 1538.[23] But Bale also preached widely in his native East Anglia.[24] Other preaching friars who went over to the Reformation

---

[20] The identification was challenged by E. G. Rupp, *Studies in the Making of the English Protestant Tradition* (Cambridge, 1947), 62–72, and in *The Work of William Barlowe, including Bishop Barlowe's Dialogue on the Lutheran Factions*, ed. A. M. McLean (Sutton Courtenay, 1983), 169–77. However, the identification is forcefully, and to my mind convincingly, defended by G. H. Duffield (ibid., 178–80) and his views were accepted by J. H. Fines, A *Biographical Register of Early English Protestants, c. 1525–1558* (2 unpaginated vols., unpublished typescript, 1981–1985). 'Jerome' may have been a name taken upon joining the Observant Franciscans, in which case he might have returned to the 'William' of his christening upon leaving the order.

[21] *The Manuscripts of Shrewsbury and Coventry Corporations. Fifteenth Report of the Historical Manuscripts Commission, Appendix, Part X* (1899), records of Shrewsbury Corporation, 32–4. See also *BRUO*, 178.

[22] Muller, *Stephen Gardiner*, 84–92. For his preaching in Worcester diocese, see Susan Wabuda, '"Fruitful Preaching" in the Diocese of Worcester: Bishop Hugh Latimer and his Influence, 1535–1539', *Religion and the English People, 1500–1640*, ed. E. J. Carlson (Kirksville, MO, 1998), 61.

[23] A. G. Dickens, *Lollards and Protestants in the Diocese of York 1509–1558* (Oxford, 1959), 141–3 (where Kirkham is called Kirkby). For Kirkham see *BRUO* and Fines, *Biographical Register*. See also Richard Rex, 'John Bale, Geoffrey Downes and Jesus College', *JEH* 49 (1998), 490–1; 'A catalogue of the deeds of surrender', Appendix II of the *Eighth Report of the Deputy Keeper of the Public Records* (1847), 19. For Bale's licences to preach in the dioceses of London (1531) and York (1534), see L. P. Fairfield, *John Bale: Mythmaker for the English Reformation* (West Lafayette, in, 1976), 31–2.

[24] See *LP* XI 111; XII (i) 40, 230, 307.

cause have left less obvious traces in the historical record, but still enough for us to see that their role was important. The aptly named Paul Luther, warden of the Greyfriars of Ware, was in trouble in 1529 for preaching against the excesses and abuses of the cult of the saints.[25] Robert Ward BD, a Cambridge Dominican, was indicted for his tendentious preaching in March 1535, but wrote to Cromwell in his own defence, denouncing the mendicant orders in general and voicing his hopes of release from his order.[26] His wish soon came true, for he was secularised on 17 July 1535.[27]

It was with the Henrician assault on the monastic life in the later 1530s that the full impact of the Reformation upon the friars became apparent. With the transfer of the papal dispensing power to the archbishop of Canterbury's Faculty Office, requests from friars for release from their vows were handled and recorded by Cranmer's staff. In the two or three years preceding the suppression of the friaries (which began in earnest in autumn 1538), more than a hundred friars were licensed to abandon the mendicant life for that of the secular priesthood. While it would be simplistic to conclude that all these men were devoted to the cause of Reformation, it is clear that with very few exceptions they were not men for whom their vows retained much appeal. One of the few was Anthony Browne, once an Observant Franciscan, who transferred to the Norwich Franciscans when the Observants were closed down in 1534, and in 1538 petitioned to be allowed to live as a hermit – a move of a kind which would have been easily granted even before the Reformation, representing as it did a transfer to a more demanding state of life. Browne's commitment to the old ways which were represented by both strict observance and the eremitical life is perhaps best illustrated by his death shortly afterwards; he was executed in Norwich for denying Henry VIII's supremacy over the Church of England.[28] On the whole, though, such friars as were out of sympathy with Henrician policy and anxious to maintain a mendicant lifestyle are unlikely to have sought dispensations from Cranmer. No doubt some of the requests for release originated either in despair at the sudden collapse of alms which the friars experienced in the 1530s (as public confidence in both the security of church property and the value of devotional expenditure was undermined) or else in the welcome opportunity of escape for those who had undertaken, or been

[25] *AM*, 1040.
[26] See *LP* VIII 625 for Ward's justification of his sermon at Mistley (Essex) on 31 March 1535, and VIII 626 (Ward to Cromwell, no date) about another controversial sermon of his.
[27] *FOR*, 30.
[28] *FOR*, 135; *LP* XIII (ii) 34, and cf. *Original Letters, Illustrative of the English Reformation*, ed. H. Ellis (11 vols., 1825–46), 1st series, ii. 85–9.

committed to, the religious life with little choice or little knowledge of what it entailed.[29] Yet perhaps the majority of these petitions came from those whose own confidence in the spiritual standing of the mendicant life had been shattered by the polemics of evangelical reformers against 'salvation by works' and 'human traditions'.

Many of the dispensed friars certainly were active evangelicals, and, while leaving their traditional religious life behind them, retained their vocation to preach. Indeed, they preached with all the fervour of the converted against much of what their previous careers had been dedicated to building up. Dr John Vyall, warden of the Bedford Greyfriars, appeared before Bishop Longland of Lincoln to answer for his preaching in 1535, and Longland formally banned him from preaching on 11 March 1536. We do not know precisely what his offences were, but we can make some educated guesses on the basis of his future career. A couple of months later he was secularised by Cranmer's Faculty Office, and soon afterwards Cranmer collated him to the rectory of Hayes in Middlesex. In 1542 Cranmer collated him to the Canterbury peculiar and early Reformation hothouse of Hadleigh in Suffolk, which he held until his death in 1544.[30] An Austin Friar named Francis Eliot was among the evangelical preachers stirring things up at Rye in 1536.[31] Another Augustinian, Thomas Cambridge, dispensed on 23 July 1536, was presumably the Cambridge who took a BD at Cambridge University in 1526, and was accounted by Foxe a disciple of his prior, Robert Barnes.[32] A warden of the Austin Friars of Northampton, named John Goodwin, had secured his dispensation and was preaching sacramentarian heresy in the town by 1538, supported by a local Dominican, Stephen Wilson, who had not yet left his order.[33] John Madowell, a former London Blackfriar, went on

---

[29] David Knowles observes that many mendicant houses were described by the royal agents who closed them down in late 1538 as wretchedly poor, but adds that this poverty should not be thought to have been their normal state. See *The Religious Orders in England* (3 vols., Cambridge, 1948–59), iii. 360, 364–6.

[30] *BRUO*, 596; *FOR*, 55. *LP* VII 665 records that John Vyall subscribed to the oath of succession as warden of Bedford on 5 May 1534: *Lincoln Diocese Documents*, ed. A. Clark, EETS o.s. 149 (1914), 195. Vyall's connection with Hadleigh was first brought to my attention by John Craig; for more on the early Reformation in Hadleigh, see his 'Reformers, conflict, and revisionism: the Reformation in sixteenth-century Hadleigh', *Historical Journal* 42 (1999), 1–23 (although Vyall is not mentioned therein).

[31] *LP* XI 1424.

[32] *FOR*, 64. See above, note 14. For his degree, see *Grace Book B, Part II*, ed. Mary Bateson (Cambridge, 1905), 130.

[33] Edward Peacock, 'Extracts from Lincoln Episcopal Visitations in the 15th, 16th and 17th Centuries', *Archaeologia* 48 (1885), 264–6, cited in Baskerville, *English Monks*, 237. 'Catalogue of deeds of surrender', 33, records the surrender of Northampton Austin Friars, with Goodwin

to serve as chaplain to Nicholas Shaxton at Salisbury, where his preaching helped divide the city in the later 1530s, before Shaxton's eventual resignation.[34] John Scory, a rising Dominican scholar at Cambridge in the 1530s, was soon putting his talents to new use after the suppression of the priory in 1539. By 1541 he was a chaplain to Cranmer, and was appointed as one of the Six Preachers in the refounded cathedral chapter at Canterbury.[35] The Dominican prior of Winchester, James Cosyn BD, was in trouble early in 1536 for preaching against such ceremonies as holy water and blessed bread. Appearing before Cromwell, he was not only vindicated, but licensed to preach and dispensed from his habit.[36]

John Barrett, a Carmelite and a close contemporary of John Bale, was the first member of his order to seek a licence of secularisation from Cranmer's Faculty Office (9 June 1535), just a couple of years after taking his Cambridge doctorate in theology.[37] He seems to have found employment soon enough. When the monastic cathedral of Norwich surrendered itself into Henry's hands in 1538 (prior to its refoundation as a secular cathedral), Barrett was employed as the community's theology lecturer. This does not mean that he had become a monk. Presumably Barrett was Cromwell's nominee at Norwich, intended to counteract the conservative influence of the successive bishops of Norwich, Richard Nix and William Rugge. Barrett remained at the new cathedral in the same capacity, was granted appointment for life in 1542, and ended as a canon of Norwich, leaving Protestant manuscripts which still survive in Corpus Christi Library.[38] Another convert was the Protestant martyr John Laurence, burned at Colchester on 29 March 1555. John Foxe tells

as prior, on 28 October 1538; ibid., 34, records the surrender of the Blackfriars, including Wilson, on 20 October 1538. Their dispensations are both recorded at 2 January 1539 (*FOR*, 180), which does not tally with the visitation account. Goodwin presumably had an earlier, and unrecorded, dispensation. The *Faculty Office Registers* do furnish occasional cases where one man received more than one such dispensation, once individually and once subsequently with his whole house.

34 Madowell was in fact a Scot by origin. His dispensation of 1 March 1536 is in *FOR*, 46. See also Fines, *Biographical Register*. There is another article to be written on Scottish friars in the Reformation. Fines lists several Scottish friars, many of whom fled to take up an active ministry in England.

35 'Catalogue of deeds of surrender', 14; Fines, *Biographical Register*; *BRUO*, 285–6.

36 *LP* X 357 notes his indictment for his preaching on 26 February 1536. *LP* X 512 forwards both the indictment and Cosyn himself to Cromwell. On 31 March 1536 William Basing (prior of Winchester Cathedral) interceded for him with Cromwell (*LP* X 588). Within a month Cromwell had discharged Cosyn and licensed him to preach (*LP* X 723). For Cosyn's dispensation for a secular habit, see *FOR*, 59.

37 *FOR*, 27. For his degree, see *Grace Book Γ*, ed. W. G. Searle (Cambridge, 1908), 274.

38 For his career at Norwich Cathedral, see Ralph Houlbrooke, 'Refoundation and reformation, 1536–1628', *Norwich Cathedral: Church, City and Diocese, 1096–1996*, ed. I. Atherton et al. (1996), 510, 521, 535.

us that he was a professed Dominican who had been ordained eighteen years before (i.e. in 1537). This means he is almost certainly to be identified with the John Laurence who was among the Dominicans of Sudbury at its suppression in December 1538. His position as last on the list of eleven names gives an impression of his relative youthfulness which sits well with Foxe's account. Laurence, however, presumably affiliated himself with evangelical doctrines after, rather than before, leaving the religious life.[39] Hugh Glasier BD, last warden of the Greenwich Franciscans (formerly Observants), was sufficiently in tune with the new ways to earn Cranmer's patronage, securing a prebend at Canterbury Cathedral in 1542. He is said to have been 'an eager man for Reformation' in the reign of Edward VI, preaching against Lent at Paul's Cross. However, Glasier never married, and he enjoyed the patronage of Mary Tudor in the 1550s, eventually dying shortly before her, having ordered a profoundly traditional funeral monument with the figure of a priest engraved upon it.[40]

One of the fascinating by-products of this investigation into the role of the friars in the English Reformation has been the discovery of how important Hugh Latimer was in the story. It is remarkable just how often the conversion of a preaching friar shows some connection with him. When he preached his notoriously controversial series of sermons in Bristol in 1533, he was at once answered by a team of local friars. Yet their leader, John Hilsey, soon came round to his way of thinking, and from 1535 enjoyed the favour of Thomas Cromwell because of his evangelical sympathies.[41] John Erley was another friar who fell under Latimer's spell. He was in trouble for evangelical preaching in Gloucestershire as early as 1533, when he was arrested on suspicion of being a disciple of Latimer. The latter's appointment as bishop of Worcester made both the county and the diocese safer for Erley, and he enjoyed the patronage and protection not only of the bishop but also of Thomas Cromwell and of the local evangelical notables Sir John Walsh and Sir Nicholas Poyntz.[42] As bishop, Latimer exerted an influence still more marked. He had a devastating impact upon the morale of the Worcester friars. John Joseph, the Franciscan warden in the town, was dispensed for a secular habit on 31 July 1536, and joined Latimer's team of preaching chaplains in that

---

[39] *AM* (1563), 1112; *FOR*, 162. There are several other men named John Laurence in the *Faculty Office Registers*, but the John Laurence of Sudbury (relatively near Colchester) is the only Dominican.
[40] *BRUO*, 234.   [41] *BRUO*, 289–90.
[42] Caroline Litzenberger, *The English Reformation and the Laity: Gloucestershire, 1540–1580* (Cambridge, 1997), 33, referring to *LP* VI 1192. See also Wabuda, '"Fruitful Preaching"', 55, 72.

diocese.[43] His predecessor, Dr Robert Knollys, who had been licensed to preach in the diocese in his capacity as warden of the Worcester Greyfriars on 4 March 1535, received his dispensation for a secular benefice on 20 July 1536.[44] Lawrence Thorold, another regular diocesan preacher, a rather older man and the former prior of the Worcester Dominicans, received his dispensation on the same day as Joseph.[45]

There are similar indications of Latimer's influence elsewhere in his diocese. The Franciscan friar Edward Large, who was dispensed on 20 September 1537, had been in trouble earlier in the year for preaching against traditional religious ceremonies, and was already serving a secular cure (which is probably why his dispensation does not attach him to any particular house). He fled the country in Mary's reign.[46] One can also speculate about Latimer's possible links with the Franciscan John Williams of Gloucester (who was secularised on 31 January 1537, and is almost certainly the John Williams BD who was deprived of benefices in Gloucester in 1554)[47] as well as with William Walton, once a Gloucester Dominican, who sought refuge abroad in the reign of Mary Tudor.[48] The Gloucester Blackfriars also held at its closure John Reynolds BD (who on 22 February 1528 had been licensed by the bishop of Hereford to preach in the Forest of Dean), another future Marian refugee,[49] and one John Hooper. While tradition makes the Protestant bishop John Hooper a former Cistercian monk, it is by no means impossible that he was in fact a former friar. His reputation as a preacher and his later appointment as bishop of Gloucester make the identification tempting.[50] Irrespective of that, Latimer's last and greatest triumph was over the warden of the

---

43 *BRUO*, 323; C. H. Garrett, *The Marian Exiles: A study in the Origins of Elizabethan Puritanism* (Cambridge, 1938), 201; *FOR*, 63; Wabuda, ' "Fruitful Preaching" ', 60, 73. The argument here about Latimer's influence on the friars of his diocese overlaps with Wabuda's general argument about his influence on the diocese through preaching.

44 *BRUO*, 331; *FOR*, 63.

45 *BRUO*, 583, as 'Twyrewolde' (cf. ibid., 561, as 'Tayorcolde'); *FOR*, 63 (as Townerolde). As Lawrence Torolde BD, prior of Worcester OP, he was licensed to preach in Hereford diocese on 15 September 1528. See *Register of Charles Bothe*, 206.

46 Garrett, *Marian Exiles*, 216. For more on Large, see Wabuda, ' "Fruitful Preaching" ', 66; Baskerville, *English Monks*, 238.

47 *FOR*, 85; *BRUO*, 630, which notes that Williams was licensed to preach in Worcester diocese on 16 February 1540 (after Latimer's resignation).

48 Litzenberger, *English Reformation and the Laity*, 89; *FOR*, 162; Garrett, *Marian Exiles*, 429.

49 Garrett, *Marian Exiles*, 270–71; *Register of Charles Bothe*, 201; *BRUO*, 477.

50 *FOR*, 162. However, the name was far from uncommon, and there are several John Hoopers in the *Faculty Office Registers*: the same page gives us a Bristol Carmelite of the same name. See also *BRUO*, 296–7, which makes the customary identification with a Cistercian of that name. But there seems to be nothing more than seventeenth-century tradition behind that identification, and Hooper's subsequent Gloucester connection perhaps renders a mendicant origin more plausible.

Exeter Franciscans, John Cardmaker, in 1537. He was reportedly converted by hearing Latimer preach in Exeter in 1537, and the date of his licence to dress as a secular priest (1 December 1537) offers some corroboration for the story.[51] Cardmaker went on to figure as one of the leading evangelical preachers in Edwardine London, and gave his life for his beliefs in 1555. It looks very much as though Latimer made a point of targeting mendicant preachers, and was frequently successful in winning them over.

While it is in general tendentious to draw conclusions about doctrinal affiliations from the marriages of priests in Edward VI's reign,[52] there is a case for seeing the marriages of former friars as indicative of a real move towards Protestantism. Friars took vows of celibacy, which differentiated them from secular priests, who were simply prohibited from marrying by Catholic canon law. Thus essentially conservative parish priests may well have found marriage an attractive option when English law made this possible in 1549. But for the ex-religious to marry was still to break a vow; this was easier perhaps for those who had ceased to believe that vows were 'good works' and had come to see the vow of celibacy, in particular, as impossible and presumptuous, an insupportable burden imposed upon the flesh by Antichrist in order to drive religious souls to despair. While this argument might apply equally well to monks, it is likely that the educational attainments of friars were in general higher. From the Catholic point of view, friars really should have known better. Moreover, many of the friars in this situation were graduate theologians. So when we find ex-friars deprived of church benefices on the grounds of marriage in Mary Tudor's reign, we are more likely than usual to be looking at men who had moved a considerable way towards Protestantism. Dr John Hardyman, last prior of the Cambridge Austin Friars, was soon ensconced in a London parish, and was prosecuted under the Act of Six Articles in 1540. In due course he married. He resigned a prebend at Lincoln late in 1553, but was given another at Westminster by Elizabeth in 1560.[53] In 1567 he was deprived of this on account of his iconoclastic excesses there. Guy Eton BD, a Plymouth Franciscan who had studied at Oxford, remained in the order until the dissolution

---

[51] Wabuda, '"Fruitful Preaching"', 54–55, notes Latimer's conversion of Cardmaker. For Cardmaker's dispensation, see *FOR*, 116. For the dating of the episode, and indeed for my knowledge of it, I am indebted to Tom Freeman.

[52] For a balanced discussion of this vexed question, see Helen L. Parish, *Clerical Marriage and the English Reformation: Precedent, Policy and Practice* (Aldershot, 2000), 198–217.

[53] Fines, *Biographical Register*, as Hardiman.

in 1538, soon found a benefice in Gloucestershire, and eventually became chaplain to Bishop Hooper. Deprived for marriage in 1554, he went into exile, returning in 1559 to serve as archdeacon of Gloucester.[54] Dr John Hurleston, Carmelite prior of Chester in 1537–8, was instituted to a London benefice (St Bride's) in 1552, and was deprived for marriage in 1554.[55] Dr Kirkham, who had opposed Bale at Doncaster in 1534, was deprived of his London benefice (St Martin's Outwich) on the same grounds in 1555. The former Dominican Clement Thredar BD was a licensed preacher under Edward VI, and was deprived of his benefices in 1555, although he soon found his way back into a parish.[56] Richard Clay, the last Dominican prior of Thetford, was recorded in Mary's reign as having contracted marriage.[57] An ex-friar named John Law (perhaps the former Oxford Dominican John Low), by now rector of St Margaret Moses, London, was one of three friars who did penance for marrying on 4 November 1554.[58]

The relatively sophisticated administrative structures of the mendicant orders, and the higher levels of educational attainment found among them, meant that ex-friars could make valuable contributions to the implementation and administration of the Reformation, whether or not they underwent any personal conversion to an evangelical theological agenda. Several of them rose to senior positions in the Reformation hierarchy.[59] The Augustinian George Browne found that his earlier assistance in the king's divorce had put him in pole position in the race for preferment once the king had assumed headship of the church. Together with the last Dominican provincial, John Hilsey, he conducted a visitation of the English friaries with a view to securing their assent to the royal supremacy. Browne became archbishop of Dublin, and Hilsey succeeded John Fisher at Rochester.[60] In 1537 John Hilsey appointed another

---

54 Fines, *Biographical Register, FOR*, 167; *BRUO*, 195; Garrett, *Marian Exiles*, 181–2, where he appears as 'Heton'.

55 For his position in 1537, see *LP* XII (ii) 597; *BRUO*, 306.

56 For Kirkham, see above, note 23. For Thredar, see *BRUO*, 565–66. Thredar was somewhat fluid in his affiliations: he had served the conservative William Rugge, bishop of Norwich, as chaplain in the 1540s.

57 G. Baskerville, 'Married clergy and pensioned religious in Norwich diocese, 1555', *EHR* 48 (1933), 53.

58 Susan Brigden, *London and the Reformation* (Oxford, 1989), 570. See also *FOR*, 145.

59 Knowles, *Religious Orders*, iii. 496, lists friars who became bishops after 1533. He omits Browne, and erroneously lists the Dominican John Hodgkins as an Augustinian.

60 Brendan Bradshaw, 'George Browne, First Reformation Archbishop of Dublin, 1536–1554', *JEH* 21 (1970), 301–26, emphasises that Browne's role in the Reformation was more that of a typical Tudor administrator than of an evangelical convert.

learned Dominican, Maurice Griffith (an Oxford BD who spoke against papal primacy at the order's chapter around 1535) to the archdeaconry of Rochester, which he held until 1554, when, apparently having undergone another change of heart, he was promoted bishop of the diocese.[61] Former Dominicans did particularly well in the scramble for preferment. Richard Ingworth, prior of King's Langley, assisted Hilsey in the visitation of 1535. A few years later, having himself by now been secularised, he played a major role in securing the final surrenders of the friaries, and wrote to Cromwell assuring him that he had lost his 'friar's heart' two years before abandoning his habit.[62] His reward was appointment as suffragan to the archbishop of Canterbury.[63] Under Queen Mary he certainly showed no inclination to take up his former habit. But he was more than keen to participate in the trial of his erstwhile superior, Cranmer. So perhaps Cromwell's suspicion about his friar's heart was nearer the truth than, at the time, Ingworth cared to admit. Dr John Hodgkins, another former Dominican provincial, may have paid more than lip-service to evangelical ideas in order to gain the favour of Thomas Cromwell in the later 1530s, having fallen upon hard times after the closure of his priory at Sudbury. He became suffragan bishop of Bedford and later a canon of St Paul's, and was deprived for marriage in 1554, before being restored to his various dignities under Elizabeth.[64] John Scory became bishop of Rochester in 1551, transferring to Chichester in 1552. He took refuge at Emden in Mary's reign before returning to spend a quarter of a century as bishop of Hereford under Elizabeth.[65] The Augustinian Miles Coverdale went on to become bishop of Exeter (1551–3).[66] Dr John Bird, the former Carmelite provincial, became bishop of Bangor (1539–41) and then Chester (1541–54) under Henry VIII. Having taken a wife under Edward VI, he was deprived of his benefices under Mary, but was in due course restored under Elizabeth.[67] Gilbert Berkeley, a member of the York Franciscans at the suppression, was deprived of his benefices under Mary, but went on to be appointed bishop of Bath and Wells by Elizabeth I.[68]

[61] *LP* VIII 472; *BRUO*, 248. See *FOR*, 11, for Griffith's licence for a secular habit, 8 September 1535.

[62] Knowles, *Religious Orders*, iii. 361, citing *Three Chapters of Letters Relating to the Suppression of Monasteries*, ed. T. Wright (Camden Society o.s. 26, 1843), 197. For Ingworth's assistance to Hilsey, see *LP* IX 373.

[63] *LP* XII (ii) 1311 (13).   [64] *LP* X 1235; *BRUO*, 291.

[65] 'Catalogue of deeds of surrender', 14; Fines, *Biographical Register*; Garrett, *Marian Exiles*, 285–6.

[66] Garrett, *Marian Exiles*, 132–4.

[67] C. H. Cooper and T. Cooper, *Athenae Cantabrigienses* (2 vols., Cambridge, 1838–61), i. 190–1.

[68] Garrett, *Marian Exiles*, 87.

Besides preaching and ecclesiastical administration, the third main field in which former friars could advance the Reformation cause was that of theological literature, both polemical and devotional. The contributions of Robert Barnes and John Bale, which hardly need to be recapitulated here, were far from alone. Miles Coverdale's contributions to the translation and publication of the English Bible make him a substantial figure in the literary history of English Protestantism, and he translated a variety of evangelical texts from German.[69] John Hilsey's Primer, compiled in the late 1530s, promoted a mildly evangelical piety.[70] Lewis Wager, a London Franciscan who abandoned his habit in 1536, imitated John Bale in composing popular plays as vehicles for the new doctrines. Wager's *Mary Magdalene*, which was printed in Edward VI's reign, is notable for its unmistakable debts to Calvin's *Institution of the Christian Religion*.[71]

One of Thomas Cromwell's most effective popular propagandists, William Gray, may perhaps have been a friar. Gray is famous chiefly for the *Fantasy of Idolatry*, a punchy and catchy ballad first published in 1538 as an accompaniment to Cromwell's obliteration of England's leading pilgrimage shrines. Gray threw himself into the religious pamphlet war which broke out in London over the next few years, offering vigorous defences of obedience to the king and the cause of the 'word of God'. Nothing certain is known of Gray before the appearance of the *Fantasy of Idolatry* in 1538. He has been conjecturally identified with a monk of Abbotsbury in Dorset who wrote to Cromwell informing against his abbot in 1535, but as that Gray was still a member of the house at its dissolution in 1539, this cannot possibly be correct.[72] Intriguingly, one of the friars who secured early release from his order before the general suppression of the mendicants was one William Gray, a Dominican from Ipswich. As his secularisation was issued on 6 April 1538, almost a year before the closure of his house, this William Gray was probably sympathetic

---

[69] See *Writings and Translations of Myles Coverdale*, and *Remains of Myles Coverdale*, both ed. G. Pearson (PS, 1844, 1846).

[70] H. C. White, *The Tudor Books of Private Devotion* (Wisconsin, 1951), 103–8.

[71] P. W. White, *Theatre and Reformation: Protestantism, Patronage and Playing in Tudor England* (Cambridge, 1993), 80–7.

[72] E. W. Dormer, *Gray of Reading: a sixteenth-century controversialist and ballad-writer* (Reading, 1923), 17. This is corrected by *The House of Commons 1509–1558*, ed. S. T. Bindoff (3 vols., London, 1982), ii. 256–7. The fact that the author of the *Fantasy* was a married man in the 1540s is not incompatible with the hypothesis advanced here. If he was a novice, he would not have taken binding vows, and if he had not been ordained to major orders, then he would not be forbidden from marriage by canon law. There were several novices still found in mendicant houses during the suppressions of 1538–9.

to reform.[73] Ipswich was a nervecentre for the early Reformation, and it was shortly after Gray's release that the shrine of Our Lady of Ipswich was taken down.[74] The religious interests and knowledge manifested by the balladeer William Gray, along with his evident popular touch, make a training in the Order of Preachers a plausible hypothesis for his early career. The friars were adept at exploiting scholarship to meet the demands of popular culture.

The argument so far can be summarised with some tentative statistics. We can identify perhaps 1,100 friars active in the 1530s, through surrender documents, dispensations at the suppression, university records and stray references (there must have been many more). An appreciable number of these men became Protestants, and that percentage is still more substantial if the statistics are confined to the priors and the theologians. There were around 200 mendicant houses, and in addition to the priors we know of many more theology graduates. Most of the evangelical friars known to us were recruited from this elite. Of a sample of perhaps 250 at the outside (we cannot identify all the priors), we know of at least twenty-five who went on to become evangelicals.[75] Ten per cent at such an early stage of the Reformation is probably a higher rate of affiliation to evangelical doctrines than can be found among any other easily identifiable group. Certainly there were more friars than monks among the early English Reformers, although there were more monks than friars in England. Affiliation to Reformation doctrines was also lower among the secular clergy as a whole than among the friars, although analysis of a more strictly comparable cohort (for example, theology graduates) might yield more comparable figures.

But no doubt the overwhelming majority of English friars remained conservative in their sympathies. This could simply be implicit, as in the case of Thomas Skevington, former warden of Nottingham Greyfriars; his entirely traditional will, dated 8 July 1540 and proved shortly afterwards, left his priestly kit to the Lady Chapel of St Peter's, Nottingham.[76]

---

[73] *FOR*, 128, 180.

[74] For the evangelical movement at Ipswich in the 1530s, see Diarmaid MacCulloch, *Suffolk and the Tudors* (Oxford, 1986), 160, 171, 174–5; and *A Reformation Rhetoric: Thomas Swynnerton's Tropes and Figures of Scripture*, ed. Richard Rex (Cambridge, 1999), 19–20. On 30 July 1538 Thomas Thacker informed Cromwell of the recent arrival of the image at Cromwell's London headquarters, the Austin Friars: *LP* XII (i) 1501.

[75] These statistics are very tentative. Gwyn, *King's Cardinal*, 275, notes two estimates for the number of friars in England on the eve of the Reformation: of 1500, proposed by Philip Hughes (Philip Hughes, *The Reformation in England* (1950) i. 70); and of 3000, proposed by David Knowles (*Religious Orders*, iii. 52).

[76] *Testamenta Eboracensia VI*, ed. J. Raine (Surtees Society 106, 1902), 98.

Other former friars kept their heads well down in the troubled mid-Tudor years, yet clearly preferred the old order. For example, John Crayford BD, last warden of the Newcastle Greyfriars, went on to serve as chaplain to the reformist Catholic Cuthbert Tunstall, bishop of Durham, and secured a canonry in the refounded cathedral there.[77] Another conservative bishop, Stephen Gardiner, also had a former friar, a man named Wygg, among his chaplains.[78] Dr John Hopton, prior of the Oxford Dominicans around 1530, went on to become chaplain to Mary Tudor, encouraging her in her resistance to the Book of Common Prayer under Edward VI. She made him bishop of Norwich (1554–8) when she came to the throne, and he showed an inquisitorial zeal against Protestants, bringing forty-six of them to the stake.[79]

In the 1520s and 1530s friars were habitually involved in the proceedings against the early English Reformers, especially outside the golden triangle of Oxford, Cambridge and London (within which there were usually plenty of well-educated secular priests to assist in heresy proceedings). The Dominican John de Coloribus and the Franciscan John Kington were among Oxford University's theological delegation despatched to London in 1521 to advise Henry VIII and Wolsey about Luther.[80] When Thomas Dusgate (alias Bennett) was hauled before an ecclesiastical court at Exeter around New Year 1531, he was engaged in debate by a team of local friars, including Gregory Bassett BD and Dr Edward Baskerville.[81] Thomas Bilney was subjected to similar treatment by the friars of Norwich at his second trial. John Bird, the prior provincial of the Carmelites; Dr William Call, the minister (i.e. provincial) of the Franciscans (who appeared in an equal but opposite capacity for the proceedings against Anthony Browne in 1538); John Hodgkins and Geoffrey Julles (Dominicans); and Dr John Stokes, warden of the Austin Friars, were all called in; and we have a lengthy record of a disputation between Bilney and John Bruisyard.[82] The Carmelite priors of both

77 Cooper and Cooper, *Athenae Cantabrigienses*, i. 70 for his career; *LP* XIV (ii) 724 for his position as Tunstall's chaplain.

78 *LP* XIV (i) 775.   79 *BRUO*, 298.

80 Richard Rex, 'The English Campaign against Luther in the 1520s', *Transactions of the Royal Historical Society*, 5th series 39 (1989), 87. De Coloribus was a member of the Truro Blackfriars when it surrendered on 22 September 1538, and was reckoned to have been a popular preacher. See A. L. Rowse, *Tudor Cornwall* (1941), 185–6. The surrender is not abstracted in 'Catalogue of deeds of surrender', but De Coloribus was also among those given their dispensations on 3 December 1538 (*FOR*, 167).

81 *AM*, 1038. I identify Foxe's 'Dr Bascauild' with Dr Edward Baskerville, who was warden of the Oxford Greyfriars when it surrendered in 1538 (*FOR*, 145).

82 *AM* (1563), 474–7 for the disputation with Bruisyard; 478b for Hodgkins, Call, Stokes and Bird; *AM*, 1010 for Julles. For Dr Call's role in the proceedings against Browne, see *LP* XIII (ii) 34.

London and York (Simon Clerkson BD) assisted at the trial for heresy of a lunatic named Cowbridge at Wycombe in 1538.[83] Perhaps it is not surprising that among those thus professionally obliged to deal with heresy, some were won over to the ideas they were supposed to refute and repress. There will always be the occasional Paul among the Pharisees. Clerkson became a licensed preacher under Henry VIII and married under Edward VI before being deprived of his benefices under Mary.[84] John Hilsey, later himself an evangelical, led the opposition to Latimer at Bristol in 1533. One of his successors as prior of Bristol, William Oliver, was reportedly an opponent of the divorce and the supremacy back in 1534, yet by 1537 was preaching against religious vows.[85] Dr Thomas Kirkham, who as warden of the Doncaster Franciscans and a licensed preacher in York diocese had spoken out against Bale in 1534, went on after the dissolution to serve as rector of St Martin's Outwich, London, and by 1549 was noted as a leading opponent of the mass. He preached against transubstantiation in 1550, and was deprived of his benefice for marriage in 1555.[86]

Resistance to the Reformation is most obvious in the more important, and better documented, orders: the Dominicans and the Franciscans. Edmund Harcock BD, prior of the Norwich Blackfriars, was informed against in 1535 when his preaching of the royal supremacy struck the Norwich authorities as too conservatively nuanced, and was again under suspicion in the wake of the Pilgrimage of Grace.[87] His conservatism was enduring. In Mary's reign he was noted for 'an honest and a catholic man' who had never married, and was licensed to preach by Mary, although he subscribed to the royal supremacy in 1559.[88] Dr Thomas Charnock was in trouble in 1534 for preaching in favour of the pope.[89] The Dominicans of Stamford (who included at least one BD) were delated

---

[83] *LP* XIII (i) 1434. For Cowbridge see *AM* (1563), 570; Margaret Bowker, *The Henrician Reformation: the Diocese of Lincoln under John Longland, 1521–1547* (Cambridge, 1981), 179–80.

[84] Dickens, *Lollards and Protestants*, 145–7.

[85] Martha C. Skeeters, *Community and Clergy: Bristol and the Reformation, c. 1530–c. 1570* (Oxford, 1993), 183–4. See *FOR*, 199 for his appearance on the list of the friars who were serving as confessors to the Dominican nuns at Dartford when it surrendered on 16 October 1539.

[86] Fines, *Biographical Register, BRUO*, 336.

[87] *LP* VIII 667. See also *LP* VII 694, Sir Roger Townshend to Cromwell, 20 May 1535; and VII 595, Ingworth to Cromwell, 1 May 1535 (both letters wrongly calendared in 1534). For later suspicions, see *LP* XII (i) 297.

[88] Baskerville, 'Married clergy and pensioned religious', 219. For his subscription, see Henry Gee, *The Elizabethan Clergy and the Settlement of Religion, 1558–1564* (Oxford, 1898), 112. As his will was proved in 1562, it is unlikely that his resignation of his benefice (St Michael Coslany, Norwich) in 1561 was a matter of conscience.

[89] *LP* VII 259; *BRUO*, 112.

to Cromwell in autumn 1535 for countering the preaching of a circle of evangelicals active in the town.[90] Dr Robert Buckenham, prior of the Cambridge Blackfriars, having already preached against Latimer as early as 1529, fled the country in 1534 (taking with him a confrère, probably one Richard Hargrave) rather than accept the royal supremacy.[91] Cranmer was soon complaining to Cromwell about the conservative sympathies of Buckenham's successor in Cambridge, William Oliver.[92] Other Dominican refugees included the prior of Newcastle, Dr Richard Marshall, who fled in 1536 and subsequently took the trouble to pen an apologia and appeal which he posted back to his brethren;[93] and another Dominican theologian and busy preacher, William Peryn (Oxford BD, 1530), who returned to England in the 1540s to serve as chaplain to Bishop Bonner in London, and to publish sermons defending traditional eucharistic doctrine. It was Peryn who presided over the London Blackfriars when it was briefly revived in the 1550s.[94] Dr John Pickering, prior of the Beverley Dominicans, was a ringleader in the Pilgrimage of Grace and was duly executed in 1537. He is remarkable for having composed one of the dissident ballads of the Pilgrims, beginning somewhat pretentiously, 'O faithful people of the Boreal region'.[95] But there is an interesting indication here that the friars retained their medieval sympathy with popular culture.

The Franciscans likewise furnished their share of opponents of the Reformation. Dr Robert Thyxtyll OFM was preaching against the new learning in Colchester in Lent 1534.[96] A Franciscan named Watts (William Watts) was accused by the Protestant ex-friar John Madowell of 'seditious' preaching at Salisbury in 1537, and two years later was preaching against Latimer in London.[97] Another Franciscan, John Arthur, was already being reported for stirring sedition (presumably regarding the king's divorce) as early as 1533, in Plymouth. In 1535 he was noted as preaching against innovations in Kent, and in 1537 he was arrested in

90 *LP* IX 611; Bowker, *Henrician Reformation*, 145.
91 Patrick Zutshi and Robert Ombres, 'The Dominicans in Cambridge, 1238–1538', *Archivum Fratrum Praedicatorum* 60 (1990), 345–8. I hazard the identification of Hargrave with Buckenham's colleague, mentioned in ibid. 345, note 139.
92 *LP* VII 308; cited in Zutshi and Ombres, 'Dominicans in Cambridge', 346–7.
93 *LP* X 594.
94 William Peryn, *Thre godlye and notable sermons, of the sacrament of the aulter* (1546); *BRUO*, 444. After being forced to recant in 1547, Peryn fled again, to return under Mary.
95 *LP* XII (i) 1021 (3).   96 *LP* VII 406; *BRUO*, 567.
97 *LP* XII (i) 746; *BRUO*, 611. See also *LP* XII (i) 755, 756, 824, 838 for further details of the furore around the pulpit conflict between Madowell and Watts. For his activity in London, see Brigden, *London and the Reformation*, 306. I identify Madowell's 'Watts' and Brigden's 'Dr Wattes' with the William Watts who took a Cambridge BD in 1533. See *Grace Book B, Part II*, 178; *Grace Book Γ*, 273.

Exeter on the orders of Cromwell.[98] Arthur's warden at Plymouth, Friar
Gawen (Gavin Jones), may have shared his views, for he was gaoled at
Launceston Castle later in 1533.[99] Five years later one 'Bachelor Gawen'
was among a group of London Franciscans implicated in seditious talk
about the king.[100] Peter Lawrence (alias Shefforde) and Giles Coventry
BD, two senior members of the Reading Franciscans, were in the Tower
of London late in 1539, implicated in the treasonous affairs of the late
abbot of Reading.[101] The monastic priory of Thetford paraded its religious preferences in its closing years by hiring a succession of heavyweight
conservative friars to preach in the town: Alexander Barclay, Edmund
Brygett, John Stokes and Peter Brinkley (all Franciscans except for Stokes,
an Augustinian).[102]

Among all the friars, it was members of the Observant Franciscans
who opposed Henry VIII's policies most promptly and most consistently,
and their resistance is so well-known as to require no more than brief
discussion. William Peto notoriously preached to Henry's face against
his divorce from Catherine of Aragon, and found it expedient to flee
the country soon afterwards, along with Friar Elstow.[103] Two Observant
wardens, Hugh Rich (of Richmond) and Richard Risby (of Canterbury),
were closely associated with the Holy Maid of Kent, and were executed
along with her on 20 April 1534.[104] And the Observants were prominent in the 'Aragonese' connection which supported Catherine's cause.
It was reported years afterwards that numerous friars had frequented
her household as confessors: Peto, Rich, Sebastian, Curson, Covert,
Robynson, Forest, Neswyk and others.[105] Many more seem to have fled
the country rather than accept Henry's changes.

The English province of the order was suppressed. The houses were
transferred to other orders (conventual Franciscans, or Augustinians),
and their members were dispersed, especially the troublemakers. Some

---

[98] *LP* VI 394; VIII 480; XII (ii) 557; *BRUO*, 14.

[99] *LP* VI 1503; *BRUO*, 322.

[100] *LP* XIII (i) 658. Gawen is presumably to be identified with Gavin Jones BD, a member of the
London house at its suppression in 1538 (*FOR*, 149).

[101] *LP* XIV (ii) 554. *FOR*, 150, notes their dispensations at the suppression of their house on
30 September 1538. See *BRUO*, 513, for Shefforde. *LP* XIV (ii) 613 is a diatribe against the
abbot of Reading which mentions both friars.

[102] Diarmaid MacCulloch, 'A Reformation in the balance: power struggles in the diocese of
Norwich, 1533–1553', *Counties and Communities: essays on East Anglian history*, ed. C. Rawcliffe
et al. (Norwich, 1996), 105.

[103] *LP* V 941.

[104] Richard Rex, 'The Execution of the Holy Maid of Kent', *Historical Research* 64 (1991), 216.

[105] *LP* XIV (i) 190.

of these were slow to learn their lesson. Gabriel Pecock, warden of Southampton, preached against the royal supremacy at Winchester on Passion Sunday 1534, and it took the mayor several days to bring him into custody because he was out on a preaching tour.[106] Hugh Payne's traditionalist preaching around Hadleigh in Suffolk attracted unfavourable attention from Cranmer and Cromwell in 1537.[107] He was shut up in the Marshalsea prison, and by early 1539 he had died there.[108] Sir Thomas Johnson, formerly Friar Bonaventure, was reported to have been involved in the Pilgrimage of Grace,[109] and Henry VIII instructed the Duke of Norfolk to arrest as many of the former Observants as he could.[110] Friar William Robynson was voicing somewhat implausible hopes in 1538 of the reestablishment of his order.[111] A former confessor of Queen Catherine, John Forest, earned the unenviable distinction of becoming the only man to be burned as a heretic in England on account of Catholic (as opposed to Lollard, Protestant or Anabaptist) beliefs.[112] That same year saw the execution for treason (denial of the royal supremacy) of another former Observant, Anthony Browne.[113]

But other orders also produced men who attempted to stem the tide of change. John Dryver, prior of the London Crutched Friars, was one such. As early as 1532 he was in trouble for describing Henry VIII as 'Destructor Fidei'. His fate is unknown, but he had certainly been replaced as prior by April 1534 (by Edmund Stretham, who was subsequently surprised in bed with a whore by one of Cromwell's agents), and neither he nor his two accusers is found among the handful of friars still there at the suppression in 1538.[114] The last prior of the Doncaster Carmelites, Laurence Cooke, was implicated in the Pilgrimage of Grace and was apparently executed in 1538.[115] Another friar, William Storme,

[106] *LP* VII 448–9, 472–3.

[107] *The Works of Thomas Cranmer*, ed. J. E. Cox (2 vols., PS, 1844–6), ii. 333–4.

[108] *LP* XIV (i) 244; also in *Works of Thomas Cranmer*, ii. 361–2. I follow *LP* and Diarmaid MacCulloch, *Thomas Cranmer: a Life* (New Haven and London, 1996), 143–4, in dating this to 1539.

[109] *LP* XII (i) 392, pp. 183–4.   [110] *LP* XII (i) 666.

[111] *LP* XIII (ii) Appendix 28 (cf. *LP* XIII (i) 1326). His preaching had been deemed suspect as far back as 1532: *LP* V 1142.

[112] Peter Marshall, 'Papist as heretic: the burning of John Forest, 1538', *Historical Journal* 41 (1998), 351–74.

[113] See above, note 28.

[114] *LP* V 1209; VII 665. See also 'Catalogue of deeds of surrender', 28 for the handful of friars left at the suppression. *STC* 14077.c.39 is a fragment of a printed indulgence from 1523 referring to John Dryver in an earlier capacity as prior of the Crutched Friars at Colchester. For Stretham's discomfiture, see *Letters Relating to the Suppression*, ed. Wright, 59–60.

[115] *LP* XII (i) 854 is Laurence Cooke's account of his actions during the Pilgrimage. *The Works of Hugh Latimer*, ed. G. E. Corrie (2 vols., PS, 1844–5) ii. 392 note 3, states that Cooke was executed

wrote to Cromwell from the Fleet prison excusing himself for preaching in defence of pilgrimage and the cult of the saints.[116] And an otherwise unknown friar named John Brynstan was preaching at Glastonbury against 'new books', 'new fangles and new men' in February 1536.[117]

The Reformation, then, produced among the friars what it tended to produce among other groups and communities: division. That many friars remained entirely traditional in their religious sympathies is hardly surprising. After all, they had dedicated themselves to a way of life which embodied much that was most distinctive in medieval Catholicism, and which fostered the diffusion among the laity of a semi-monastic piety through preaching, penance, confraternities and indulgences. It may seem more surprising that so many friars were so readily attracted to religious ideas which at a stroke evacuated of all spiritual meaning and value that way of life to which they had hitherto devoted themselves. Yet on reflection, this should occasion no surprise. The relative success of the Reformation among the friars is merely a particular instance of the general truth that support for the new religion came not from those most alienated from the old religion, but precisely from those who had hitherto been most engaged in it.[118]

What rendered the friars especially susceptible to the ideas of the Reformers was, of course, that preaching and doctrine were their vocational concerns. They were thus more likely to come across the teachings of Luther and his followers – not least, in the first instance, from being called upon to refute them or to prosecute them. As popular preachers they would be obliged to answer evangelical challenges from the pulpit, as in Bristol and Exeter. And as expert theologians in episcopal courts they would be entrusted with the task of trying to win heretics back to the consensus of the Church. In short, the friars were, because of their education and employment, more likely and more prompt than others to take sides in the polarising religious situation of the sixteenth century. Where friars led, others would follow.

Lollardy had failed in Plantagenet England to a large extent because it had failed to win significant and lasting support among the friars, whose preaching reached the masses and whose work in hearing confessions

in 1538, but the authority for this is not clear. The surrender of the house, dated 13 November 1538 ('Catalogue of deeds of surrender', 19), lists no Laurence or Cooke, neither is there a dispensation for any such man (*FOR*, 160). The Duke of Norfolk advised Cromwell to exclude Cooke from the royal pardon for the Pilgrims (*LP* XII (ii) 291), so execution seems likely.
[116] *LP* VI 1690. [117] *LP* X 318.
[118] See Peter Marshall's essay in this volume.

gave them enormous influence among the nobility and gentry. The ultimate triumph of the Reformation in England certainly had something to do with the early enthusiasm for Protestant doctrines among the friars, whose participation in the political process of the Reformation was especially valuable thanks to their influence among both gentry and people, and their ability to negotiate the emerging division between popular and elite culture. Stephen Gardiner was being characteristically acute when he pointed out both the irony and the importance of the transformation of old 'friars' into new 'brethren'.[119]

[119] See above, note 15.

CHAPTER 3

Clement Armstrong and the godly commonwealth: radical religion in early Tudor England[1]

Ethan H. Shagan

I

Clement Armstrong, an eccentric London grocer and occasional decorator for Henry VIII's court, is a well-known walk-on character in Tudor historiography. As a minor member of the 'commonwealth' school of economic thought in the 1530s, Armstrong earned the attention of social historians interested in early responses to capitalism.[2] As a decorator for the Field of Cloth of Gold, he made a cameo appearance in A. W. Reed's classic *Early Tudor Drama*.[3] As a fringe member of Thomas Cromwell's clientage, his activities were described by S. T. Bindoff and G. R. Elton.[4] But Armstrong is almost wholly unknown to scholars of the English Reformation, despite his voluminous writings on religious subjects, in part because he died in 1536 just as things were really getting fascinating, and in part because his writings are nightmares of convolution even by the self–indulgent standards of the sixteenth century.

Yet for historians of early English Protestantism, Clement Armstrong may be of very great interest indeed. Certainly there is *prima facie* evidence that his ideas were taken seriously by contemporaries, since he was notably well connected in both political and evangelical circles. Armstrong was a close friend and business associate of John Rastell, and it was

---

[1] An earlier version of this paper was presented at the religion department colloquium at Northwestern University, and I would like to thank the participants for their comments. I also owe thanks to Tom Freeman, Richard Kieckhefer, Peter Lake, Diarmaid MacCulloch, Peter Marshall, Bill Monter, Ed Muir, Christopher Rowland, Alec Ryrie and Regina Schwartz for their help at various stages in the evolution of this article.
[2] Three of Armstrong's treatises and some other fragments were printed in *Drei Volkswirtschaftliche Denkschriften aus der Zeit Heinrichs VIII von England* ed. R. Pauli (Göttingen, 1878). Two of these tracts were then reprinted in *Tudor Economic Documents: Being Select Documents Illustrating the Economic and Social History of Tudor England*, ed. R. H. Tawney and E. Power, (3 vols., 1924), iii. 90–129.
[3] A. W. Reed, *Early Tudor Drama: Medwall, the Rastells, Heywood and the More Circle* (1926), 13, 26.
[4] S. T. Bindoff, 'Clement Armstrong and His Treatises of the Commonweal', *Economic History Review* 14 (1944), 64–73; G. R. Elton, *Reform and Renewal: Thomas Cromwell and the Common Weal* (Cambridge, 1973).

almost certainly Rastell who introduced him to Thomas Cromwell in the early 1530s. When he died in 1536, Armstrong's will was witnessed by one Thomas Gibson, a printer associated with Bishop Hugh Latimer who worked as an unofficial propagandist for Cromwell. He was wealthy enough that an abortive financial deal involving Bishop Stephen Gardiner resulted in Armstrong claiming to Cromwell that he was owed the lordly sum of £363. Moreover, after sending numerous writings to the government, at least one of his Latin works was translated into English by Ralph Sadler, Cromwell's secretary. Clement Armstrong, then, was obscure but hardly a nonentity – he knew the right people, he circulated his writings, and he was a successful enough hanger-on at Henry VIII's court to have had a career that can be followed in the State Papers from 1516 onwards.[5]

It is therefore of no small significance that in a series of tracts written no later than 1533, Armstrong produced what may be the most comprehensive and radical justifications for the royal supremacy over the Church ever written in England.[6] Armstrong defined the powers of kingship in such a way that he not only granted Henry VIII authority over the Church and its temporalities but also granted him sacerdotal and even sacramental powers, a theological imperative to monitor the morality of his people, and a unique and startling role in the redistribution of his subjects' wealth. Along the way Armstrong also revealed himself to be a theological fellow traveller with spiritualist radicals on the Continent such as Hans Hut and Caspar Schwenckfeld. Whether through direct influence or parallel evolution through the Lollard tradition, he came to share many of their ideas, producing an elaborate theology of spiritual rather than physical sacraments, questioning the authority of worldly law to punish the godly, and stripping the clergy of all institutional authority, to name just a few similarities.

This article will argue that Armstrong's productive interweaving of religious radicalism and the royal supremacy forces us to question some of our most basic assumptions about the early Reformation. First, it suggests

---

[5] This biographical sketch is based on Bindoff, 'Clement Armstrong'. Thomas Gibson's writings for Cromwell are in BL Cotton MS Cleopatra E.vi, 401–6.

[6] Of Armstrong's religious tracts, nine are in PRO E 36/197 and one is in PRO SP 6/11, 102–33. All of these which can be dated are no later than 1533, based on their references to the ongoing divorce crisis and their use of the term 'pope' rather than 'bishop of Rome'; they are probably no earlier than 1532, since Armstrong stated in 1536 that he had been writing tracts for Cromwell for three years. Another brief tract on tithes is in PRO SP 6/2, 43–4; this is dated no later than the beginning of 1534, when the London tithe issue was temporarily settled. The tracts printed by Pauli, which are more economic in character and which I use only incidentally in this article, are probably from 1535. For all of these issues of dating, see Bindoff, 'Clement Armstrong'.

that we need to reconsider the idea that the 'radical Reformation' almost by definition 'bore patent anti-institutional consequences'.[7] The divergence between the 'magisterial' Reformation and its 'radical' cousin has been reified by George Williams and others as an embodiment of the classic Christian dichotomy between the authority of the institutional Church and the authority of the Holy Spirit.[8] Revisionist historians reacting to Williams's theological focus have suggested that the 'radical Reformation' should instead be defined by its socially revolutionary character.[9] But whether theological or social in orientation, most historians since the 1960s have accepted that radicalism was incompatible with the growth of ecclesiastical and political institutions. While magisterial reformers sought to build a new institutional Church on the model of the scriptures and thus could align themselves with princely authority, this argument goes, radicals located Christianity in the spiritual rebirth of individual believers and thus subordinated worldly institutions to the community of the faithful.[10] Yet for Armstrong this apparently simple dichotomy breaks down. In a world where religious radicalism normally went hand in hand with the erosion of institutional authority, Armstrong favoured vastly expanding the powers of the crown. While most religious radicals identified the Church with gathered communities of the faithful, Armstrong defined the spiritual community through the political structures of the English state. He produced a theology that was at once virulently spiritualist, deeply anti-Catholic and blatantly authoritarian,

---

[7] S. Ozment, *Mysticism and Dissent: Religious Ideology and Social Protest in the Sixteenth Century* (New Haven, 1973), 117. Interestingly, this quotation refers to Thomas Müntzer, who was among the *most* institutionally minded of the radicals.

[8] G. H. Williams, *The Radical Reformation* (Philadelphia, 1962). For some examples of broadly similar categorisation, see Ozment, *Mysticism and Dissent*; P. P. Peachey, 'The Radical Reformation, Political Pluralism and the Corpus Christianum', *The Origins and Characteristics of Anabaptism*, ed. M. Lienhard (The Hague, 1977); 'Introduction', *Profiles of Anabaptist Women: Sixteenth Century Reforming Pioneers*, ed. C. A. Snyder and L. A. H. Hecht, (Waterloo, Ontario, 1996).

[9] See for example *The German People and the Reformation*, ed. R. Hsia (Ithaca, 1988); P. Blickle, *Communal Reformation: The Quest for Salvation in Sixteenth-Century Germany*, trans. T. Dunlap (Atlantic Highlands, New Jersey, 1992). Hans Jürgen-Goertz described the radical Reformation as 'the force which aimed to destroy the fundamental order of sixteenth-century society and was most clearly expressed by the "Revolution of the Common Man" of 1525'. See *The Anabaptists*, trans. T. Johnson (1996), 134.

[10] There has been some dissent from this view, noting that a few radicals – especially Thomas Müntzer, Balthasar Hubmaier and Jan van Leiden – admitted the possibility of alliances with princely power. See J. M. Stayer, *Anabaptists and the Sword* (Lawrence, Kansas, 1972); A. de Groot, 'The Radical Reformation Revisited?', *Nederlands Archief voor Kerkgeschiedenis* 73 (1993), 199–207; H. Hillerbrand, 'Radicalism in the Early Reformation: Varieties of Reformation in Church and Society', *Radical Tendencies in the Reformation: Divergent Perspectives*, ed. H. Hillerbrand (Kirksville, MO, 1988). But even these dissenting opinions do not seem to allow for radical royalism and institution-building of Armstrong's calibre.

suggesting a possible alternative trajectory for religious 'radicalism' in its English context.

Perhaps more importantly, Armstrong's writings also force us to re-assess the institutional centrepiece of the English Reformation: the royal supremacy over the Church. Historians basing their analyses on the pro-nouncements of the Tudor regime and its apologists have seen the break with Rome as a fundamentally political manoeuvre, unconnected to the broader stream of European Protestantism. In Armstrong, however, we see something of how the king's antipapal and anticlerical manoeuvres in the early 1530s were interpreted by members of London's evangelical community. For Armstrong the break with Rome was not a simple act of jurisdictional realignment but rather presaged the establishment of a true Church for the first time in human history(!). Nor was this mere toadying to the regime; Armstrong's tracts are filled with gratuitous and patently seditious references to the spiritual blindness of Henry VIII and his parliament. We can only conclude, then, that even before the royal divorce was completed, Armstrong had linked in his mind the king's assumption of ecclesiastical authority with the spiritual rebirth of the English people. And given that Armstrong sent these tracts to Thomas Cromwell, it could not have escaped the government's attention that the king's ecclesiastical rumblings were threatening to unleash forces which he would soon be unable to control.

II

Virtually nowhere in more than 500 pages of extant manuscripts does Clement Armstrong tell us about his theological influences, so our first job is to place him within the larger framework of religious controversy in the early 1530s. This is no easy task, as Armstrong specifically denied affiliation with either the Catholic Church or the movement begun by Luther. He described how over the past '12 or 13 years' (in other words since the Diet of Worms) 'the clergy of the East parts on one side and the clergy of the West parts on that other side . . . have accused the one that other with heresy, and hath written books the one against that other which hath caused errors throughout all Christendom'. He claimed that if the emperor were to ask clerics on both sides 'to set forth the very person of Christ, that all men might see his lively face' those clerics would produce only 'words and writings . . . by men's teaching and not by God's teaching'. Indeed, 'when the Emperor hath done his best to have Christ to be openly known to all men by God's teaching, after he hath examined both parties, [he] may go home again and say he is never the wiser of the knowledge of Christ by none of all their teachings'.[11]

This argument, however, amounted more to a spiritualist critique of worldly reason than a genuine claim of neutrality, and there can be no doubt that Armstrong was in a general sense an evangelical. He was, to begin with, stridently antipapal, calling the pope 'antichrist' and 'a minister of the wicked synagogue of sin of Satan of which the head is the devil's spirit'.[12] On confession, Armstrong argued, 'What need then hath man to show sin to the priest, that cannot forgive him?'[13] Echoing Luther's earliest rebellion, Armstrong wrote, 'Whatsoever pardons, absolution, dispensations, forgiveness, and mercy we believe in and trust to have without the righteousness of God by this judgment of son of man, we must needs be deceived.'[14] On salvation through faith, Armstrong rejected the efficacy of works and argued that 'the most wretched sins of the world may outwardly work as much holiness as the pope and all his ministers, and yet no man therewith [is] never better inwardly'.[15] Faith can save men even if they 'have no deeds'.[16] Armstrong also took the conventional Protestant view that the existence of purgatory would imply that Christ was 'no savior but came into this world and died in vain'.[17] On the issue of free will, Armstrong again took an evangelical position, arguing that Adam had free will through his 'pure innocency' in paradise but then 'sank out of freewill' with his fall.[18] And showing his spiritualist rejection of worldly learning, he extended this denial of free will to attack self-proclaimed intellectuals (presumably Erasmus) who dared to use reason to interrogate issues of faith:

Many high arguments and dispositions hath been to prove man to have freewill. O lord, how are lettered men's minds blinded with the fleshly lusts and desires living in this vain life under the sun, and over natural reason cannot rise by faith? . . . Who in proving himself can over himself stand in pure innocency, without knowledge and temptation of sin, so pure without sin like as good angels in heaven [have] been? Who without that pureness of life can prove himself to have freewill?[19]

On the role of the clergy, too, Armstrong echoed evangelical complaints that priests had 'crept in office between God and man' and he

---

[11] PRO SP 6/11, 118v.

[12] PRO E 36/197, tract 9, 353. Throughout this article I will cite this main Clement Armstrong manuscript by tract number and page number, e.g. 9: 353. The page numbers of the tracts are: tract 1: 3–55; tract 2: 59–110; tract 3: 115–52; tract 4: 155–200; tract 5: 208–43; tract 6: 250–76; tract 7: 289–95 (bound upside down and back to front); tract 8: 294–318; tract 9: 322–54.

[13] 9: 341.   [14] 4: 157.   [15] 2: 91.   [16] 1: 4.   [17] 4: 199–200.   [18] 1: 39–40.   [19] 1: 37.

insisted that priests had no authority except 'to minister the lively word'.[20] But in the context of defending Henry VIII's incipient divorce, he also adopted more radical Lollard positions to argue that priests had no business even involving themselves in worldly marriages. He suggested that the role of the clergy is to provide 'knowledge to man's soul . . . [to] lead all men by grace to do good'. This is, for Armstrong, a purely spiritual office. The clergy have no title over men's bodies and cannot enforce the law, since that would be carnal; they can merely preach the law, which then can 'by power of God's grace lead the soul from falling into the will of the flesh'.[21] Since marriage is a carnal union, then, it is outside clerical jurisdiction. By extension, this argument has significant consequences for the temporal state of the clergy. Since priests are 'no ministers of man nor man's law but . . . ministers of God and God's law', it follows that 'they should receive no living of no gift of man but only of the gift of God'.[22] The nature of God's gift to the clergy, moreover, is clearly laid out in scripture: 'Of all lively things that God every year giveth increase, they [are] to have thereof a tenth part.'[23] Armstrong thus glossed Matthew 10: 9–10 to argue that the clergy are to live on tithes and tithes alone: they may possess no lands, no silver, no gold, not even a second coat besides the one on their back. Armstrong even took this line of argument to its logical conclusion, suggesting that in principle no separate clergy is necessary at all: 'priests needeth not where every man is a priest, and the person of a priest is no matter'.[24] These positions push against the limits of evangelical orthodoxy, imagining a world where the Protestant mantra of a 'priesthood of all believers' is actually put into practice and the institutional basis of the worldly Church is stripped away.

Armstrong also takes what appears at first to be a strictly reformed view of the sacraments, arguing that there are only two: the sacrament of baptism and the sacrament of 'bodily life of Christ'.[25] Yet when he explains his reasons for denying sacramental status to marriage, the ears of a Reformation historian begin to prick up. His argument is not based on the lack of direct scriptural institution but rather on the theory that 'matrimony between man and woman in flesh after Adam's fall can be no sacrament that cometh out of heaven'.[26] This suggestion that flesh is incompatible with the sacraments implies a starkly different sacramental theology than either Catholics or most Protestants would have accepted, imagining sacraments neither as efficacious nor as signs of

---

[20] 8: 310 and 2: 78.   [21] 8: 306–7.   [22] PRO SP 6/2, 43r.
[23] 8: 311.   [24] 8: 312.   [25] 4: 162.   [26] 1: 50.

Christ's promise, but as spiritual links between fallen man and his prelapsarian union with God. Here, then, we begin to sense that Armstrong is not the conventional reformer that he at first appears to be.

This spiritualist view of the sacraments is reflected most strongly in Armstrong's exotic view of the Lord's Supper. Like most evangelicals, Armstrong condemned the 'mass, whereby . . . priests saith they consecrate and make their maker, which no man can so do'.[27] Yet Armstrong's reasons for denying transubstantiation were extremely unusual: 'Christ's flesh' cannot be mixed with the worldly flesh of the communicant because 'Christ's flesh [was] pure without sin', and to accept the real presence of Christ in the sacrament would 'counteth Christ to be a sinner'.[28] This is clearly a version of a radical Christological doctrine common to many Lollards and Anabaptists, the 'celestial flesh of Christ'. Moreover, unlike other evangelicals who became obsessed with the issue of the communion wafer and whether Christ's body was really, carnally, or merely symbolically present in it, Armstrong rejected the whole connection between the sacrament of Christ's body and the necessity of a physical ceremony. Man cannot 'receive grace . . . through a vile, stinking, sinful body', nor can the 'grace of God's Holy Spirit' come 'into health of man's soul through such vile bodies'.[29] The real sacrament, in which the body of Christ is consumed in the symbolic form of bread, is rather the sacrament represented in the Lord's Prayer, when Christ told us to pray for our daily bread.[30] This 'daily bread' is seen by Armstrong as a purely spiritual gift, the only kind that can be efficacious since the fall of man. The actual receipt of communion in any physical form is therefore irrelevant, so that, for instance, when England was placed under interdict in the reign of King John, it was 'better that services were put away' so that 'every man himself out of sin, worthily by his faith . . . [could] offer at the altar in his spirit to receive grace of God's Holy Spirit'.[31] Indeed, there can be no physical communion on earth after the Fall of man: 'The life of Christ's body is not received in this world in form of flesh. After Adam's Fall it is received in spirit.'[32] The true sacrament consists of a spiritual union with Christ which the pope and his clergy 'to this day never yet ministered'.[33]

This radicalism is more than matched by Armstrong's views on the law. In the context of his bizarrely nationalist theology, Armstrong argued that 'all men in England', through their allegiance to the king, 'shall be

---

[27] 9: 331–2.   [28] 4: 199.   [29] 9: 334–5.   [30] 9: 331–2.
[31] 9: 350.   [32] 9: 340.   [33] 9: 329.

delivered out of all the laws of this world out of sin into grace, to live by faith'. It is the king's job in this system to prevent God's elect 'from falling into sin, to keep them out of his law of rigour in this world'. Certainly this implies a sort of perfectionism, and it is significant that in this context Armstrong glosses the biblical precept: 'If ye be lead by the spirit then are ye not under the law.'[34] Similarly, Armstrong argued that when one neighbour wrongs another, according to the biblical precept that without charity he can profit nothing, he should be excommunicated 'out of Christ's Church as no member of his body, to be judged and condemned under laws of rigour made in this world'.[35] The clear implication here is that those who *are* members of Christ's body are not subject to worldly law.

Armstrong also offered an exotic, tripartite Christian anthropology, proposing 'three regions of life' which humanity might inhabit. The first region is that of the 'good angel in heaven of everlasting light invisible, which life is of grace without any sin'. This is the region from which Adam fell. Second, there is the 'life of sin and darkness of flesh', the region into which Adam fell. Third, there is the 'region of life of man, in light visible . . . between both the other two regions of the two contrary angels good and ill'. This third region is located 'right at the sun, otherwise (it may be said) at the soul; at that point is the very judgment of all men by God's law of grace and of faith'. Here Armstrong is punning on the words 'sun', 'sol' and 'soul', making a series of connections between the sun in the sky (Latin *sol*) and the souls of men.[36] The human soul, in other words, exists in a liminal state 'between God's law of grace and of faith in the spirit of man above the sun, and man's law of knowledge of sin that by lively reason rose out of lust and will of sin in flesh from under the sun'. This system reconfigures some elements of Manicheism in its location of the evil force in the cosmos on earth and in human activity; Armstrong repeats many times that the devil is lord of this world. Yet it also suggests that however reprobate human existence may be, the human soul still contains a spark which can partake of divinity. When this positive principle is released, human beings can transcend the carnal world: 'At this point in the middle of the region of man's life is the knowledge to see how man hath diversity of life of both spirit and soul. . . . At that point between is the window through which man, with the eye of faith, must see and believe into God by his Holy Spirit.'[37]

This anthropology is highly developed in Armstrong's writings and can be found at the bedrock of many of his ideas about Church and state. Yet

[34] 2: 68–9.   [35] 2: 73–4.   [36] 1: 9–10.   [37] 1: 11.

in obvious ways it also contradicts another of Armstrong's core notions: his denial of free will.[38] Already it is clear, then, that Armstrong's theology is far from internally consistent, and once this initial contradiction is exposed, others quickly become apparent. At one point, for instance, he described altars in church as sites for 'the offering up of our Lord' but then crossed out 'our Lord' and replaced it with 'our right life of grace'.[39] This nimble save prevented him from implying that there was any physical presence of Christ in communion, but the mere fact that he identified the altar as a proper place for the Lord's Supper contradicts his notion of a purely spiritual sacrament. Another contradiction lies in Armstrong's reference to excommunication, where he claims that sinners are excommunicate 'out of Christ's Church as no member of his body, to be judged and condemned under laws of rigour made in this world'.[40] This implies a definition of the Church which is limited to the body of the faithful rather than encompassing all of Christian society, and like the Anabaptist 'ban' it provides for a strict separation between the Church and the world. Yet elsewhere, in his discussion of the royal supremacy over the Church, Armstrong insists that the king's job is to 'lead all men, elected and unelected, faithful and unfaithful, good and ill, all together to be saved from falling into outward works of sin'.[41]

Armstrong's spiritualism and anti-intellectualism also produce bizarre contradictions. He claimed that 'fleshly reason living in the fleshly body ... wherein is no spirit, life, nor light' could discover nothing in matters of faith, and that 'it is not for blind reason to argue the clear knowledge of Christ's bodily life in spirit'.[42] He thus glossed John 6: 45 ('all men shall be able to be taught of God') as evidence that men cannot be taught *except* by God and that therefore 'no credence nor trust should be given to men's word or writing'.[43] Yet of course Armstrong himself produced more than 500 pages of discourses on matters of faith. As if pre-empting charges of hypocrisy, Armstrong excused his own author-ship on the rather bizarre grounds of worldly ignorance: his work was

---

[38] Armstrong makes one attempt to resolve this glaring contradiction: 'Some saith man of himself hath freewill. It may be said that man hath in himself choice, lust, and consent, but to say that man hath freewill, where should that will of man have any place everlasting but either in will of spirit of God or of the Devil? At the first beginning, when God by making everlasting light made angel's spirit in heaven, then was [there] but the only will of God, before a contrary will rose out of the deepest darkness, which comprehended Lucifer, which with all his consenters turned out of light into darkness cast down out of heaven by God dividing light from darkness, by which fall then was two contrary wills ... so as man made to live between both wills must follow that one or that other, of God's spirit or of the devil's spirit'. See PRO SP 6/11, 109v. This seems to imply that man can and indeed must choose between God and the devil, but that in making this choice he follows one of their two wills rather than creating his own. This argument is far closer to the position of the supporters of free will than Armstrong seems to understand.

[39] 4: 170.   [40] 2: 73-4.   [41] 4: 193.   [42] 4: 183.   [43] 8: 294.

'a little light and knowledge, running out of a rude blind wit, somewhat scribbling as fast as the pen can race across the paper, without any study or advisement'.[44] This characterisation is wholly believable to anyone who has read the tracts.

III

Given Armstrong's evident departures from the mainstream, 'magisterial' Reformation, it would be useful to determine whether Armstrong was directly influenced by Continental radicalism. Yet in practice, without clear statements of intellectual influence, it is almost invariably futile to try to determine which aspects of Armstrong's theology were outgrowths of indigenous medieval Lollardy, which aspects were borrowed from Lutheran or Reformed theology, and which aspects may have been drawn from Anabaptists and other 'radicals'. On virtually every point such efforts prove impossible, both because of Wyclif's powerful influence on central European thought through the Hussite movement, and because in practice the Wycliffite tradition was so rich and varied that an Englishman immersed in late Lollardy could have developed virtually any hodgepodge of doctrines in the Reformation repertory.

For example, Armstrong's implicit definition of sacraments as marks of unity between mankind and God echoes the Wycliffite definition of sacraments as 'turnings of man to God' so that 'any good, sensible deed that we do, or that springeth of man's charity, may be called a sacrament'.[45] In his descriptions of communion, moreover, Armstrong invoked the doctrine of the 'celestial flesh' of Christ, for instance in his statement that Christ's 'pure life of divinity turneth not into corruption of flesh'. As has been recently noted, the presence of this quintessential radical doctrine in Henrician England is not solid evidence of Anabaptist influence because it, too, can be found in the Wycliffite tradition.[46] Armstrong's denial of the necessity of a physical sacramental ceremony again could have its origins in various Continental radicals (especially Caspar Schwenckfeld), but also in more extreme forms of Lollard sacramentalism. But on the other hand Armstrong referred to 'both sacraments, of baptism and of bodily life of Christ'.[47] While many Lollards denied the validity of

---

[44] 5: 218.
[45] *The English Works of Wyclif Hitherto Unprinted*, ed. F. D. Matthew, (2nd edition, 1902), 341.
[46] PRO SP 6/11, 123v. See D. A. Penny, *Freewill or Predestination: The Battle Over Saving Grace in Mid-Tudor England* (Woodbridge, Suffolk, 1990), 18–21; J. F. Davis, *Heresy and Reformation in the South-East of England, 1520–1559* (1983), 36–8, 104–5. These scholars provide an important corrective to I. B. Horst, *The Radical Brethren: Anabaptism and the English Reformation to 1558* (Nieuwkoop, 1972).
[47] 4: 162.

particular sacraments, and every sacrament was attacked by Lollards at one time or another, the firm limitation of the sacraments to two is a position central to the Continental Reformed and radical traditions which is not attested within English Lollardy.[48] It seems likely from this realignment that Armstrong had been drawn away from the Lollard tradition by more recent theological initiatives. But which initiatives, and to what degree?

Another powerful piece of evidence against imagining Armstrong as merely a 'late Lollard' is his evocation of the king's ability to 'see all the inward knowledge of scripture, and therein judge and discuss all the inward secrets which is not possible to be learned by no men's teaching'.[49] This implies the existence of an inward or hidden scripture lying behind the readable scripture, a position characteristic of Hans Hut and other radicals of the 1520s yet antithetical to basic Lollard (and Lutheran) scripturalism. This appearance of non-Lollard influence is strengthened by Armstrong's habitual citation of the Bible in Latin rather than English and his lukewarm reaction to Tyndale's translation project. While he admitted that Tyndale had done 'much good to the common people of this realm for the knowledge of such things which the papists did what they could to hide', he thought it was inappropriate for books to be printed outside the kingdom and smuggled in, and he wanted 'all haberdashers' to be 'commanded not once to bring any manner of primers from any place beyond the sea, nor no other book to sell here within this realm'.[50] Yet on the other hand Armstrong clearly favoured English scripture in principle (he merely thought it should be printed in England), and while the idea of a hidden scripture *seems* to oppose the main thrust of Lollard biblicism, several Lollard sermons take positions that could be read as supporting a mystical scripture as well. One sermon, for instance, glossed Christ's simile that 'the realm of heaven is like to treasure hid in the field':

This field is understanden the faith of holy writ, and God's Word is hid everywhere in this field. . . . Man findeth this treasure when he taketh the faith of God's Son of heaven, that is yet hid; for belief is a thing hid to men that believe, since belief is a thing that men kindly see not.[51]

---

[48] The spectrum of Lollard views on the sacraments is discussed in A. Hudson, *The Premature Reformation: Wycliffite Texts and Lollard History* (Oxford, 1988), 290–4.

[49] PRO SP 6/11, 120r.

[50] Cited in Pauli, *Drei Volkswirtschaftliche*, 58–60. Armstrong makes it clear that he wants Bibles printed in England primarily because of the economic rather than the spiritual benefits of the project. See also Andrew Pettegree's essay in this volume.

[51] *English Wycliffite Sermons*, ed. A. Hudson and P. Gordon (5 vols., Oxford, 1983–96), ii. 167–8.

Another sermon stated that while 'holy writ containeth all truth', some of this truth is shown 'expressly' and 'some truth privily'.[52] The problem is that it was wholly conventional for Christians to argue that the true meaning of scripture cannot be gleaned without a special act of divine grace; this doctrine only became radical when put to particular uses. Some Continental thinkers in the 1520s used it for expressly spiritualist and anti-institutional ends, while Armstrong used it to give the king unique power in interpreting scripture for his people; both are in some sense radical, but there is no proof that one position influenced the other, and neither is necessarily incompatible with the Wycliffite tradition.

Armstrong's tripartite anthropology creates perhaps the thorniest intellectual thicket. The idea of a tripartite human condition was common, although by no means ubiquitous, in the Middle Ages. The fourteenth-century theologian Johannes Tauler used a tripartite anthropology delineating first an outward, animal man, second a rational man, and third what he called the '*gemuete*', the highest part of the soul.[53] In a somewhat different vein, Erasmus wrote that 'not every human inclination is "flesh": there is "soul" and there is "spirit", by which we strive towards goodness. This part of the psyche is called reason or the ruling principle.'[54] Even Wyclif argued that 'the intellectual and rational soul', when subsumed by the body, was unified with both the immortal spirit and the brute flesh.[55] These persistent references to man's *rational* nature all had clear platonic roots, in Erasmus's case mediated through the Christian humanist tradition. As Pico Della Mirandola put it in his *Heptaplus*:

Antiquity imagined three worlds. Highest of all is that ultra-mundane one which the theologians call the angelic and philosophers the intelligible, and of which, Plato says in the *Phaedrus*, no one has worthily sung. Next to this comes the celestial world, and last of all, this sublunary one which we inhabit.[56]

But there was also precedent for a tripartite anthropology that rejected the resources of human knowledge as Armstrong did. The Anabaptist Balthasar Hubmaier argued that mankind's 'three special and essential substances – soul, spirit, and body – are made and unified in every human

---

[52] *English Wycliffite Sermons*, ii. 224.
[53] S. Ozment, *Homo Spiritualis: A Comparative Study of the Anthropology of Johannes Tauler, Jean Gerson and Martin Luther* (Leiden, 1969), 2.
[54] *Collected Works of Erasmus*, ed. R. J. Schoeck et al. (84 vols., Toronto, 1974–), lxxvi. 61. See also Erasmus's anthropological discussion in his *Enchiridion Militis Christiani*, in ibid., lxvi. 65.
[55] John Wyclif, *De Compositione Hominis*, ed. Rudolf Beer (1884), 115.
[56] G. Pico Della Mirandola, *On the Dignity of Man and other Works*, trans. C. G. Wallis et al. (New York, 1965), 75.

being according to the image of Holy Trinity'. Before the transgression of Adam, all three of these substances 'were good', but since the Fall 'the flesh has irretrievably lost its goodness . . . and has become entirely and wholly worthless and hopeless unto death'. The spirit, on the other hand, 'before, during, and after the Fall remained upright, whole, and good'. The soul occupies an intermediate position. It was wounded and bound in the Fall and 'become sick unto death so that it can on its own choose nothing good. . . . Only the flesh can act, without which the soul is outwardly able to do nothing, for the flesh is its instrument.' Yet the soul is not wounded beyond healing; it is 'reparable through the word of God'. Christ's death and resurrection freed the soul from its bondage so that 'it can now freely and willingly be obedient to the spirit'.[57] This position sounds suspiciously close to Armstrong's, but certainly there is no proof of a connection.[58] At least in this case we can be sure Armstrong did not get his anthropology from Luther, who wrote in response to Erasmus, 'I, too, know of Origen's fancy about the "threefold affection", one called "flesh", another "soul", and the other "spirit", the soul being in the middle between the other two, and able to turn either flesh-wards or spirit-wards. But these are just his own dreams; he retails them, but does not prove them.'[59]

A host of other issues can also be seen where Armstrong seems to be drawing on Continental influences but where, upon more careful attention, his ideas could have emerged from the later Lollard morass. While most Lollards accepted the existence of purgatory, for instance, there is evidence of occasional Lollard arguments that 'there is none other place of purgatory but only this world', a position extremely close to Armstrong's view that if 'purgatory is where sin is' then it must be 'in this world'.[60] To take another example, Wyclif defended free will in plain

---

[57] *Balthasar Hubmaier: Theologian of Anabaptism*, ed. H. W. Pipkin and J. H. Yoder (Scottdale, PA 1989), 432–9.

[58] Another Continental radical with an anthropology similar to Hubmaier's was Melchior Hoffman. It is perhaps more than a coincidence that besides this similarity, Hoffman and Hubmaier were also like Armstrong in that (very unusually for radical reformers) they approved of the use of state power for spiritual ends. See K. Deppermann, *Melchior Hoffman: Social Unrest and Apocalyptic Visions in the Age of Reformation*, trans. M. Wren, ed. B. Drewery (Edinburgh, 1987), 223–9, 263–4. For Hubmaier see his 'On the Sword', *Balthasar Hubmaier*, ed. Pipkin and Yoder, 492–523.

[59] *Martin Luther on the Bondage of the Will*, ed. J. I. Packer and O. R. Johnston (1957), 300. According to Steven Ozment, the revolution in Luther's thought was directly connected with his recon-figuration of Tauler's tripartite anthropology, changing the *gemuete* into the 'spiritual man who relies on faith', a formulation which denied that any intrinsic anthropological resource could have soteriological utility for fallen man. See Ozment, *Homo Spiritualis*, 2, 16 and *passim*.

[60] 4: 199–200; Hudson, *Premature Reformation*, 309.

terms: 'God giveth to each man a free will to choose good or evil, and God is ready to give him grace if they will receive it.'[61] Yet at the same time he defended a rigorous form of predestination that could easily be misread as a denial of free will. Armstrong skirted the same line in opposite fashion: he denied free will in plain terms yet his anthropology seemed to allow significant soteriological resources to fallen man.

So in other words, while there is much evidence of theological eclecticism, there is no smoking gun to link Armstrong to Continental radicalism, in large part because there is no doctrine so unique to the Continental Reformation that indigenous English sources for it could not be found. We know that Armstrong was active in London evangelical circles, that he hobnobbed with merchants and printers, that he read Latin, and that he travelled at least once to the Continent; certainly he *could* have had access to radical Reformation tracts, and without question he knew of Anabaptists and other radicals by word of mouth. But lacking the evidence of any actual avowal of Continental influences, we can say no more than that in the milieu of early Reformation London, Armstrong combined and reconfigured many aspects of Lollard and Protestant theology in ways that were characteristic of Anabaptism and the emerging radical tradition in central Europe.

This, however, is enough for me to make my central claim: that we may think of Clement Armstrong as both an English radical reformer and an English Reformation radical, even if not technically an English member of the 'radical Reformation'. Like so many lay activists in the early Reformation, he evolved a spiritualist theology that could be deployed to undermine virtually any aspect of outward, corporate religiosity. And following in the footsteps of Thomas Müntzer, he felt comfortable enough with his divine calling to send tracts to Henry VIII's chief minister lamenting that 'the king is so blind' and suggesting that his tracts might be 'a school for a king whereby to be taught of God'.[62] Armstrong was thus almost an ideal Reformation-era type, surprising only because we find him in England rather than in the Holy Roman Empire. He was that most dangerous of creatures, a literate layman, amateur preacher[63] and theological omnivore, the sort of instinctive radical whom the magisterial reformers at first embraced, then feared, and eventually sought to destroy.

---

[61] *English Works of Wyclif*, 110. [62] 9: 324; 8: 295.

[63] Tract 5 is clearly written in the generic form of a sermon on Psalm 7: 15. We have no evidence that it was ever preached orally, but Armstrong argued in several places that preaching was an activity proper to those chosen by God rather than those ordained by the worldly Church.

IV

By 1533, then, Clement Armstrong had developed a theology that slashed and burned its way through the institutional underbrush much as did the theology of the Continental Anabaptists. He stripped from the clergy their lands, their legal system and their authority to enforce worldly morality. He eliminated the need for any institutional Church in the performance of the sacraments. He rejected the utility of academic theology and the Church's 1,500 years of doctrinal detritus. His *modus operandi* for reforming the Church was, in a word, radical. For Armstrong, however, the next step was not the withdrawal of the elect from the corrupt world; he wrote on the contrary that 'Christ left the form of his law behind him from his ascension . . . so as the good may live with the ill'.[64] Rather, building on Lollard ideas, Armstrong proposed the erection of a new and remarkable institution: the royal supremacy over the Church. He defined the Church in hyper-royalist fashion as 'the congregation of all men in a realm congregated as in the body of one man, which one man is the king's body wherein all people his subjects are as his bodily members'. Thus, as he put it elsewhere, 'like as the king is the Church, so the Church is the king'.[65]

Of course, it is no coincidence that in the context of Henry VIII's divorce from Catherine of Aragon the English government was simultaneously devising its own theology of a royal supremacy. To Armstrong the deepening English schism was the catalyst for a fundamental transformation of the Church, and to further this goal many of his tracts were ostensibly written in support of the regime, defending the theological and legal legitimacy of the king's divorce. Yet while Armstrong's vision of the royal supremacy was in principle consistent with the official break with Rome, in practice the system he proposed was strikingly different from anything the regime was willing to support in its public statements.

Armstrong's conception of the royal supremacy was based not in any notion of *imperium*, as it would soon be defined in the government's official pronouncements, but rather in his exotic and deeply spiritualised vision of a subject that we have not yet addressed: human economy. As we have seen, Armstrong adopted a spiritualist view of the sacraments, but within this spiritualism the idea of Christ's body symbolised in the form of bread remained fundamental. When Christ told us in the Lord's Prayer to pray for our 'daily bread', it was a plea at once for physical sustenance and for spiritual salvation through Christ's body. When Paul said that

---

[64] 4: 197.   [65] 9: 332–3; PRO SP 6/11, 119v.

'if any would not work, neither should he eat' (2 Thessalonians 3: 10)
this was a recognition that the Holy Spirit cannot enter human souls
unless bodily discipline is maintained: 'Who that work not to receive the
meat that the son of man shall give, shall not have no life in him nor
else cannot eat the flesh and blood of Christ.'[66] Thus in Armstrong's
view economics, the harvesting of God's bounty and the distribution of
that bounty through human exchange, is a crucial component of godly
discipline.[67] Yet because most human beings did not possess their own
land, the king, as principal holder of all land in England and the arbiter of
all property disputes, held a unique position in God's plan as the provider
of spiritual sustenance for his subjects. As Armstrong put it, God's law:

bindeth all men to live and work bodily the meat that the son of man shall give,
but by his gift God in heaven giveth no meat to no man in this world. Therefore
the king in his head office over the body of his realm doth see, but if [i.e. unless]
he in the form of son of man doth give bodily living to all his people, else they
cannot receive it of God's gift.[68]

With the king's charge to 'give bodily living to all his people' thus not
merely an economic expediency but a spiritual prerogative, Armstrong
called for major alterations in the use of land in England. Landlords,
Armstrong tells us, are 'bound by God's laws to lead people to work the
earth, as much as every possessioner hath in possession', and therefore
'no possessioner may not take the earth from the works of the common people'.[69] In other words, Armstrong would effectively ban enclosure. Moreover, while he does not quite advocate the redistribution

---

[66] 3: 115. I take Armstrong's term 'meat' to refer generically to agricultural produce, for instance in
his reference to the 'meat' which 'riseth out of the herb growing in earth' (4: 164). In Tyndale's
translation of Genesis, God told Adam that the 'herbs that sow seed which are on all the earth'
would be 'meat' for him (Genesis 1: 29), a sufficiently similar phrasing to make us suspect
Armstrong to have had a copy. See William Tyndale, *The Pentateuch* (Antwerp, 1530), B2r.

[67] Despite his usually strict separation of flesh and spirit, Armstrong imagined bread to have a
spiritual as well as a carnal component, as evidenced by Christ's repeated references to it: 'The
meat that men receive into their earthly bodies, the material substance thereof, is earthly. But
the inward gift in the outward form thereof, which inwardly sustaineth and feedeth the body
with strength, wealth, and health, is given of God by the son of man by influence of grace out of
heaven descending' (2: 103).

[68] 2: 59. This seems superficially similar to the Wycliffite emphasis on the indivisibility of royal
power, and may indeed be derived from it. But on the other hand Armstrong argues that kings
possess all land in England by virtue of their office, a position deeply inimical to the essential
Wycliffite belief that no one in a state of sin can have true dominion and that the faithful share
all true dominion in common. See John Wyclif, *Tractatus De Civili Dominio Liber Primus*, ed. R. L.
Poole (1885), p. 1, ch. 14 and *passim*.

[69] 2: 100. Armstrong's use of the term 'possessioner' is an almost sure sign of Wycliffite influence,
but his use of it to describe lay landlords rather than prelates represents a significant divergence.

of land (under his system 'mean holders of lands of the king's' would lose 'not one penny' of their titles)[70] he certainly gives the king prerogative to redistribute the *fruits* of the land. The king should 'search, see, know, and discern what rich commodious gifts . . . God yearly giveth to all people in his realm': in other words, take annual inventories of his subjects' agricultural production. Then, just as Christ did with the loaves and the fishes, he should 'receive' that bounty into his possession and 'minister gift thereof to all his people, to feed them that followed with works to receive it of Christ'. After England's produce has been redistributed to the nation's labourers, the king should then take the 'overplus' and 'assign it to feed all such as were not able to work' because of age or infirmity.[71] Here we have an effective communism of goods (if not of land) which is in some ways analogous to Anabaptism, but is also starkly different, in that it envisions the 'community' not simply as the faithful brethren but as the whole realm under the auspices of the king.

From this starting point of sacred kingship based upon the crown's ownership of property, Armstrong embarks on a more comprehensive, heavily spiritualised redefinition of royal power. He is careful to deny that kings are in any sense immune from the fall of man and the bondage of the will; on the contrary, he writes that no king 'born in sin since Adam's Fall should think and believe himself to be a like lord as Adam was without sin before his Fall; that is not possible'.[72] But that he felt it necessary to make so defensive a statement implies that this view was dangerously close to the mark. Elsewhere, for instance, he writes that the king, by virtue of his anointment, plays a double role just as Christ was at once God and man: 'The king by his birth of flesh is but as a subject and an earthly man, and by his birth of Holy Spirit is a right born king and a head lord in Christ over all lordship in this world in form of son of man.'[73] This is in effect a remarkably productive intersection of the Pauline opposition of spirit and flesh with the medieval political theory of the king's two bodies.

When combined with Armstrong's antinomianism, this vision of the king's 'body politic' as a spiritual body produced a striking conclusion:

The king by grace and mystery of the Holy Spirit shall lead all men of a forewit to save them from falling into sin, to keep them out of laws of rigour in this world; as Paul saith, "If ye be led by the spirit then are ye not under the law."[74]

---

[70] PRO SP 6/11, 127v.   [71] 3: 119.   [72] 1: 17.   [73] 2: 68.   [74] 2: 69.

The king, in other words, provides access to the Holy Spirit which frees the elect from the moral law. When combined with Armstrong's spiritual sacramental theology, moreover, his vision of the king's two bodies produced an even more remarkable result: since the clergy 'will never receive the body of Christ's flesh and blood given of God out of heaven by his lively Word above, therefore the king in form of son of man must minister the body of Christ in form of bread to all men'.[75] Here the king is unquestionably given sacramental powers.

The maintenance of the king's new ecclesiastical and spiritual power is imagined by Armstrong in the workings of his most remarkably creative flight of fancy, something which he calls 'the king's ordinary head seal'. This 'seal' clearly refers to a wax seal such as those used by kings and leading subjects to authenticate their documents, and the term 'ordinary' used here has a double meaning in Tudor parlance: it both provides 'good order' and symbolises ecclesiastical jurisdiction (in the sense of an 'ordination'). The king's ordinary head seal, then, is Armstrong's ultimate metaphor for royal authority over the Church, and in its mysteries lie Armstrong's most extraordinary claims for royal power.

The king's ordinary head seal is, according to Armstrong, divided into three parts which signify the spirit, the soul and the body; it is through this seal, then, that the king claims rightful jurisdiction over all three parts of mankind's tripartite nature. The three sections of the seal, moreover, imprint three different colours of wax. The highest part of the seal imprints white wax, 'signifying the everlasting mercy of God in Holy Spirit'. The middle part of the seal imprints red wax, 'forasmuch as Christ through His passion shedding his blood redeemed and raised all men out of life of sin under the sun into life of grace and faith in spirit over the sun'. The lowest part of the seal imprints green wax, 'signifying that part of the seal always must lead all bodies to work the meat of the gift of son of man that riseth out of the herb growing in earth'.[76] The two highest parts of the seal work together in Armstrong's vision, representing 'the mercy and righteousness of God in the two spirits of God and man

---

[75] 4: 188. This idea of the king acting 'in form of son of man' seems contrary to Wyclif's argument, derived from Augustine, that kings are vicars of God the Father just as bishops are vicars of Christ the Son. See John Wyclif, *Tractatus De Officio Regis*, ed. A. W. Pollard (1887), 10. On the other hand Armstrong writes elsewhere that 'the ministers of God ... are and ought to be in office over a king'. See PRO SP 6/11, 127r. This position, far from contradicting Armstrong's notion of the royal supremacy, shows his indebtedness to Augustine (possibly through Wyclif) and to the view that kings are owed a higher dignity in the world and should rule over priests even though priests have a higher impalpable or spiritual dignity. See Wyclif, *Tractatus De Officio Regis*, viii.

[76] 6: 263; 4: 164.

knit together in unity of one person'.[77] The lowest part of the seal (which according to Armstrong's oft-repeated allegory 'signifieth the moon') works separately and is responsible for 'the son of man's law under the sun', in other words the positive law which acts as a 'helper of all men to live in the law of Holy Spirit'.[78]

The king's use of the two higher parts of the seal clearly connotes spiritual authority. But it is in his description of the lowest part of the seal that the metaphor does the most work for Armstrong, allowing him to create an elaborate and frankly revolutionary apparatus for the king to maintain godly discipline among his subjects. Under the authority of the lowest part of the king's seal, according to Armstrong, once a month (i.e. on a lunar calendar, corresponding to our world below the sun) the king's officers must 'search throughout all bodies of people in his whole realm, to see that all bodies have works bodily to work the earth, whereby to receive bodily living rising out of the herb in the earth'. These royal officers, since they work according to the cycle of the moon, Armstrong dubs 'lunators'. The goal of these monthly investigations by the 'lunators' is to 'see who worketh for the meat of gift of God or of the devil, by grace or by sin, by faith or by falsehood', so as to 'help all people to live in the law of grace of God'.[79] The king's headship, in other words, extends to moral authority over his subjects, especially concerning their willingness to work for the fruit of the earth, which has both economic and sacramental significance.

But how can a few royal officers really investigate the morality of all English subjects once a month? Armstrong proposes a remarkable answer. He argues that out of the 'king's head seal' there should proceed other 'lesser head seals, to be in the head houses over all bodies of shires'. Then from those lesser, countywide seals should proceed still lesser seals 'into the head house over the body of every parish and cure, that is the church, which seal shall be print, parchment, and paper with ink'. Then in turn each householder would receive every Easter a parchment under the parish seal which he would carry with him 'all the whole year, wheresoever he ride' to prove that 'he liveth in cure'. Those householders would then provide 'cure' for their 'servants and other such' who live under their roofs. In this way 'there shall be not one soul of lawful age . . . left out of cure and knowledge of the soul in the king's head seal'.[80]

---

[77] 2: 72.   [78] 6: 261–2.   [79] 6: 265.
[80] 2: 71–2. This explanation is repeated with minor differences in 6: 266–7.

Once every month, the curate of each parish would ride to the chief town of the hundred, where he would meet with the 'lunator' for the county; each hundred would hold its meetings with the 'lunator' on consecutive days, so the 'lunator' would essentially make the rounds of the county once a month, like the moon revolving around the earth. In preparation for these monthly meetings with the county 'lunator', each curate would 'search throughout the body of their parish and of all souls and bodies in their cure' and write a report on each person, 'whether they live either as faithful or unfaithful'. Through these reports, given by every curate in England to his 'lunator' once a month and then passed on to Westminster, the king 'shall have all people as members in the whole body of his realm . . . [and] have knowledge of all members in his body in his head'. With this system in place, then, 'in England shall not be suffered thief, vagabond, whore, nor harlot, nor idle people without office or labour'.[81]

Here, then, developed in the early 1530s by a grocer and amateur theologian, is a comprehensive moral and economic surveillance system that would make Foucault blush. It is a system remarkable in part for what it takes for granted: that ecclesiastical and civil officers might combine into one administrative apparatus under the authority of the king. But Armstrong's vision is more remarkable for its apotheosis of kingship, embodied in the king's ordinary head seal, in which the monarch's power as priest-king vastly surpasses the sum of its parts. As Armstrong puts it in one of his loftiest passages:

This ordinary head seal is the very kingdom of a right Christendom that never yet was ministered in earth until now. This mystery is the very face of Christ in the ordinary head of son of man that is the light of all this world. But only in this seal, no king nor no man can live in Christ's life, whereby to enter into heaven.[82]

V

It is a commonplace of scholarly analyses of the 'radical Reformation' that radical theology required churches to be organised 'on the principle of voluntary association',[83] that radicals 'disdained a settled relationship with secular society',[84] and that radicals 'faced the institutions of their day with a spectrum of rejections ranging from outright rebellion to barely

---

[81] 6: 266–9.   [82] 8: 314–5.
[83] Williams, *Radical Reformation*, xxviii.
[84] E. Cameron, *The European Reformation* (Oxford, 1991), 319.

feigned acceptance'.[85] Yet in Armstrong's case we have what seems to be an authoritarian and hyper-institutionalist concoction mixed from many of the same elements found in the Anabaptist theological brew. Armstrong was deeply suspicious of worldly learning, respecting only those insights provided by the direct inspiration of the Holy Spirit. He experimented freely with antinomianism. He rejected the ritualised institution of the sacraments in favour of a spiritual sacramental theology that was in many ways even less 'institutional' than adult believers' baptism. His 'commonwealth' economic views included a form of redistribution of worldly goods. Yet out of these elements he did not proceed to imagine the Church as a gathered community of the faithful, set apart from the world through the characteristic radical apparatus of believers' baptism, godly communism and exclusion of the unworthy. He imagined instead a world where a Christian king made the world safe for the godly through a programme of moral surveillance and provided his subjects with the means to obtain Christ's spiritual sacraments.

One result of this analysis is clearly that, at least in the English Reformation, 'radical' and 'magisterial' cannot function as simple antonyms. In small and more or less autonomous cities like Zürich and Strassburg, where Protestants quickly acquired the reins of government, this binary opposition might be useful. But England in the early 1530s was very different. There the hopes of a small evangelical minority lay in the policies of a mercurial king who had begun making dark threats against the pope and the clergy. Moreover, the social and economic context was not a self-governing city but an enormous, sprawling, largely agricultural nation where the most pressing social problems involved disputes between landlords and tenants. In these circumstances it was comparatively easy for Armstrong to divide worldly institutions into those which partook of the Holy Spirit (such as a strong, centralised monarchy that was embroiled in conflict with a popish Antichrist) and those which partook of the devil (such as the Church and the capitalist market for agricultural commodities). From there it was a simple manoeuvre to imagine the ministry of the Holy Spirit through the authority of the king; indeed, for Armstrong the Holy Spirit *was* authoritarian. I would suggest, therefore, that if we want to talk about a 'radical Reformation' based on the authority of the Spirit rather than the authority of the Church, we are going to have to construct an understanding of 'radicalism' that is less dependent on *a priori* assumptions about what the Holy

---

[85] Ozment, *Mysticism and Dissent*, 246.

Spirit has on his agenda. In practice this points to the difficulty of trying to deploy political terms in a theological setting. It has been relatively easy for historians of Anabaptism to use the term 'radical' because the prototypical Anabaptist was simultaneously spiritualist in theology, communist in economics and populist in politics. This is about as left-wing as you can get.[86] But Clement Armstrong was clearly no leftist, except in the sense that, like some of the twentieth century's more infamous 'left-wing' totalitarian regimes, he imagined that a comprehensive system of moral surveillance could liberate people from the ravages of their own sinfulness.

Beyond the question of religious radicalism, however, Armstrong forces us to reconsider the meaning of Henry VIII's break with Rome and the royal supremacy over the Church. To many of its supporters and public apologists the break with Rome was to be a simple act of jurisdictional realignment, concerned only with matters of Church governance that were spiritually indifferent. There is no question that Henry VIII himself would have balked at any suggestion of doctrinal innovation, although his definition of 'doctrine' was notoriously idiosyncratic. But regardless of the regime's stated objectives and rationales, it is clear that Thomas Cromwell and his evangelical colleagues in the government knew how their actions were being interpreted by London radicals, and they made no effort to suppress those interpretations.

Moreover, a growing body of evidence suggests that while the details of Armstrong's theology were unique, he was part of a wide circle of evangelicals who elaborately overinterpreted the government's reforms and contested the narrow interpretation of the royal supremacy peddled by conservatives like Stephen Gardiner. For instance, a brief memorandum that found its way into the State Papers, probably from 1536, declared that it is:

manifest in scripture that all princes upon monition and warning given unto them ... by our sovereign lord the king's majesty, be bounden to make war against the said forsaken Antichrist [the pope] ... or else if they omit or refuse so to do, they show and declare themselves to be of his damnable synagogue and disobedient unto God and his Word.

The tract also called for the wholesale disendowment of the Church, arguing that lands formerly belonging to the pope or 'any of his orders or synagogue ... do appertain and belong to the king's highness'. Most

---

[86] The idea of Anabaptism as the 'left wing' of the Reformation was first canvassed in R. Bainton, 'The Left Wing of the Reformation', *The Journal of Religion* 21 (1941), 124–34.

interestingly, it ended by endorsing an extreme version of sacerdotal monarchy: 'The property, custody, and keeping of the testimonies of scripture, called the book of life, is given to the possession of the king's majesty.'[87]

As another example, an anonymous tract from 1534 argued that princes not only wield the power of the sword to correct the errors of priests but also have the right to preach God's Word to the people when priests are negligent. This argument, which even the author admitted 'seemeth strange', was based on the idea that bishops and priests are merely deputies of the king, like judges in common law, who perform their functions as a direct extension of royal power. This assertion was based on a variety of proof texts, particularly Exodus 18, where Jethro told Moses (the 'true image of a king') to delegate his authority as God's messenger.[88] Another anonymous tract, probably from 1536, announced that the 'Aaronite priesthood is now translated away with full abrogation of Mosaical ceremonies and legal shadows', and that the new, spiritual priesthood 'is represented by Melchizedech, king of Salem, *qui erat rex et sacerdotes*, by whom all Christian people are made *sacerdotes*'.[89] Besides these manuscripts, there were also printed tracts produced in 1532–3 by the MP Jasper Fyloll, another member of Thomas Cromwell's circle, which advanced conceptions of the royal supremacy imbued with extremely radical, Wycliffite anticlericalism.[90]

The conclusion to be drawn from this evidence is obviously not that the royal supremacy over the Church was part of an evangelical conspiracy to overthrow Catholicism in England. For every document that can be found ascribing radical significance to the royal supremacy, another can be found tightly circumscribing its significance. Rather, the conclusion suggested is that the royal supremacy was a deeply contested process, amenable to a wide array of interpretations. Furthermore, Thomas Cromwell knew that the government's actions were being interpreted in far more radical terms than the king would approve, and at least in some circumstances he encouraged those interpretations. We might speculate that given the blatantly radical interpretations of the royal supremacy in some of the documents that crossed Cromwell's desk,

---

[87] PRO SP 6/3, 47r (*LP* X, 253).   [88] PRO SP 6/7, 159r–162r (*LP* VII, 1384).

[89] PRO SP 6/2, 94r–96r. For the dating of this manuscript, see Richard Rex, 'The Crisis of Obedience: God's Word and Henry's Reformation', *Historical Journal* 39 (1996), 863–94.

[90] Richard Rex, 'Jasper Fyloll and the Enormities of the Clergy: Two Tracts Written During the Reformation Parliament,' *Sixteenth Century Journal* 31 (2000), 1043–62.

some of these interpretations may have lodged themselves in Cromwell's mind and played a role, if only whispered in the king's ear, in the formulation of English policy. But even without this speculation, it seems certain that the relationship between early English Protestantism and the royal supremacy over the Church was far more complex than historians have supposed. To see in the royal supremacy some intrinsic *via media*, the origins of a moderate solution to the problem of authority within the Church, is severely to misunderstand the almost messianic role of monarchy in the minds of some radical English reformers in the 1530s.

CHAPTER 4

Counting sheep, counting shepherds: the problem of allegiance in the English Reformation[1]

Alec Ryrie

I

Did the English jump into their peculiar Reformation, or were they pushed? The answer seems clear: the moving force behind religious change was obviously political pressure. We might ask, though, whether the English were so easy to push because they were already preparing to jump. A distinguished line of Protestant historians from John Foxe onwards has suggested that this was indeed the case. However, this argument would find few defenders today. Its key ingredients have come under sustained and more or less effective attack for a generation. In particular, the idea that there was widespread anticlericalism in late medieval England has been discredited.[2] We are reduced, therefore, to asking how quickly, and in what numbers, the English came to cooperate with the political forces propelling them. They *were* pushed; but a time came when most of them stopped resisting. As Patrick Collinson has suggested, in the 1570s – when both Catholic England and Catholic Europe were fading from living memory – insomniac historians begin to count Catholics rather than Protestants.[3]

This much is reasonably clear. More intractable is the question of how this transition from the Catholic nation of the 1520s to the more or less Protestant nation of the 1580s took place. The nature and meanings of conversion to evangelical ideas are discussed elsewhere in this volume by Peter Marshall. This essay is concerned with the linked and equally problematic question of the scale and speed of that conversion. With reference principally to the period before 1553, it will consider how many

---

[1] Among those who have assisted at various stages in my work on this article, I would especially like to thank Caroline Litzenberger, Diarmaid MacCulloch, Peter Marshall and Penny Roberts.
[2] Christopher Haigh, 'Anticlericalism and the English Reformation', *The English Reformation Revised*, ed. Christopher Haigh (Cambridge, 1987).
[3] Patrick Collinson, *The Birthpangs of Protestant England: Religious and Cultural Change in the Sixteenth and Seventeenth Centuries* (Basingstoke, 1988), ix.

evangelical sympathisers there were in England, and how rapidly their numbers grew. This question has been investigated with more diligence and ingenuity for England than for anywhere else in Europe: a result, no doubt, of the ideological temperature of the debates over the English Reformation. At the height of the 'revisionism' arguments, the question of whether Protestants or Catholics were better at filling pews was a key battleground. Nevertheless, the evidence remains fragmentary enough for scholars to continue to disagree wildly with one another. Geoffrey Elton could argue that, by 1553, England was so infected by a 'powerful heresy' that it was 'almost certainly nearer to being a Protestant country than to anything else'. Yet J. J. Scarisbrick could counter that most English people accepted the Reformation slowly and reluctantly, and Christopher Haigh could add that mid-century evangelicals were 'always an unpopular minority'. As Rosemary O'Day has pointed out, none of these assertions can be quantified.[4]

This is not for want of trying. Most historians who have tackled this question have tried to find some statistical or systematic evidence for their views, and have done so with varying levels of sophistication. The most obvious way to quantify religious allegiance is, of course, to count heads. The late John Fines's invaluable register of some 3,000 early English evangelicals has seemed a good starting point for this;[5] but his list is based largely on chance survivals of evidence and represents, as many have observed, the tip of an iceberg whose overall size is unknown and unknowable.[6] The majority of Fines's reformers are known only because they fell foul of the heresy laws under Henry VIII or Mary Tudor. We are therefore dealing only with the very hardest core of outspoken reformers – the committed, plus a handful of the unlucky. An attempt to count religious conservatives by the same means would be equally futile. Around such visible figures lies a penumbra of reformers whose commitment may have been real, but was never publicly tested; of fellow travellers, persuaded by reformist ideas but unwilling to put themselves

---

[4] G. R. Elton, *Reform and Reformation* (1977), 371; J. J. Scarisbrick, *The Reformation and the English People* (Oxford, 1984), 1; Christopher Haigh, *English Reformations: Religion, Politics and Society under the Tudors* (Oxford, 1993), 202; Rosemary O'Day, *The Debate on the English Reformation* (1986), 146.

[5] I am grateful to Professor Fines for providing me with a copy of his register. For attempts to use it in this way, see A. G. Dickens, *The English Reformation* (1964; 2nd edition 1989), 325–6; Diarmaid MacCulloch, *Tudor Church Militant: Edward VI and the Protestant Reformation* (1999), 109–10.

[6] A. G. Dickens, 'The early expansion of Protestantism in England, 1520–1558', *The Impact of the English Reformation 1500–1640*, ed. Peter Marshall (1997), 92. Haigh's optimism that the surviving evidence reveals most of the major reformist groups does not explain away Dickens's evidence that there were significant groups which we know about only through chance survivals of documentation. Haigh, *English Reformations*, 198–9.

in danger; of sympathisers, ready to listen to reformist preachers but not yet fully persuaded; of reformers of convenience, whose family, business or political connections were such that drifting into reformist circles was the path of least resistance. This penumbra may have been large or small, but it is invisible, at least by such direct means, and it is a critical part of the evangelical movement's shape.

The obvious unreliability of such direct methods of quantification has led historians, over the past forty years or so, to investigate other sources which might yield a clearer picture of religious allegiance in England. Sources such as churchwardens' accounts and rates of clerical marriage have their uses, of a somewhat oblique and limited kind.[7] The most intense and sustained research, however, has been devoted to wills, in the hope that changes in the pieties expressed by testators can be used to trace the process of religious change. From the 1530s onwards wills across England progressively abandoned the traditional pious formulæ which cite the Virgin Mary and the saints, replacing them with more ambiguous or – in some cases – apparently evangelical formulæ.[8] However, while wills constitute an invaluable window on to the lives and even the beliefs of individuals, the problems of using them to build a systematic representation of the shifts in English religious culture are legion. It is not merely that the pious formulæ were usually composed by a scribe, not the testator. J. D. Alsop and Christopher Marsh have shown that many testators did not even have much interest in the form of words the scribe used.[9] Nor is it clear whether the gradual transition from one theologically ambiguous set of formulæ to another represents

---

[7] Ronald Hutton, 'The local impact of the Tudor Reformations', *English Reformation Revised*, ed. Haigh; MacCulloch, *Tudor Church Militant*, 106; D. M. Palliser, 'Popular reactions to the Reformation during the years of uncertainty 1530–1570', *English Reformation Revised*, ed. Haigh, 100; Helen L. Parish, *Clerical Marriage and the English Reformation: Precedent, Policy and Practice* (Aldershot, 2000), 198–217.

[8] A. G. Dickens, *Lollards and Protestants in the Diocese of York 1509–1558* (Oxford, 1959), 172, 215; Peter Clark, *English Provincial Society from the Reformation to the Revolution: Religion, Politics and Society in Kent 1500–1640* (Hassocks, Surrey, 1977), 58; Claire Cross, 'The development of Protestantism in Leeds and Hull, 1520–1640: the evidence from wills', *Northern History* 18 (1982), 231–2; Jennifer Ward, 'The Reformation in Colchester, 1528–1558', *Essex Archaeology and History* 3rd series, vol. 15 (1983), 93; Elaine Sheppard, 'The Reformation and the citizens of Norwich', *Norfolk Archaeology* 38 (1983), 54–6; Susan Brigden, *London and the Reformation* (Oxford, 1989), 382–3; Caroline Litzenberger, *The English Reformation and the Laity: Gloucestershire 1540–1580* (Cambridge, 1997), 179–87.

[9] J. D. Alsop, 'Religious preambles in early modern English wills as formulae', *JEH* 40 (1989), 19–27; Christopher Marsh, 'In the name of God? Will-making and faith in early modern England', *The Records of the Nation*, ed. G. H. Martin and Peter Spufford (Woodbridge, Suffolk, 1990).

a change in religious beliefs or one in scribal fashions.[10] The changes in testators' religious bequests, apparently almost as dramatic,[11] can also be interpreted, according to taste, as evidence of changing religious opinions or of realism in the face of a rapacious regime.[12] At best, wills tell a very partial story;[13] and bequests, importantly, can rarely tell us anything about positive allegiance to evangelical ideas. In investigating religious allegiance historians have to search for their evidence where the light is best, but wills have not repaid the attention which has been lavished on them. If the shift in preamble formulæ, from time-honoured phrases to new and more opaque ones, can be taken to mean anything at all, it is a sign neither of enthusiastic conversion nor of diehard conservatism, but rather of turbulence and confusion.[14]

The haphazard nature of almost all sixteenth-century documentation, and the elusive nature of religious belief in any era, makes any application of statistical methods to such questions distinctly limited. As Geoffrey Elton wrote a generation ago, 'A few examples prove nothing one way or another.... The only remedy, however, is to produce many examples.'[15] The promise of a statistical foundation to our understanding of the religious complexion of England is alluring, but we are in the end forced to turn to unashamedly anecdotal evidence.

II

Contemporaries did not treat the question of religious allegiance as seriously or as systematically as we might have wished. Even so, it was a subject which caught the attention of a number of commentators; in particular, as we might expect, that of the evangelicals themselves. In many cases their opinion was thoroughly 'revisionist'. Repeatedly they claimed that evangelical sympathisers were very rare creatures, and that most English people remained resolutely conservative. In 1539 George Constantine lamented that although the Gospel was openly preached:

[10] Brigden, *London and the Reformation*, 380; Eamon Duffy, *The Stripping of the Altars: Traditional Religion in England 1400–1580* (New Haven and London, 1992), 507–8; Alsop, 'Religious preambles', 20–2.
[11] Ward, 'Reformation in Colchester', 87–8; David Marcombe, *English Small Town Life: Retford 1520–1642* (Nottingham, 1993), 221–2.
[12] Duffy, *Stripping of the Altars*, 504–5; G. R. Elton, *Policy and Police: the Enforcement of the Reformation in the Age of Thomas Cromwell* (Cambridge, 1972), 67–71.
[13] Clive Burgess, 'Late medieval wills and pious convention: testamentary evidence reconsidered', *Profit, Piety and the Professions in Later Medieval England*, ed. Michael Hicks (Gloucester, 1990), 15–18.
[14] Brigden, *London and the Reformation*, 383. [15] Elton, *Policy and Police*, viii.

How unthankfully, how rebelliously, how carnally and unwillingly do we receive it! Who is there almost that will have a Bible, but he must be compelled thereto? How loath be our priests to teach the commandments, the articles of the faith, and the Paternoster in English! Again, how unwilling the people to learn it! Yea, they jest at it, calling it the new Paternoster and new learning.[16]

The publisher John Gough agreed that the common people were 'full of hatred and malice . . . against this most holy word and the lovers therof'.[17] Gough's pessimism was echoed by his most prolific author, the evangelical cleric Thomas Becon. In 1541–2 Becon wrote that, while there was an English Bible in every church:

how many read it? Verily, a man may come into some churches and see the Bible so enclosed and wrapped about with dust, even as the pulpit in like manner is both with dust and cobwebs, that with his finger he may write upon the Bible this epitaph: *Ecce nunc in pulvere dormio.*[18]

Indeed, his assessment has a note of bitterness which perhaps reflects his experience as a parish priest in Norfolk:

If they have a ghostly and learned curate . . . him they do hate, they wish the pulpit a coalpit. They think it a hundred years, if he preacheth but half an hour, so little pleasure have these assheads in hearing the glorious and blessed word of God.[19]

A London evangelical writing during 1543–6 gave the mirror image to Becon's lament, describing the continued influence of traditionalist priests in the country at large. He painted a vivid picture of such a priest coming to the house where his people were gathered on a holy day, when they are:

at the hottest in their ale. One biddeth Master Parson welcome; off goeth every man's cap. 'Come hither, Sir John!' 'To me!', saith another; and well is he that can soonest get a chair and a cushion to the highest end of the table for the priest to sit in.

He even ventured to put numbers to the question, claiming (with slightly shaky syntax) that reformers and conservatives were 'two parts

---

[16] 'A Memorial from George Constantine to Thomas Lord Cromwell', *Archaeologia* 23 (1831), 59.
[17] John Gough, *The dore of holy scripture* (1540), A5v-6v.
[18] 'See, I am sleeping in the dust.' Thomas Becon, *Newes out of heauen* (1542), A6r-v; cf. Job 7: 21.
[19] Becon, *Newes out of heauen*, A8r. Cf. Becon's *The new pollecye of warre* (1542), I1r; and his *A new yeares gyfte more precious than golde* (1543), E8r.

far unequal, for the tenth man in London, neither the hundredth man in the whole realm, knoweth not the gospel'.[20] The view that the evangelical message had made few converts and many enemies was the reformers' conventional wisdom.

It is a view that should be treated with caution, however, as is suggested by a reformist polemic from 1546 which argued that the monasteries still held a special place in English hearts. If the king were to restore even one monastery, so permitting others to do the same, then, it suggested:

> you should easily perceive which way they are bent. We doubt not but for these seven years following, masons' occupation, with other belonging to building, would be the best handicrafts within this your realm.[21]

This should warn us against taking such reformist doomsaying too seriously. Within ten years of this tract monasticism was indeed restored, and the response was far less enthusiastic than this author predicted. Evangelicals conceived of themselves as an exclusive minority whether or not this was true. They used such gloomy depictions of their circumstances as a polemical weapon, in order to stir their audiences to action. Elizabethan and Jacobean Protestants continued to speak of their following as a tiny minority, by which they meant not that the mass of the people were actual Catholics, but that their adherence to Protestantism was insufficiently deep.[22] Moreover, reformers and conservatives shared a rhetoric in which denunciations of the impiety of the masses were little more than a mannerism. It is unsurprising that those historians who have emphasised the strength of popular conservatism in these years have been tempted to quote statements such as John Hooper's claim in 1546 that traditional ceremonial was 'never before held by the people as of greater value than at the present', but to take such hyperbolic rhetoric at face value is not really sustainable.[23]

Indeed, just as reformist writers tended to emphasise popular conservatism, so traditionalists warned of popular support for heresy. The most excitable and least reliable conservatives were the foreign ambassadors in London: good Catholics willing to be shocked, and often ill-informed. The Imperial ambassador van der Delft's claim in 1549 that 'the common

---

[20] BL Royal MS 17.B.xxxv, 9r, 10v.   [21] *A supplication of the poore Commons* (1546), A8r.

[22] Patrick Collinson, *The Religion of Protestants: The Church in English Society 1559–1625* (Oxford, 1982), 189–91, 200–2; Alexandra Walsham, *Church Papists: Catholicism, Conformity and Confessional Polemic in Early Modern England* (Woodbridge, 1993), 100–8.

[23] *Epistolae Tigurinae de rebus potissimum ad ecclesiae Anglicanae reformationem* (PS, 1848), 23 (my translation; cf. *Original Letters relative to the English Reformation*, ed. H. Robinson (2 vols., PS, 1846–7), i.36); Haigh, *English Reformations*, 158.

people are badly infected' should not be ignored, but for van der Delft even a small minority would constitute a serious infection.[24] Yet English conservatives agreed. The balladeer Thomas Smith wrote in 1540 that heresy was more deeply rooted than he had feared:

> Of late I well trusted, they had been over blown
> But now I well perceive, that neither favour nor smart
> From the body can expel, that is rooted in the heart.[25]

Soon afterwards, another poet – John Huntingdon, himself soon to convert to reforming ideas – wrote of reformers as being far commoner than they appeared:

> For without doubt
> There is a rout
> Of these same sleepers
> And corner creepers
> That bear a fair face
> In every place.[26]

Conservative preachers lamented the unorthodoxy of their audiences. William Chedsay feared in 1544 that 'the devil hath marked the greater part to him, and putteth Christ to the smaller', and Cuthbert Scott preached in the same year that:

the lay people do grudge against the clergy, disdaining to be taught of them, challenging unto themselves a more perfect knowledge in scripture then the other have, and say that the mysteries of scriptures be opened unto them, by I cannot tell what spirit.[27]

William Peryn's ostensible reason for publishing his sermons defending the mass was that heresy had 'crept secretly in to the hearts of many of the younger and carnal sort'. He decided to act when he saw that 'this dangerous contagion drew toward none end, but rather seemed to take secretly force and strength, and was likely to fasten daily upon more and more'.[28]

---

[24] *Calendar of State Papers, Spanish, 1547–1549*, ed. M. A. S. Hume and Royall Tyler (1912), 463. Cf. MacCulloch, *Tudor Church Militant*, 107–9.

[25] Thomas Smith, *A lytell treatyse agaynst sedicyous persons* (1540).

[26] Reprinted in John Bale, *A Mysterye of inyquyte contayned within the heretycall Genealogye of Ponce Pantolabus* (Antwerp, 1545), 71r.

[27] William Chedsay and Cuthert Scott, *Two notable sermones lately preached at Pauls crosse* (1545), D8v, H7r.

[28] William Peryn, *Thre godlye and notable sermons, of the sacrament of the aulter* (1546), *2v-3r.

Looking back from Mary's reign, Miles Huggarde agreed that 'a great part of this realm', in particular 'the vulgar people', had been allured by the reformers' doctrines.[29] In 1557 the veteran Bristol preacher Roger Edgeworth wrote that during his twenty-year preaching career, heresies:

had so sore infected the Christian flock... that the king's majesty, and all the catholic clerks in the realm had much ado to extinguish them, which yet they could not so perfectly quench, but that ever still... they burst out afresh, even like fire hid under chaff, which sometimes among will flame out and do hurt if it be not looked to.[30]

Both conservatives and reformers saw their enemies more clearly than their friends – or, when convenient, professed to do so.

However, there are more level-headed and circumstantial contemporary assessments of the shifts in the religious divisions in these years. In 1532 Thomas More, not usually a man to play down the threat of heresy, described the hard core of reformers as 'a few ungracious folk'.[31] Political support gave their ideas a chance to spread, but this did not happen overnight. In 1533 Hugh Latimer's preaching in Bristol caused uproar, but he does not seem to have won many converts. One of his partisans there claimed that he could raise 400 signatures in Latimer's defence, but when put to the test only managed 25. Latimer's opponent William Hubberdine – another man not given to understatement – apparently put the number of heretics in Bristol no higher than thirty.[32] A decade later the mood was shifting. For all his despair, Thomas Becon admitted in 1542 that the common people were learning the Commandments, the Creed and the Pater Noster in English, and that 'many savour Christ aright, and daily the number increaseth'.[33] Likewise, in 1539 Richard Morison wrote that 'the people begin to know what they that be curates ought to preach, and what they are bound to follow, and yet they do but begin'.[34] By 1543 the veteran evangelical George Joye was writing, as if it were surprising, that 'thou shalt find even among the people many that abhor and detest these said holy popes' decrees, laws etc.,

[29] Miles Huggarde, *The displaying of the protestantes, with a description of diuers their abuses* (1556), 6r, 7r, 93v, 95r-v.

[30] Roger Edgeworth, *Sermons very fruitfull, godly and learned: preaching in the Reformation c. 1535–c. 1553*, ed. Janet Wilson (Cambridge, 1993), 95.

[31] Thomas More, *The confutacyon of Tyndales answere* (1532), Bb2v.

[32] Martha C. Skeeters, *Community and Clergy: Bristol and the Reformation, c. 1530–c. 1570* (Oxford, 1993), 43.

[33] Thomas Becon, *A newe pathway vnto praier, ful of much godly frute and christen knowledge* (1542), R5r.

[34] Richard Morison, *An invective ayenste the great and detestable vice, treason* (1539), D6r.

as rotten, stinking running sores'.[35] In the following year John Bale alleged that the 'lousy legerdemain' of the clergy 'is almost perceived of all men'. Bale was also confident that the sporadic persecution during these years strengthened the reformist cause: Anne Askew's martyrdom, he asserted hyperbolically, had converted a thousand people from popery.[36] A decade later Huggarde agreed that martyrdom was capable of stirring up considerable dissent, describing with contempt the 'brainsick fools' who cried out encouragement in the streets as Protestants were being taken to the stake, and who attended executions in huge numbers to be outraged and edified.[37]

In other words, if the reformers' numbers remained small, they remained confident that the tide was moving in their direction. Morison even believed that England's conservative heartlands were ripe for conversion. Arguing in 1539 that there was a backlash against the Pilgrimage of Grace, he claimed, 'I have heard divers men say, that three or four preachers may do more good in the north country in two or three months, than hath been done in these south parts, these two or three years.'[38]

Perhaps this was wishful thinking. Yet several reports tend to confirm his point. In the same year John Marshall wrote a series of reports on the state of Nottinghamshire and Lincolnshire which depict a population thoroughly pacified. 'The commons', he wrote, 'say it is a good world, for the poor men may now live in peace by the great men, for now (thank God) their great ruffling is past.' In addition, he claimed that the people were responding surprisingly positively to the changes in religion and, despite some initial opposition, were warming to the new English texts of the Pater Noster and the Creed.[39] Other conservative regions displayed the same benevolent curiosity. Latimer's early preaching tours may not have won many converts, but they certainly drew crowds. When one open-air sermon in Exeter was interrupted by rain, his substantial audience apparently refused to disperse and stayed to hear him out.[40] Even the abrasive William Barlow, bishop of the Welsh diocese of

---

[35] George Joye, *Our sauiour Iesus Christ hath not ouercharged his chirche with many ceremonies* (Antwerp, 1543), A2v.

[36] John Bale, *The epistle exhortatorye of an Englyshe Christiane unto his derely beloued contraye of Englande* (Antwerp, 1544), 5r; Anne Askew and John Bale, *The first examinacyon of Anne Askew, latelye martyred in Smythfelde* (Wesel, 1546), 43r.

[37] Huggarde, *Displaying of the protestantes*, 43r, 49r-v.

[38] Morison, *Invective ayenste treason*, D7r.

[39] PRO SP 1 / 143, 81r (*LP* XIV (i) 295); SP 1 / 150, 187r (*LP* XIV (i) 839).

[40] Devon Record Office, ECA Book 51, 342r.

St David's, conceded in 1538 that his people were receptive to the reformist gospel:

The people, now sensibly seeing the long obscured verity manifestly to display her brightness, whereby their inveterate accustomed superstition apparently detected, all popish delusions shall soon be defaced.[41]

This optimism was echoed by Becon after an extended visit to Derbyshire and Staffordshire in the mid-1540s. The East Anglian boy clearly regarded venturing into the Peak District as stepping beyond the bounds of civilisation. When he wrote an account of his travels in a fictionalised dialogue in 1550 he had the other characters ask, 'Into the Peak? Lord God, what made you there?... I think you found there very peakish people.' But in the event he was pleasantly surprised. Although the area was dominated by 'popish pedlary', 'the people where I have travelled, for the most part, are reasonable and quiet enough, yea and very conformable to God's truth. If any be stubbornly obstinate, it is for fault of knowledge.'

Staffordshire, he added, 'savoured somewhat more of pure religion', because travellers passing through the region had brought with them ideas and books from the south-east. Indeed, Becon wrote, one Derbyshire magnate who sheltered him owned a solid library of English evangelical texts, including works by Tyndale and Frith as well as (we are told with some satisfaction) Becon's own complete works.[42] Such books were clearly available well beyond London.

If remote regions had the potential for reform, unmistakable evangelical support was visible in other areas. In London the preacher Robert Wisdom blamed his arrest in 1543 on clergy alarmed by his popular following. According to Wisdom, the bishop of Hereford had said that 'great resort was to my sermons, rather than to others, better learned than I, that had not half the audience'. Wisdom smugly summed up his opponents' view of him as follows: 'Lo, all the world goeth after him. What shall we do? This fellow hath an exceeding audience. If we let him alone thus, all will believe him.'[43]

Wisdom's impartiality is certainly open to question; but an order of the Court of Aldermen in the same year that two of the sheriff of London's men should attend every sermon at Paul's Cross suggests

---

[41] BL Cotton MS Cleopatra E.iv, 316r.
[42] Thomas Becon, *The iewell of ioye* (1550), B7v, C1v, C3r-4v, C8r.
[43] BL Harleian MS 425, 7v. Cf. ECL MS 261, 91r.

genuine concern about the size of crowds at sermons, and the consequent potential for public disorder.[44] It was not a new problem: conservatives had shown periodic concern about violence and other disturbances during sermons in London since 1540.[45] Most reformist protest, however, was of a more subtle nature. About a third of the lay people arrested in the last, abortive attempt at a universal purge of heretics in London in 1540 were charged with failing to attend their parish churches or with irreverence in church.[46] In 1537 the London conservative Rowland Phillips claimed that there were many who 'in mass do use to clap their finger upon their lips and say never a word'.[47]

It was not only in London that such problems could be found. The heretical seed which Latimer had sown in Bristol grew quickly. In 1537 it was reported that one Bristol priest's failure to pray for the king during the Pilgrimage of Grace had offended 'all the parishioners'. This was an exaggeration, but his parish was clearly divided, with the reformers apparently in a majority. Indeed, passions had risen to such a point that the priest himself had been physically attacked. He was charged with saying that:

he had not his black face for nothing. . . . For all that they be twenty-seven with a captain, and I have but seven of the old fashion with me, I trust some honest men and women will take my part.[48]

There were similar divisions in Gloucester, where an impromptu reformist sermon in 1540 was met with 'murmur' and 'unquietness' rather than outrage and disbelief.[49] Seven years later an evangelical preacher visiting Salisbury also found noticeable support, financial as well as numerical, from the townspeople.[50] In Kent in 1543 the reformers themselves boasted of their numerical strength. In May of that year, the parson of Wychling is said not only to have reviled a neighbouring priest as 'a false heretic and a popish knave', but to have added a threat: 'I shall make forty in the parish of Doddington to

---

[44] Corporation of London Record Office, Repertory 11, 13v. There were similar problems in Norfolk; see 'Great Yarmouth assembly minutes 1538–1545', ed. P. Rutledge, *Norfolk Record Society* 39 (1970), 38.

[45] Charles Wriothesley, *A Chronicle of England during the Reigns of the Tudors*, ed. W. Hamilton, vol. 1 (Camden Society n.s. 11, 1875), 115; Guildhall Library, London, MS 9531/12, 40r.

[46] *AM* (1570), 1376–80.

[47] *Miscellaneous Writings and Letters of Thomas Cranmer*, ed. J. E. Cox (PS, 1846), 339.

[48] PRO SP 1/119, 192v–193r (*LP* XII (i) 1147).

[49] Worcester County Record Office, MS BA 2764/802, 137.

[50] *Reformation Narratives*, 74–6.

bark at thee, and I shall make ten thousand of my set against thee in Kent.'[51]

We do not need to take such numbers literally to recognise the confidence that reformist support in Kent was significant and widespread. Likewise, down the coast in Brighton the parish priest lamented during the 1540s that 'in this town . . . many a rude person sticketh not to call a priest knave', and insisted that this was not simple anticlericalism but rather 'new learning and lately crept up'.[52] Even in the most reformist areas, however, widespread sympathy for reform did not equate to majority support. In 1539 the evangelical Anthony Pickering was forced to temper his optimism with realism as he wrote that 'there is of both sorts in London . . . but I trust the most part good; or else I would they were good, as knoweth our Lord'.[53] A reformist majority was not unthinkable, but it was a long way off.

In 1545 the botanist and radical polemicist William Turner responded to Bishop Gardiner's allegation that the realm was essentially at peace within itself with one of the longest contemporary analyses of the state of the religious parties. Gardiner could not have been more wrong, he argued:

The third part of the realm dissenteth from the other two parts in the cause of religion. There are ten thousand and more honest men in England which in their consciences dissent from you, and hate with all their hearts your false doctrine. . . . There is not a city nor a great town in all England wherein are not many that dissent from you in doctrine and would openly speak against you if they durst.

In addition, 'the most part' of scholars of the universities 'which have been brought up in the bosom of the holy scripture' despised traditional ceremonial. The one great bastion of conservatism, he claimed, remained the nongraduate clergy who held the vast majority of English curacies.[54] This was, no doubt, partly mere snobbery, but many reformers seem to have been cold-shouldered by clerical neighbours. Turner wrote:

If a preacher comes from Oxford or Cambridge, freely to preach the word of God to the people, and requires to be heard, the priest uses to give this answer to the preacher, if he smell anything of the new learning: 'We must this day read

---

[51] CCCC MS 128, 84 (*LP* XVIII (ii) 546, p. 316).
[52] PRO SP 1/244, 139r (*LP* Addenda 1597).
[53] PRO SP 1/143, 72r (*LP* XIV (i) 283).
[54] William Turner, *The rescuynge of the romishe fox* (Bonn, 1545), A8r-v.

the Six Articles, otherwise called Gardiner's Gospel', and so the preacher goeth away.[55]

Likewise, in an unpublished tract, Richard Morison deplored the clergy who justified their refusal to preach against the pope on the grounds that 'since your Majesty hath abolished him, the people need not talk of him, but if they would hold their tongues, every man would soon forget him.' Morison was surely right to see such an approach as disingenuous.[56] Such minimal obedience seems to have been common practice among the clergy. Even in Kent there were repeated claims that only Archbishop Cranmer's appointees were preaching the gospel and obeying the royal injunctions.[57] At the other end of the country, Bishop Bird of Chester – by no means a hot-gospeller – was shocked by the extent of noncompliance from his clergy.[58] To enforce the injunctions, a London reformer claimed, was to risk an accusation of heresy.[59] Indeed, a 1546 tract claimed that the clergy had deliberately ignored the official English Primer, issued the previous year, which was ambivalent towards the cult of the saints and prayers for the dead. By contrast, this author argued, should any new official publication seem to favour traditional religion, 'it shall be swung in every pulpit, with, "This is the king's gracious will, and yet these heretics will be still doing in the Scriptures." '[60] By November 1546, according to Richard Cox, conservative clergy were actually burning official publications such as the Primer and the *King's Book* of 1543, using as a justification the general purge against heretical books which followed the proclamation in August of that year.[61]

Even among the nongraduate clergy, however, there are indications that Turner's picture of massed ranks of traditionalists is an oversimplification. Becon was as critical of the clergy as the next evangelical, but he characterised their traditionalism as being motivated not by loyalty to Rome but by simple sluggardliness and self-interest:

God saith: Lift up thy voice as a trump. But they say, whist, not a word, unless we be suspect to be fellows of the new learning. . . . It is good sleeping in a whole skin. He is not wise that will cast himself into trouble when he may live in rest.[62]

55 Turner, *Rescuynge*, A6v-7r.
56 BL Cotton MS Faustina C.ii, 15r. I am grateful to John Jackson and John Cooper for this reference.
57 PRO SP 1/152, 2r (*LP* XIV (i) 1053); SP 1/160, 5r (*LP* XV 645).
58 PRO SP 1/168, 8r (*LP* XVI 1377).   59 BL Royal MS 17.B.xxxv, 8v.
60 *Supplication of the poore Commons*, A7v.   61 PRO SP 1/226, 16r (*LP* XXI (ii) 321).
62 Thomas Becon, *An Inuectyue agenst the moste wicked & detestable vice of swearing* (1543), 4r.

Becon had nothing but contempt for this attitude, but he clearly believed that only pragmatic considerations prevented many clergy from openly siding with reform. Beyond the ranks of the committed stood what was probably a larger number of sympathetic onlookers. George Joye was also convinced in the 1540s that such conformism was widespread. While he deplored fainthearts 'that will not believe the gospel till they see every man agree thereupon', he was willing to accept that in some circumstances indecision was understandable:

There be yet many of us which have not heard the gospel openly and freely preached which bear good zeal thereto, but yet are they but tender and weak, and not waxen so strong branches in the vineyard of Christ as some others be: which must with great diligence, cure and study be planted, watered and rooted with continual reading and teaching till they be strong and constant.[63]

One particular consideration which restrained such people from giving their open support to reform, Joye felt, was the need for public unity in religion, and he appealed to:

the learned and prudent, which yet for the study and zeal of peace ... would appear to abhor and eschew these new fashions and sudden mutations (as they call them)... lest their rashness (as they pretend it) should confirm the enemies of the gospel. Therefore decree they thus to stand still... looking upon and beholding the brunt of the battle, no hands putting forth, nor yet once (when they might) to help any amendment or reformation. But the matter is too manifest and too far gone.[64]

Similarly, John Bale chided the 'soft wits' who felt that his polemic was too violent.[65]

If reformers were impatient that such temporisers dragged their feet, conservatives were thoroughly alarmed by their readiness to dally with evangelical ideas. William Peryn's avowed aim in preaching was to 'reclaim ... such as were not too far gone' in heresy, rather than to reconvert obstinate opponents.[66] One of the most disturbing manifestations of this phenomenon was a widespread reluctance to support vigorous prosecution of the heresy laws.[67] In 1546 the conservative scholar and

---

[63] George Joye, *A present consolation for the sufferers of persecucion for ryghtwysenes* (Antwerp, 1544), B2v, C7r-v.

[64] George Joye, *The exposicion of Daniel the Prophete* (Antwerp, 1545), 210r-v.

[65] Askew and Bale, *The first examinacyon*, 44r.   [66] Peryn, *Thre godlye sermons*, *3r-v.

[67] See, for example, *AM*, 1202; Askew and Bale, *The first examinacyon*, 37v; Muriel McClendon, *The Quiet Reformation: magistrates and the emergence of Protestantism in Tudor Norwich* (Stanford, 1999), 14–5.

polemicist Richard Smith was horrified by the indulgent approach which many took towards evangelicals:

laughing merely for pastime at their sayings, reading very gladly their very naughty and railing, pestiferous books and writings, without rebuke or controlment of them, and advancing some of them to right honest and good promotions.[68]

Moderation of this kind was to become increasingly difficult as confessional identities hardened in the decades to come, and the sectarian historians of both sides shared an interest in writing such compromisers out of the record.[69] Nevertheless, it seems likely that by Edward VI's reign this fringe of 'soft', uncommitted reformers and reformist sympathisers was numerically significant; certainly far more than Turner's figure of 10,000 committed evangelicals, and possibly as many as his other guess of a third of the nation.

III

If we can tentatively conclude that a significant minority of English people became sympathetic, on a range of levels, to novel religious views, it is less easy to understand why this might have happened. The clearest achievement of so-called 'revisionism' has been to demonstrate that the English did not see themselves as groaning under a papal yoke in the generations before the Reformation. If English Protestantism had not existed, it would not have been necessary to invent it. Yet if the evangelical movement was not rooted in a pre-existing dissatisfaction with traditional religion, it becomes harder to explain how this decidedly nontraditional religion managed to establish a mass following of any kind within a generation of its arrival in England.

Part of the answer to this question must be logistical. The reformist message was being spread by some extraordinarily able preachers; and as A. G. Dickens has pointed out, in a country whose entire population was comparable to that of Wales today, such individuals might have more influence than we would be inclined to ascribe to them.[70] They seem to have had some success in turning the sermon into a form of mass entertainment.[71] The power of a sermon could be strongly reinforced

---

[68] Richard Smith, *The assertion and defence of the sacramente of the aulter* (1546), 10v.
[69] Andrew Pettegree, *Marian Protestantism: Six Studies* (Aldershot, 1996), 86–117.
[70] Dickens, 'Early expansion of Protestantism', 93.
[71] Huggarde, *Displaying of the protestantes*, 86v–87r.

by visual displays such as iconoclasm: the exposure and destruction of allegedly fraudulent relics before an audience seems to have been particularly effective.[72] In this period reformers were also eager to use the stage to spread their message.[73] In addition, of course, evangelicals produced a flood of printed religious polemic, to which conservatives were woefully slow to respond.[74] English evangelicals managed to disseminate their message remarkably quickly, through a remarkable range of media, against remarkably little organised opposition. This did not guarantee that that message would be well received, but it was perhaps a necessary condition for its success.

To most contemporaries, however, such functional approaches to the spread of the new ideas would seem to miss the point; as would the suggestion that popular dissatisfaction with the pre-Reformation church might have predisposed the English towards heresy. Both evangelical and conservative partisans at the time would have preferred to explain the change in religious rather than social terms. If moderns have focused on explaining the fertility or otherwise of the soil on to which the evangelical seed fell, contemporaries paid more attention to the intrinsic power of the seed itself, for good or ill. Reformers, of course, argued that through the preaching of the true gospel God had opened their eyes.[75] Yet conservatives agreed that evangelical preaching was at the root of the problem of heresy, and were quite clear as to how it had succeeded in inflicting such deep wounds on traditional religious practice. For Miles Huggarde the difference between the Catholic message and that of the reformers was that between the narrow and broad roads:

The one exhorteth all men to bear Christ's cross, in hard life, trouble, and affliction: the other persuadeth to embrace liberty, belly-cheer, and all pleasure. . . . The one subjugateth the affections: the other unbridleth the appetites.[76]

This is obviously polemical, but the charge that the evangelicals attracted converts or sympathisers through promising 'liberty' should not be dismissed. It was a claim which conservatives made repeatedly and at length. At times it was no more than a way of accusing their opponents of loose morals. Bishop Gardiner threw back at the reformers the oft-cited example of the penitent thief on the cross, claiming that they wished

[72] Peter Marshall, 'The rood of Boxley, the blood of Hailes and the defence of the Henrician Church', *JEH* 46 (1995), 689–96; *Calendar of State Papers, Spanish, 1547–1549*, 219–20.
[73] Ruth Blackburn, *Biblical Drama under the Tudors* (The Hague, 1971).
[74] See Andrew Pettegree's essay in this volume.
[75] See Peter Marshall's essay in this volume.
[76] Huggarde, *Displaying of the protestantes*, 34v–35r.

to follow his example by living an immoral life then repenting at the last minute.[77] The Christian freedom which the reformers claimed was merely 'carnal liberty'.[78] However, there was more to this than simple insult. In 1552–3 Roger Edgeworth claimed that in his congregation there were:

> a great many I am sure, that would haue said once within these twenty years, that no man living, no, nor an angel of heaven or all the devils in hell, should never have perverted you from the sure affiance and fast faith that you had toward the blessed sacraments of the church. But after that there came among you a great multitude of pleasant preachers, preaching liberty, and so pleasures following of such lewd liberty: how soon you have been overthrown and turned another way.[79]

The throwaway accusation of 'lewd liberty' cannot conceal his genuine dismay that the words of the 'pleasant preachers' had seduced his flock from the truth. Other conservatives agreed that those who came preaching justification by faith alone were all too persuasive. In 1540 John Standish described the doctrine as 'venom . . . which to the taste seemeth sweet and delicious'. Richard Smith and Miles Huggarde used very similar terms. Even Gardiner admitted that the doctrine had 'a marvellous appearance of plainness'.[80] He complained that, 'in a miserable state of iniquity and sin, some would have nothing preached but mercy, with only Christ, and how he beareth all sin, payeth all, purgeth all, and cleanseth all'.[81]

Of course evangelical preachers were popular, he argued: their theme was always forgiveness, and never sin.

The accusation that evangelical doctrine fostered a lax attitude to sin may be unjust, but many evangelicals took it extremely seriously. Almost every reformist treatment of justification during this period included a denunciation of the 'gross gospellers' who abused evangelical liberty.[82]

---

[77] Stephen Gardiner, *A declaration of such true articles as George Ioye hath gone about to confute as false* (1546), 50v; cf. Luke 23: 39–43.

[78] Edgeworth, *Sermons*, 127; CCCC MS 128, 10 (*LP* XVIII (ii) 546, p. 292); Huggarde, *Displaying of the protestantes*, 22v. For the potency of this charge of 'carnal liberty', see also Thomas Freeman's essay in this volume.

[79] Edgeworth, *Sermons*, 364.

[80] John Standish, *A lytle treatise against the protestacion of Robert Barnes* (1540), C2r; Richard Smith, *A defence of the blessed masse, and the sacrifice therof* (1546), 13v; Huggarde, *Displaying of the protestantes*, 113v; Gardiner, *Declaration of such true articles*, 267v.

[81] Stephen Gardiner, *A detection of the Deuils Sophistrie* (1546), 114v.

[82] See for example Thomas Becon, *A Christmas bankette* (1542), O4v; Richard Tracy, *The profe and declaration of thys proposition: Fayth only iustifieth* (1543), D3r–4r; Katherine Parr, *The Lamentacion of a Sinner* (1547), F1r–v.

Although couched in vague terms, these passages clearly aimed to describe real people rather than a hypothetical problem. I know of no case of an evangelical denying that such people existed; and occasionally they were more precise. Thomas Becon's 1550 tract, *The fortress of the faithful*, was a response to the rebellions of the previous year, which he blamed mainly on seditious papists. However, he apparently felt he could not dodge the charge that it was reformers, preaching 'indiscreet sermons', who had provoked the rising in Norfolk. Such preachers, rumour alleged, had 'caused the common people to aspire and breathe unto carnal liberty'. Remarkably, Becon did not attempt to deny this, stating instead that:

I will not excuse all preachers. For some, as I have heard, have taken upon them the office of preaching uncalled, unsent, and such disordered preachers for the most part, bring all things to a disorder, yea to an utter confusion.

However, he argued at length that those whom he called 'godly preachers' could not be blamed and had been cruelly slandered. He asked, 'Can the sermons of them which teach all obedience, humility, and patience, move men unto disobedience, haughtiness of mind, and desire of revenging?'[83] It is not the most convincing defence. The implication is not merely that reformist preachers were up to their necks in the risings in the southeast in 1549, including the one in Norfolk that developed into open rebellion.[84] This rare glimpse of the world of disreputable evangelicalism suggests that the conservative accusations were not unfounded. If a partisan as biased as Becon was forced to concede that there were reformers who tended towards libertinism, and that their audiences were ready to hear and act on this message, we may perhaps believe him.

However, the accusation that the reformers preached liberty did not simply mean that they were immoral. For most reformers evangelical liberty meant liberty from the ceremonial, ritual and regulation of traditional religion. They attacked customs which were a powerful social lubricant as superstitions, and in so doing attempted to redefine social morality. It is clear that this was deeply shocking to many people. Yet such challenges to the legitimacy of time-honoured practices can be hard to resist if they once establish themselves in a society, as the shifts in social

---

[83] Thomas Becon, *The fortresse of the faythfull* (1550), D1 v-8v.
[84] It has in any case become increasingly clear that these risings, although largely secular, had an evangelical tinge to them. Ethan Shagan, 'Protector Somerset and the 1549 rebellions: new sources and new perspectives', *EHR* 114 (1999); Diarmaid MacCulloch, *Thomas Cranmer: a Life* (New Haven and London, 1996), 432–8.

morality during the twentieth century show. It is well known that many English people whose religious conservatism was impeccable joined in the plunder of monastic property once it had become clear that the plunder was going to go ahead in any case. Likewise, as traditional practices were eroded, abandoning them looked steadily less revolutionary and more pragmatic. In the four years after clerical marriage was legalised in 1549, some 15 per cent of English parish clergy married. It would be foolhardy to suggest that they married because they were evangelical sympathisers.[85] Yet one might well drift into evangelical sympathies as a consequence of marriage; for significant areas of traditional religious practice were widely seen as incompatible with clerical marriage,[86] while the reformers defended and justified it.

Evangelicalism laid a similar trap for the laity by its rejection of set fasts. In the Swiss Reformation Lent-breaking had been a revolutionary act. In England Lent was not so much broken as whittled away. From 1538 the Lenten fast was partially relaxed by the crown, ostensibly on purely pragmatic grounds.[87] By Edward VI's reign traditional fasts were being justified simply as a gesture of support for the fishing industry.[88] Not all English people were quick to take advantage of the new freedoms, but those who stuck to the old rules must have seemed increasingly quixotic.[89] John Feckenham lamented in 1547 that those who still observed fasts were ridiculed.[90] All the while, evangelicals were insisting that fast days could simply be ignored. It was an extremely simple message, and one with an obvious and immediate appeal. As early as the late 1530s Roger Edgeworth was alarmed by how quickly this insidious idea had spread in Bristol, yet there was little he could say to stop it. He tried to associate fast-breaking with incest, but few can have been persuaded.[91] By the 1540s Lent-breaking was an endemic problem across the kingdom.[92]

When Miles Huggarde denounced Protestants as libertines in 1556, the specific areas he singled out as evidence of this were Protestant opposition

---

[85] Parish, *Clerical Marriage*, 198–217.   [86] Ibid., 161–79.

[87] *Tudor Royal Proclamations 1485–1553*, ed. Paul L. Hughes and James F. Larkin (New Haven, 1964), i. 260–61.

[88] *Calendar of State Papers and Manuscripts existing in the archives and collections of Venice . . . 1534–1554*, ed. Rawdon Brown (1873), 347.

[89] PRO SP 1/150, 187r (*LP* XIV (i) 839).   [90] PRO SP 1/228, 55v (*LP* XXI (ii) 710).

[91] Edgeworth, *Sermons*, 128.

[92] See, among many examples, *APC* i. 104–6, 114–5; CCCC MS 128, 45, 72 (*LP* XVIII (ii) 546, pp. 306, 312); PRO SP 1/146, 252r-v (*LP* XIV (i) 684), SP 1/176, 156r (*LP* XVIII (i) 327); Corporation of London Record Office, Repertory 10, 90v, 169v, 324v, Repertory 11, 176r; *AM* (1570), 1376, 1378.

to clerical celibacy and opposition to fasting. Sermons against fasting, he suggested, had been received as a 'pleasant matter', as well they might have been.[93] Bishop Gardiner's lament in 1546 that the reformers' ideas appealed to a wide section of people rings true:

> You promise them liberty of all things. . . . You flatter the covetous master with pulling away holy days, that he may have the more work done him for his year's wages. You flatter again the servant with pulling away all opinion of fast by abstinence from any meat either in Lent or otherwise. You offer priests wives, to wit, and they can win them to you. You rid all of confession, and weeping for sin.[94]

It was the evangelicals' good fortune to be preaching against practices which could be maintained only by constant and conscious effort, and which made less and less sense as fewer and fewer people observed them. The offer of liberty was real. While we should beware believing the propaganda of either side, we should not allow such wariness to blind us to the real force which these ideas could have. Of course, one did not become an evangelical because one broke a fast, much less because one accepted official relaxation of fasts. However, by breaking a fast or abandoning any of these other traditional strictures one aligned one's life with those who were preaching in defence of what you had done and against those who had denounced it.

Attacks on fasting and celibacy, for all the impact they may have had, were hardly the heart of the evangelical message. However, it is arguable that one element which was far more central had a similar impact. From the beginning the reformers had suggested, with a devastating simplicity, that purgatory did not exist. The huge intercessory effort which was one of the organising principles of late medieval piety was dismissed simply as a confidence trick. As the blunt-speaking polemicist Henry Brinklow put it, prayers and masses for souls in purgatory 'availeth the dead no more than the pissing of a wren helpeth to cause the sea to flow at an extreme ebb'.[95] The argument which was put endlessly by evangelical authors and preachers was that purgatory was a sham, maintained by the clergy to line their own pockets and to distract good Christians from the truly charitable work of giving to the poor. Like most conspiracy theories, this must have seemed inherently improbable at first, but it had an insidious quality to it. The late medieval devotional system built around prayer for the dead depended, among other things, on a sense that the Church

---

[93] Huggarde, *Displaying of the protestantes*, 30v.   [94] Gardiner, *Declaration of such true articles*, 82r-v.
[95] Henry Brinklow, *The Lamentacion of a Christian, against the Citie of London* (Bonn, 1542), A3v.

militant was united in communion with the Church triumphant. When it interceded for the dead, the Church spoke with one voice. The breaking of that unity by even a small dissenting minority gravely undermined the social legitimacy of such intercession. Henry VIII's successive attempts to circumscribe prayer for the dead only accelerated the process.

Diarmaid MacCulloch has suggested that many English people did indeed become convinced that the old Church had played them for fools.[96] In individual cases it is unclear whether this conviction precipitated a conversion to other evangelical views, or merely followed it. However, just as the evangelical message of liberty had an appeal that was more than merely doctrinal, so the evangelical attack on purgatory seems to have caused ripples among those who may not have been convinced by the theology behind it. Purgatory was not merely a doctrine but a living system of devotion, and one which required a great deal of effort and expense to maintain. From the mid-1530s onwards that system of devotion was under steady attack by Henry VIII's and Edward VI's regimes; and at the same time evangelicals were denouncing the entire system as fraudulent. Fear of endowments being seized; the niggling suspicion that the evangelicals might be right; and common sloth and avarice united to form a powerful alliance against spending time or money on intercession for the dead.

Roger Edgeworth's accusation that 'this opinion of no purgatory' is 'grounded on ... carnal liberty' may be opportunist, but it is not implausible. Perhaps, as he argued, those who doubted purgatory hoped for repentance without penance.[97] It is equally likely that they were glad of an excuse not to spend significant amounts of their wealth on intercession. Patrick Collinson has compared the abolition of purgatory to the forcible closure of hospices for the terminally ill; this vividly conveys the extent to which it would have horrified those who continued to believe.[98] But unlike a hospice, purgatory is intangible. Faced with a choice between the bleak belief that souls are being abandoned to their torments by a society that has turned its back on them, and the more comforting alternative that no such torments exist, few people would have the moral courage to resist the lure of the latter. For many, purgatory might seem less like a hospice than like a contributory pension: a burden borne willingly for the community and for one's own future, but which could quickly become intolerable if a suspicion arose that no such provision

---

[96] MacCulloch, *Tudor Church Militant*, 115–6.   [97] Edgeworth, *Sermons*, 128, 132.

[98] Patrick Collinson, 'England', *The Reformation in National Context*, ed. Robert Scribner, Roy Porter and Mikuláš Teich (Cambridge, 1994), 88.

was needed, and that the contributions were merely lining the pockets of the salesmen.

Respectable evangelicals, of course, had no truck with such worldly or mixed motives. They went out of their way to distance themselves from the avarice, gluttony and lechery to which their doctrines could be seen as appealing. This was of course politically necessary, but it is safe to assume they meant it. We are familiar with their self-image as an elect minority, and with their readiness to fall out among themselves regardless of their wider circumstances. Yet from a historical point of view, this does not convince. The committed core of reformers may have been uncomfortable with the broader penumbra of sympathisers and opportunists, but that penumbra was an inseparable part of their movement. Most English people never experienced a dramatic, individual conversion; Protestant England was formed by pragmatic gospellers. Equally importantly, the presence of this reformist penumbra was deeply damaging to traditional religion and to its attempts at self-defence. The leaders of early evangelicalism were highly moral and responsible people. Nevertheless, their message had a dangerous, irresponsible, reckless appeal. While traditional religion offered community, responsibility, virtue, prudence and asceticism, evangelicalism offered liberty. It was an offer which gave the reformers allies they may not have wanted, yet that offer and those allies were important ingredients of their eventual success.

IV

By 1553, then, a small, noisy and well-documented minority of English people had clearly experienced a shift in religious identity towards evangelicalism which we might well call conversion; and a much larger and more amorphous body of people, although still clearly a minority, seem to have been attracted by evangelical preaching and writing such that their religion was no longer wholly traditional. This is not to try to reintroduce a 'Whig-Protestant' interpretation of the English Reformation by the back door. Rather, it is to suggest that religious change under Henry VIII and Edward VI cannot be understood simply as a process of changing Catholics into Protestants. The problem of allegiance remains, but must be addressed qualitatively as well as quantitatively. We may regret, with A. G. Dickens, that there is 'little prospect of establishing tolerably hard statistics concerning...even the rough percentage of the English population which at any stage [early Protestants] attained'.[99] Living in an age of mass politics, we are accustomed to thinking in such terms. However, to attempt to compile such figures for early modern England is not merely futile – it is counterproductive.[100] The concentration on numerical support is misleading in a hierarchical society; and in such a society, to attempt to draw clear dividing lines is to mask the nature of religious change.

Committed reformers were undoubtedly a small minority. Yet it is less clear whether this matters, for in early modern Europe small minorities might have a vastly disproportionate influence. In France Huguenot allegiance at its height was perhaps one tenth of the population, yet the determined dissidence of this tiny minority was enough to sustain four decades of civil war.[101] The quality of dissidence mattered as much as the quantity, and quality can be measured in several ways. First, and simplest, is the level of commitment. One of the characteristic fallacies of a democratic age is the assumption that each individual has the same political weight. Yet revolutionaries have always known that a determined minority can overthrow a confused, divided or disorientated majority. As Rosemary O'Day has put it, 'cadres are decisive';[102] and the commitment of the evangelical cadres is not in doubt. The effectiveness of their propaganda; their refusal to compromise with opponents, especially after 1547; and their willingness to stamp out dissent among themselves all bear testimony to this.[103] Equally important was their conviction that providence was on their side. The day of the Lord, they insisted, was at hand.[104] The very persecution that they endured was the devil's last, desperate and doomed ploy; it was both a sign that the end was near, and the means by which they would attain victory.[105] A reformer burned in 1546 is said to have shouted as he was taken to the stake, 'Fight for your God; for he hath not long to continue.'[106] These are the kinds of prophecies which tend to become self-fulfilling.

However, the evangelicals had more than prophecy to fall back on. As minorities go, they were singularly well placed and well connected.

[99] Dickens, 'Early expansion of Protestantism', 89.
[100] Collinson, 'England', 83–84; O'Day, *Debate on the English Reformation*, 146.
[101] Mark Greengrass, *The French Reformation* (Oxford, 1987), 43.
[102] O'Day, *Debate on the English Reformation*, 146.
[103] See Thomas Freeman's essay in this volume.
[104] Thomas Becon, *A pleasaunt newe Nosegay* (1542), A7r; ECL MS 261, 114v.
[105] Joye, *Present consolation*, C6v; Joye, *The refutation of the byshop of Winchesters derke declaration of his false articles* (1546), 190r; John Bale, *Yet a course at the romyshe foxe* (Antwerp, 1543), 96v; Miles Coverdale, *A confutacion of that treatise, which one Iohn Standish made agaynst the protestacion of D. Barnes* (Zürich, 1541), C4r-v.
[106] *AM*, 1232.

Their strongholds were in the areas of the country which mattered polit-ically – the south-east, East Anglia, the Thames valley, and towns rather than the countryside; their weakness in the north, the south-west and Wales may have been a cause for pastoral concern, but politically it was much less important. More significantly still, like their Huguenot counterparts a generation later, English evangelicals had friends in high places. Under Henry VIII, when their political favour was only ever par-tial, they had powerful patrons in Anne Boleyn and Thomas Cromwell. Henry's diocesan bishops included nine clear evangelicals and several more fair-weather friends.[107] There were prominent evangelical sym-pathisers among the lay nobility, in successive parliaments and, espe-cially, in royal service at court. Politically the patronage and influence of these men and women was worth more than any number of re-formist converts in the 'dark corners of the land'. Moreover, evangel-ical influence had already reached deep into the universities, especially Cambridge.[108]

Under Edward VI, in addition to these advantages, the evangelicals found themselves in power, and able to use the machinery of the English state to further their aims. Perhaps this resembles a Reformation 'from above'; yet, as Nicholas Tyacke has pointed out, the distinction between 'above' and 'below' depends upon the straw man of truly 'popular' Reformation. This was a rarity across Europe, and was only likely to appear when political as well as religious authority was threatened. In a stable polity such as England, religious change could only ever be medi-ated through the existing structures of power, and in particular through the university and clerical elites.[109] To see 'above' and 'below' as op-posites is to apply the standards of a democratic age to a hierarchical society; and to apply either label to this core of convinced reformers is misleading.

What, then, of broader public opinion? It is unclear how relevant the term is to early modern Europe. The concept of 'public opinion' presupposes a 'public' which believes it has a right to an opinion; and in mid-Tudor England this 'public' was a small proportion of the population. The beliefs and preferences of the people as a whole were usually irrelevant or marginal to politics. The potential power of their

---

[107] The nine were William Barlow, Thomas Cranmer, Edward Foxe, Thomas Goodricke, John Hilsey, Henry Holbeach, Robert Holgate, Hugh Latimer and Nicholas Shaxton.
[108] Alec Ryrie, 'English evangelical reformers in the last years of Henry VIII', D.Phil thesis, University of Oxford (2000), 203–22.
[109] Nicholas Tyacke, 'Introduction', *England's Long Reformation 1500–1800*, ed. Nicholas Tyacke (1998), 4–5.

numbers was considerable, but in practical terms nearly impossible to wield: mass rebellion is a blunt political instrument. This is not to argue that the people at large were unimportant. Rather, if we are to appreciate their place in events we need to see those events through their eyes. From the perspective of most English subjects, government was something one experienced, not something in which one participated. The normal opinion of the public was one of acquiescence and obedience. In such circumstances the people did not need to be persuaded that a proposed change was right, merely that it was inevitable. This is to an extent true of all societies, but in early modern England the population positively expected to have its opinions led in this fashion. As good subjects they had had obedience to the higher powers drummed into them; and as good Christians they trusted that providence would act through those powers. As such, their personal hopes and fears regarding the changes which they experienced usually mattered less than where they believed those changes to be going. If we are trying to assess mid-Tudor public opinion, the question of what the people wanted to happen is secondary to the question of what they believed was happening; for this, too, is the kind of prophecy that is inclined to be fulfilled.

This does not mean that the people would inevitably acquiesce in the destruction of traditional religion. In France the determination of the Huguenot minority could not achieve this, largely because the population was galvanised to believe that a Huguenot victory was neither inevitable nor favoured by God. In England, by contrast, the population was not called to the barricades. For the committed evangelicals the religious tensions were an apocalyptic conflict between the earthly representatives of Christ and Antichrist. It was a view shared by their fiercest opponents; by their successors, in particular the martyrologist John Foxe; and by many subsequent historians who have continued to see the Reformation era as one of trench warfare between Protestant and Catholic. Yet the reformers' achievement in mid-Tudor England is that this did not happen. Catholic England did not unite against them. There can be no doubt that the religious changes imposed on parish life under Henry VIII and Edward VI were profoundly disturbing to most English people.[110] However, their piecemeal nature, and their imposition in the king's name, meant that the response was not resistance but rather disunity, controversy and confusion. Such confusion was, it seems, only

---

[110] Margaret Spufford, *Contrasting Communities: English Villagers in the Sixteenth and Seventeenth Centuries* (Cambridge, 1974), 240–2.

exacerbated by evangelical preaching. The *King's Book* of 1543 claimed that 'the heads and senses of our people have been much imbusied, and in these days travailed with the understanding' of doctrinal controversies.[111] Indeed, conservatives claimed that the reformers' gospel was 'the original of all dissension, schisms and contention', although, significantly, Henry VIII chose to share the blame equally between evangelical and traditionalist.[112] Whoever is to be blamed, by the 1540s all observers agreed that religious discord had become endemic.

One of the more well-known and memorable examples of this discord comes not from London's pulpits and printing presses, but from one of the most isolated and conservative places in England: Bodmin, in Cornwall, where there was a free school. According to a later account, not long before the 1549 rising:

The scholars, who used customably to divide themselves for better exploiting their pastimes, grew therethrough into two factions, the one whereof they called the old religion, the other the new. This once begun, was prosecuted among them in all exercises, and now and then handled with some eagerness and roughness, each party knowing, and still keeping the same companions and captain. At last one of the boys converted the spill of an old candlestick into a gun, charged it with powder and stone, and (through mischance or ungraciousness) therewith killed a calf: whereupon the owner complained, the master whipped, and the division ended.[113]

The significance of this darkly comic episode is not that the school was genuinely torn by religious divisions, as some have argued.[114] Schoolboys' gangs have always been able to find names for themselves without taking on the causes behind them. The choice of the terms, old and new religion (if they date back to the boys themselves), indicates where their real religious sympathies lay.[115] The point is that even in so remote a region as this, the division between reformers and conservatives was the most obvious dispute on which the boys could model their gangs. By the time of Henry VIII's death, every adult in England and Wales would have been touched by the religious changes which he introduced, in some form or other, and most must at least have been aware of 'the new religion', of people who wished to take the process of change further.

---

[111] *A necessary doctrine and erudition for any christen man* (1543), A3r.
[112] Parr, *Lamentation*, F2v-3r; PRO SP 1/212, 112r (*LP* XX (ii) 1030).
[113] Richard Carew of Antony, *The Survey of Cornwall*, ed. F. E. Halliday (1953), 196.
[114] Dickens, *English Reformation*, 328; Palliser, 'Popular reactions', 107; Robert Whiting, *The Blind Devotion of the People: Popular Religion and the English Reformation* (Cambridge, 1989), 235.
[115] Richard Rex, 'The New Learning', *JEH* 44 (1993), 26–44.

During the reign of Edward VI, both the impact of religious change, and the regime's zeal for more, would have become unavoidable. By then a good majority of the population probably had more detailed knowledge or experience of evangelicalism, through direct or indirect encounters with evangelical preachers or books, or through meeting with reformist sympathisers. Some may even have managed to absorb something from the official homilies. A minority – perhaps, in some areas, as many as William Turner's estimate of a third of the nation – were in sympathy with at least some of the reformers' ideas; a much smaller minority had become committed supporters. Another minority was passionately opposed to some or all of the reformers' changes. However, just as important as the presence of such committed groups was the fragmentation and dissension they engendered, and the confusion and uncertainty of most of the nation as to the future. This confusion was, of course, only exacerbated by the bewildering shifts in royal policy.

In such an atmosphere the position, influence and self-belief of the committed vanguard of reformers gave them a certain momentum. Their dominance of the religious scene was out of all proportion to their numbers. They had not converted the nation; indeed, they had scarcely begun, and by their own standards they would never succeed. But their achievement is nevertheless remarkable: by 1553 the English had come, like the schoolboys of Bodmin, to see themselves as a nation divided by religion.

CHAPTER 5

Sanctified by the believing spouse: women, men and the marital yoke in the early Reformation

Susan Wabuda

I

'Women are subjects; ye be subjects to your husbands.' Quoting from some of the most famous and influential passages in St Paul's epistles, Hugh Latimer's last sermon before Edward VI's court in 1550 rehearsed many of the standard sentiments the Christian Church had to offer about women. Women's subjection had been established by God in an unalterable warrant, following Eve's original transgression, 'after that she had given credit to the serpent', a just punishment that extended through all generations, a perennial truth that encompassed the pains of childbed, sobriety of dress and silence, in addition to obedience. This is no trifle, Latimer argued, but 'a godly matter, a ghostly matter, a matter of damnation and salvation'. All women must learn 'ye are underlings, underlings, and must be obedient'.[1]

Latimer's sermon fits into a long tradition (stretching back to the recesses of the early Church and Middle Ages, and forward into some of the dark corners of the twentieth century) of clerical denunciations of the essential weaknesses of womankind. Spiritually equal women might be, in keeping with the apostle Peter's observation that husbands and wives were heirs together of the grace of life, or with Paul's Epistle to the Galatians, that all who have been baptised into Christ have 'put on Christ'. There is 'neither man nor woman', for all are one in Christ Jesus. But women were still inferior in most ordinary terms, since the punishments imposed by God as their portion of Eve's legacy had never been superseded.[2]

Women stood at a further remove from God, and men were their intermediaries. Male and female he created them, but God made Eve

---

[1] Hugh Latimer, *Sermons*, ed. George Elwes Corrie (PS, 1844), 252–4.
[2] For scriptural references to women, see Genesis 1: 27, 2: 18–25; 1 Corinthians 11: 3–16 (headship), 14: 34–5; Galatians 3: 28; Ephesians 5: 22–33. See also Anthony Fletcher, *Gender, Sex and Subordination in England 1500–1800* (New Haven, 1995), 60–82.

for Adam. The man was not of the woman, Paul wrote, but the woman was of the man. He was not created for her, but she had been made for him. A woman 'hath a superior above her, by whom she ought to be ruled and ordered', Latimer advised, 'for she is not immediately under God, but mediately'.[3] Patriarchy was the standard for the world at large, and the smaller political framework of the family. The husband was the head of his wife, Paul wrote, just as Christ was the head of his Church. In a society where authority was defined as headship, women were consigned to the role of the silent body, as the body of the Church, a member of the body politic, the body in the marriage: always a member, not the head, usually in subjection, not in rule. St Paul 'maketh many heads', Bishop John Fisher proclaimed in his 1521 sermon against Luther, defending Peter as the head of the apostles, and the pope as the head of the Church, and 'here be three heads unto a woman, God, Christ, and her husband. And yet beside all these she hath a head of her own.' But just as it would be 'a monstrous sight to see a woman without an head', it would also be unnatural to perceive a woman without a master. Female subjection was one of the cornerstones of society. She should use her own head to govern herself 'according to the will and pleasure of her husband'. Her husband should be her head, Christ was to be 'her head, and God to be her head', in a graduated series of steps of ever-increasing authority, with God the Father as the ultimate superpatriarch over her and all humankind.[4]

Women's submission had its symbolic expression for all to see in the trimming of the head. If a man should not cover his head because he was made in God's image, according to Paul, then a woman needed a covering, for she was merely the glory of the man, created from his bone and flesh. Where the apostle castigated plaited hair, or gold and pearls, Latimer fulminated against laying out the locks in showy 'tussocks and tufts'. What women needed were not the fashionable French hoods, the bonnets and caps whose names belonged so much to the mysterious realm of women that the ever-unmarried Latimer professed he did not know what to call them. Rather, a woman required what Paul termed 'a power on her head', the supreme symbol of her submission, of her obedience to her earthly master, and to her God. 'I would wish', Latimer said, 'the women would call the covering of their heads by the terms of

---

3 Latimer, *Sermons*, 252–4.
4 *The English Works of John Fisher*, ed. John E. B. Mayor, EETS, extra series 27 (1876), 321; Maria Dowling, *Fisher of Men: a Life of John Fisher 1469–1535* (1999), 72–89.

the scripture: as when she would have her cap, I would she would say, "Give me my power".'[5]

'Give me my power': surely this sentence marks a supreme paradox, at once a symbol of submission and strength, a summation of the Pauline trope that 'when I am weak, then am I strong', that the strength of God is made perfect through weakness.[6] Encrypted here we have one of the most profound inversions of the entire Christian Church. Women, in their dress, even as the most dependent and vulnerable members of society, spoke to the subjection that all humanity owed to the will of God. 'Give me my power' also hints at profound challenges to patriarchy in marriage and society, through faithful absorption in service to the Almighty, the sixteenth century's application of wifely obedience to undermine the husband's power and authority.

If we revise Joan Kelly's haunting question – did women have a Renaissance?[7] – to embrace the early years of doctrinal change in England, the evidence suggests that women did have a Reformation, especially as its early effects were literally 'domesticated', striking at that one unquestioned female space, the household. As Eamon Duffy tells us, the suppression of the cult of the saints deprived women of talismanic safeguards 'in the domestic intimacies of pregnancy and childbirth'. And churching rituals, those links between the darkened birth chamber and the public celebration of a safe delivery, as David Cressy reminds us, were subject to divisive controversies.[8] The deposition of female saints as intercessors, the loss of shrines as places of pilgrimages, and (in paramount) the eclipse of the role of the Virgin Mary as salvatrix, second only to her son, were important changes, which deserve continued exploration to gauge the effect they had upon women's lives.[9]

---

[5] Latimer, *Sermons*, 252–4. Scriptural references against plaited hair: 1 Timothy 2: 9–15; 1 Peter 3: 1–9.

[6] 2 Corinthians 12: 10; see also Susan Wabuda, 'The Woman with the Rock: the Controversy on Women and Bible Reading', *Belief and Practice in Reformation England: a Tribute to Patrick Collinson from his Students*, ed. Caroline Litzenberger and Susan Wabuda (Aldershot, 1998), 40–59.

[7] Joan Kelly, 'Did women have a Renaissance?', in her *Women, History, and Theory* (Chicago, 1984), 19–50. See also Euan Cameron, *The European Reformation* (Oxford, 1991), 402–5.

[8] Lyndal Roper, *The Holy Household: Women and Morals in Reformation Augsburg* (Oxford, 1989), 3–55, 252–67. For England see Eamon Duffy, *The Stripping of the Altars: Traditional Religion in England 1400–1580* (New Haven, 1992), 385; David Cressy, *Birth, Marriage and Death: Ritual, Religion and the Life-cycle in Tudor and Stuart England* (Oxford, 1997), 197–229.

[9] Eamon Duffy, 'Holy Maydens, holy wyfes: the cult of women saints in fifteenth- and sixteenth-century England', *Women in the Church*, ed. W. J. Sheils and Diana Wood, *SCH* 27 (1990), 175–96; Marina Warner, *Alone of All her Sex: the Myth and Cult of the Virgin Mary* (New York, 1976), especially 296–7; Margo Todd, 'Humanists, puritans and the spiritualised household', *Church History* 49 (1980), 18–34.

So, too, was the loss of the cycle of fasting and feasting in the Catholic Church's calendar, in which women necessarily played a leading role, as the preparers and withholders of food.

Marriage, as the mirror of the relationship that bound Christ to his Church, was deeply affected; the subtle shifts that accompanied the transformation of matrimony from a sacrament to 'an holy ordinance of God' were written in the lives of women and men who entered into that blessed union.[10] Once Protestants embraced Christ as the sole mediator between a sinful humanity and a reconciling God, and argued that faith meant placing active confidence in Christ's promises (trusting to God's goodness alone), the prestige of a host of mediators was reassigned. The existence of purgatory was impugned, and thus the entire structure of the traditional economy of salvation, and above all the mass, which had been the central redeeming ritual in the life of the traditional community. The celibate priesthood, whose propitiations were offered on behalf of the rest of society, were now supposed to become preaching ministers who taught their flocks and raised their families. Cloistered nuns, whose prayers had been uttered for the alleviation of the sufferings of others, were now considered redundant, and forced to surrender their houses. The saints, pleading the causes of their clients at the celestial court, were now to withdraw to the backdrop, to be regarded as those honourable men and women in the history of the Church who had lived and witnessed for their faith, without any intercessory powers. The Reformation also redefined the mediation that husbands and wives were to offer for each other, reducing the husband's power slightly, while preserving wifely subordination in a revised form.[11] Each partner was supposed to become less of a spiritual mediator for the other, and more of an earthly comforter, for their mutual care and consideration.

The crucial texts for the standard of Christian matrimony on all sides of the doctrinal divide were taken from Paul's seventh chapter of his first Letter to the Corinthians, written for the primitive Church when troubling marriages were first being entered into between newly made

[10] James Calfhill, *An Answer to John Martiall's Treatise of the Cross*, ed. Richard Gibbings (PS, 1846), 235–41.

[11] The literature on marriage in the early modern period is vast. For a sample of some of the most recent essays and studies, see Cameron, *European Reformation*, 117–20; Eric Josef Carlson, *Marriage and the English Reformation* (Oxford, 1994); Patrick Collinson, *The Birthpangs of Protestant England: Religious and Cultural change in the Sixteenth and Seventeenth Centuries* (Basingstoke, 1988), 60–93; Cressy, *Birth, Marriage and Death*, 294–7; Anthony Fletcher, 'The Protestant idea of marriage in early modern England', *Religion and Culture in Early Modern Britain*, ed. Anthony Fletcher and Peter Roberts (Cambridge, 1994), 161–81; Steven Ozment, *When Fathers Ruled: Family Life in Reformation Europe* (Cambridge, MA, 1983), 9–49.

Christians and the unconverted. As with much of the rest of Paul's writings on the respective duties of men and women, the apostle had issued a complicated and ambiguous series of directives. These verses had been interpreted by the Catholic Church to argue that the marriage was a sacrament and its promises were unbreakable. The husband should not put the wife away, for the unbelieving husband is sanctified by the believing wife, and the unbelieving wife is sanctified by the believing husband. 'How knowest thou, O woman,' Paul asked, 'whether thou shalt save thy husband? Or how knowest thou, O man, whether thou shalt save thy wife?'

Paul's writings were used in the sixteenth century to validate an arrangement of power inside the marital union where the man was the ultimate authority for his wife, but she acted as a sanctifier within their marriage, best seen, for our purposes, in *The Instruction of a Christian Woman* by Juan Luis Vives. Through utter selflessness, the wife developed for herself a small measure of agency. Vives's book became the great template for female behaviour for the whole of the sixteenth century and beyond. Mrs Jane Ratcliffe, the godly seventeenth-century gentlewoman from Chester, with all of her convoluted struggles to gain some slight autonomy for herself, would have recognised Vives's contention that through lowly obedience the wife might rule her husband.[12]

Another of Vives's important truisms was that a wife must not do things that are against the laws of God, even if her husband commanded her to perform them. This was the same wedge that the Protestant reformers developed to compress and delimit the power of the husband over the wife, especially in extreme cases. By stressing Christ as the sole mediator, reformers adumbrated the saintly actions of the wife. The theory of what it meant to be a wife moved from Vives's portrait of a chaste cipher (an evaporated presence in her own marriage, Kelly would maintain),[13] to a companion, if not an equal. Because a wife did not have to obey a husband who wished her to do things against the laws of God, she might leave him if necessary, and permanent separations became possibilities on a narrow scale that would have been unthinkable before.

---

[12] See Patrick Collinson, '"A magazine of religious patterns": an Erasmian topic transposed in English Protestantism', in his *Godly People: Essays on English Protestantism and Puritanism* (1983), 499–526; Peter Lake, 'Feminine piety and personal potency: the "Emancipation" of Mrs Jane Ratcliffe', *The Seventeenth Century* 2 (1987), 143–65; Jacqueline Eales, 'Samuel Clarke and the "lives" of godly women in seventeenth-century England' and Susan Wabuda, 'Shunamites and Nurses of the English Reformation', *Women in the Church*, ed. Sheils and Wood, 335–44, 365–76.

[13] Kelly, 'Did women have a Renaissance?', 19–50.

II

Among the great goals of the humanists was to extend the sanctity which permeated churches and allow it to infuse daily life. They wished to make households holy and to domesticate devotion. Every person could pause, Fisher counselled: the man who 'goeth to his pastures to see his cattle'; the 'poor women also in their business'; or the sleepless, lying awake at night, and direct their thoughts to a meditation upon the crucifix, to examine the full implications of what the sacrifice of Christ meant in every life, for each soul.[14] Heavily illustrated books of hours catered to an eager readership, and enabled their purchasers to follow the monastic round of prayer in the Hours of the Blessed Virgin Mary, and to lose themselves in their contemplation of the Passion of Christ. All 'householders', or those men and women who had 'governance', could teach their children and servants, the humanist monk Richard Whitford advised, how to approach the basic tenets of Christian belief, and to assist them in the making of their prayers.[15]

Vives's *Instruction of a Christian Woman* was an important part of that shift. Its scope was ambitious, for Vives soldered classical models for behaviour on to accepted Christian truths, and he aimed at the highest in the realm. Prepared under the patronage of Catherine of Aragon as one of several books on matters of conduct and education, *De institutione foeminae Christianae* was printed in Antwerp in 1524 and became something of an international bestseller. It was soon Englished by Richard Hyrde, a member of More's household, and went through nine print runs in English from the end of the 1520s until 1592. Hyrde's spirited translation, full of pithy colloquial expressions, no doubt helped its success.[16] His book was a compendium of what virtuous women of the upper classes (and generally all women, but with a definite stress upon great ladies and gentlewomen) should know, a shrewd conflation of the fundamentals of scriptural learning plus the antique, a didactic contrast between the

---

[14] Fisher, *Works*, 391–6; Wabuda, 'The woman with the rock'.

[15] Richard Whitford, *A Werke for Householders or for them that haue the gydynge or governance of any company* (1530); Duffy, *Stripping of the Altars*, 86–7, 209–65; J. T. Rhodes, 'Syon Abbey and its religious publications in the sixteenth century', *JEH* 44 (1993), 11–25.

[16] Juan Luis Vives, *De institutione foeminae Christianae* (Antwerp, 1524), translated by Richard Hyrde as *A very frutefull and pleasant boke called the Instruction of a Christen woman* (1529?). See the *STC* for later editions. Also, see Maria Dowling, *Humanism in the Age of Henry VIII* (1986), 124, 147–50, 176, 181–3, 223, 227; Diane Valeri Bayne, '*The Instruction of a Christian woman*: Richard Hyrde and the Thomas More circle', *Moreana* 45 (1975), 5–15; Todd, 'Spiritualised household', 21. For the modern translation, see *The Education of a Christian woman: a sixteenth-century manual*, ed. and trans. Charles Fantazzi (Chicago, 2000).

saintly and sinful. To the Christian standard for a virtuous woman, Vives annexed the realm of classical thought, by distilling the ideas of Aristotle, Tacitus and Xenophon. It was a library in itself of most of the important references to women from the Bible, the writings of the early Fathers of the Church (including Jerome and Chrystostom), and the classics, a useful handbook for those who wished to introduce their daughters to the authoritative sources concerning their roles in life. It presented a vision of womanhood that infused Pauline tropes and the mandates of Genesis with the breath of Aristotelian moderation. Restraint, obedience, silence, modesty, and above all chastity, were the qualities that Vives elevated.[17]

Vives hoped chastity would be the maiden's lifelong companion and chief attribute. In contrast with well-established conventions that divided men's lives into the Seven Ages, Vives related the woman's life into her sexual and marital status, arranging his work into three books, on the maiden, the wife and the widow.[18] A man needed many things, he advised, including wisdom, eloquence, a means of livelihood and a sense of justice, and if some of these were missing, 'it is not to be disliked, so that many of them be had'. But in a woman no one would seek these qualities beyond 'her honesty', and if that one were missing, it 'is like as in a man, if he lack all that he should have'. Take from a woman her beauty, kin, riches, eloquence, 'sharpness of wit' and her livelihood, but give her chastity, 'and thou hast given her all things'. Give her all these but call her 'a naughty pack', a shameful bundle dragged along in secret behind a sinful man, and all is taken away, leaving her 'bare and foul'.[19]

The married woman 'ought to be of greater chastity than an unmarried' one. At the time she entered holy wedlock, she 'must ponder higher things in her mind', a clear allusion to the solemnity of the Virgin Mary, whom the woman must emulate in her pure devotion to the will of God. Her marriage would reflect, on a small and earthly scale, the mystic union between Christ and his Church. The good woman must remember that she represents the Church in her marriage,

---

[17] Collinson, ' "Magazine" ', 499–526; Linda Pollock, ' "Teach her to live under obedience"; the making of women in the upper ranks of early modern England', *Continuity and Change* 4 (1989), 231–58.

[18] Merry E. Wiesner, *Women and Gender in Early Modern Europe* (Cambridge, 1993), 16, 41–2, 127; Fletcher, *Subordination*, 376–82.

[19] Vives, *Instruction of a Christen woman*, F2r. 'Naughty pack' ('natoghte pake') can be found in a 1538 court case in the diocese of Lincoln, referring to a former serving woman who was designated as the cause of a priest's incontinence. See Lincolnshire Archives Office Vj 10, 82r. I am indebted to Rosmarie Sunderland for discussion on this point.

and that her husband bears the image of Christ. She must bring her chastity with her to their union, and then develop that 'great love toward her husband' that is the guarantor of a 'light, sweet, and happy' marriage.[20]

For Vives, as for other Catholic writers, sexuality was suspect, and must not form part of the Christian wife's character.[21] Vives here may have been more restrictive than Erasmus, who asked, 'For what thing is sweeter' than to live coupled with the 'benevolence of the mind' and in the 'conjunction of the body'? What one needed in a spouse, Erasmus maintained, was someone with whom one could share the mind's 'secret affections' and the 'permixtion of bodies', in fellowship under the 'confederate band of the sacrament'.[22] Vives argued that the wife should rely upon friendship, bearing in mind that all people are bound together in 'universal friendship' as 'brethren' who are descended of God. Wedlock 'was not ordained so much for generation, as for certain company of life, and continual fellowship'. He held up for admiration the example of learned Queen Zenobia of Palmyra, who resorted to her husband's bed only in the hope of conceiving.[23] In marriage, as throughout the rest of Christendom, *agape* should win out over *eros* every time.

The ultimate happiness of the marriage rested with the wife, and the source of her power lay not in sensuality but in common Christian fellowship. With 'pure charity' and meekness, and by 'buxom using of thyself', the wife could encourage her husband to be 'pleasant and loving'. She should also cultivate that indefinable quality of 'buxomness' in all her dealings with her husband. Here we would be wrong if we discerned more than a hint of physical enjoyment inside wedlock, at least on the part of the wife. The word 'buxom' has suffered in dignity over recent centuries, and it was abandoned by Archbishop Thomas Cranmer in his marriage ritual when he replaced the bride's vow to be 'buxom in bed and at the board'. Here, as Hyrde used it, buxomness meant a wandlike tractability that combined the emotional strength every wife needed with pliability. Without buxomness the husband would be 'froward and crabbed', and

---

[20] Vives, *Instruction of a Christen woman*, Riv-Sir.

[21] See also Roger Edgeworth's exposition of 1 Peter 3, which discussed standards for sexual propriety inside marriage. Edgeworth, *Sermons very fruitfull, godly and learned: preaching in the Reformation c. 1535–c. 1553*, ed. Janet Wilson (Cambridge, 1993), 270–9.

[22] Erasmus, *A ryghte frutefull Epystle . . . in laude and prayse of matrymony*, trans. Richard Taverner (1536?), C6r-v.

[23] Vives, *Instruction of a Christen woman*, R1v-R2r, R3r, Aa3r-Aa3v; Todd, 'Spiritualised household', 21–2.

continual strife would mar the household. A 'grievous torment' would be the legacy of such a match. Christ 'openly forbiddeth divorcement', Erasmus observed in his *Prayse of matrimony*. Relief could not come even in the separation of death, since failure led to eternal damnation. The success of the marriage could not be measured by earthly considerations alone. Marriage had a bearing upon the hereafter in any life's story. The choices lay largely 'in thy hand', Vives told his reader, for if by virtuous living and 'buxomness' she caused her husband to love her in return, 'thou shalt be mistress in a merry house', and bless the day she was wed. 'The wise sentence sayeth: A good woman by lowly obeisance ruleth her husband.'[24]

Obedience was the chief tool the wife needed to surmount all of the disadvantages of her married life, and the human condition in general. It was the way that she turned convention on its head, by revealing herself to be the strong and capable partner in the union. It was the means by which she gave the lie to the legacy of Eve. Through wifely obedience she proved herself to be the wiser yokefellow, she turned pettiness into generosity, she transformed submission into glory. Her obedience was the means by which she saved her husband, from himself if necessary, physically and even spiritually. Was he difficult? With 'courtesy and gentle means' she was to advise him to 'amend his living', and if he abided by her words, then she had succeeded in profiting them both. Was he 'foolish and witless'? Then she needed to treat him as if he were 'a wild beast tamed', or as a mother dealt with her children. Was he ill? Here Vives invoked the story of his wife's mother, Clara, who nursed her much older husband, Bernard Valdaura of Bruges, with unwearying devotion, bearing him two children who were remarkable for their good health, despite the loathsomeness of his diseases. Was he unfaithful? She should continue to love him, and forgive him when he returned from his straying. Was the husband violent? She should think his blows 'the correction of God', and be grateful 'if thou mayest so with a little pain in this life, buy out the great pains of another world'.[25]

Although a wife should obey her husband's commandment 'as a divine law', his power was not completely unlimited, for he should not constrain his wife to do anything that was against the will of God, or put her soul in danger, even if it was inside his purview to prevent her from going to

[24] Vives, *Instruction of a Christen woman*, R1v-R2r, R3v-R4r; Erasmus, *Prayse of matrimony*, C2r. For 'buxom' see Diarmaid MacCulloch, *Thomas Cranmer: a Life* (New Haven and London, 1996), 420–1; *Oxford English Dictionary*.
[25] Vives, *Instruction of a Christen woman*, S4r-X3v; Fantazzi, *Manual*, 8, 200, 202.

church. In Vives's thinking the authority of the husband was bounded by all the laws that God had imposed upon mankind. 'For those things that be against the laws of God she ought not to do, though her husband command her never so much.' The man may be the head of the woman, but 'Christ is the head of the man'. In cases of conflict the wife 'must acknowledge one far better than her husband'. She must keep Christ, her heavenly lord, 'more in price' than her earthly spouse. Loyalty to God came before even her wifely duty.[26] But these ideas occupied a small space in the broad span of his advice for a wife. Her main task was to know how to obey.

In synthesising a template for women's roles out of the scriptures and classics, Vives encapsulated patriarchy as the standard for the small political framework of the family. Here the theory of the king's two bodies worked on a miniature scale: in this case the husband, the head, the symbol of Christ, had a corruptible body and nature; while the submissive wife, the representative of the Church, and the literal body politic of the marriage, was of such spiritual excellence that she made possible, through her good care, the physical survival of her husband's body, and she ultimately eased the salvation of his soul. Breathtaking convolutions and a deep bow to the double standard were necessary to make this argument convincing. If men were so weak that they surrendered to the illicit demands of the flesh, they had to be indulged. It fell to the watchful wife to accept him back from the fatal embraces of a concubine, or to maintain her chastity even in their marriage bed, out of her greater love for him and her overarching respect for God. For Vives the good woman was the living salvatrix of her husband, physically, morally and spiritually, for she would not allow even his abuse towards her to become the cause of his perdition. The final goal was always the same for herself and her spouse: the preservation of the soul, even if it entailed every type of self-denial, inconvenience or agony in earthly life. God preferred the lowly and meek. If the husband did wrong, 'himself shall bear all the blame', and 'the wife shall be out of fault'. Obedience spelled power on the cosmic scale, for it spurned human weakness in all its manifestations and made the ultimate victory hers – but at a price.[27]

---

[26] Vives, *Instruction of a Christen woman*, X3v-Y1r.

[27] Vives, *Instruction of a Christen woman*, X4v-Y1r. See also Ernst Kantorowicz, *The King's Two Bodies* (Princeton, 1957); Keith Thomas, 'The double standard', *Journal of the History of Ideas* 20 (1959), 195–216.

III

An apprehension of the pains of purgatory was always just below the surface in Vives's thought, and the belief that a chaste marriage was less glorious than pure and perpetual virginity. Heinrich Bullinger's *The christen state of matrimonye*, printed in English under Miles Coverdale's translation for the first time in 1541, challenged most of these basic assumptions. Wedlock defiled no one and was forbidden to no one, Bullinger argued – a clear assault upon the ideals of clerical celibacy and the cloistering of women in convents. Marriage was an antidote to adultery and whoredom, the substitution for the false notions of faithful living that had been promoted by the regular religious orders.[28] It is 'a very peevish saying', Hugh Latimer complained, to lament that, '"All religious houses are pulled down"', for the married couple who lived together 'godly and quietly', going about their usual work with the fear of God, hearing and keeping his word, 'that same is a religious house', the new type of religious house that had been built with the reforms, and 'that house pleaseth God'.[29] God had ordained marriage as a covenant between a man and a woman, Bullinger argued, as the pure and 'goodly' symbol of Christ's love for his congregation. Here the emphasis was upon the earthly realities of marriage. Someone about to marry should choose a spouse, not accept a mate without due consideration. Making a wise choice was the best means to avoid all of the ills that marriage could bring. The prospective partner should be meet, honest, virtuous and healthy. Bullinger even advised that there should be a comely soberness in male raiment.[30]

When Bullinger retold the creation story from Genesis, he stressed the companionate aspects of the relationship between Adam and Eve by drawing on Peter Lombard's observation that Eve had been taken from Adam's side, not from the earth (lest anyone think womankind had proceeded from 'the mire'). She was not made from his feet that he should 'spurn her', nor from the head to rule him, but from the side, to be 'his help and companion'. He should be her 'strength, help, and comfort'.[31] In balance, the new ideal for fellowship was expressed

---

[28] Cf. Erasmus, *Prayse of matrymony*, C1v; and the homily against adultery, whoredom and uncleanness in the Edwardine Book of Homilies, *Certayne Sermons, or Homilies* (1547), S4v-X3v.

[29] Latimer, *Sermons*, 391–2.

[30] [Heinrich Bullinger], *The christen state of matrimonye*, trans. Miles Coverdale (Antwerp, 1541), A2v, A8r, 27r–31r, 40r-7v; similarly William Tyndale, 'The Obedience of a Christian Man', *Doctrinal treatises . . . by William Tyndale*, ed. Henry Walter (PS, 1848), 171–6.

[31] Bullinger, *Matrimonye*, A4v; Ozment, *When Fathers Ruled*, 63–4.

in Cranmer's innovative declaration that marriage was for the mutual society, help and comfort that the partners should have for each other, in prosperity and adversity, a tacit freighting of the husband's vow to love, comfort, honour, and keep his wife in cherishing her.[32]

The emphasis upon the husband's dutiful consideration of his wife also points towards important limits upon his authority. Obedience should be extended only to the good, not to the wicked. A husband must not 'turn his authority unto tyranny'. Kindness must be extended to the wife, not force or wilfulness.[33] Nor was the wife to sacrifice herself unduly for her husband. Bullinger drew a new thread of thought from Paul's first Letter to the Corinthians. Against the older idea that a wife must not depart from her husband, because the partners were, in some sense, necessary for each other's salvation, Bullinger demurred: 'And verily what woman so ever taketh an unbelieving man must draw after him in unbelief, yea and do, see, and hear that which is clean contrary unto faith, and hurtful to her soul.' If the unbeliever left, then let him go. The believing spouse should not be under servitude in such cases.[34] Both spouses, man and woman alike, were responsible for their own spiritual sanctification, through their own individual faith. What each spouse offered the other, according to Bullinger, was a sanctified life together, in accordance with the new understanding of God's ordinance. 'To draw one yoke, is a manner of speaking, and is as much to say, as to have fellowship, and to yoke themselves together in wedlock.'[35]

As Thomas Freeman has recently established, women were doubly disadvantaged once households began to be divided along doctrinal lines, cruelly caught between their obedience to their husbands and their loyalty to God, accused of a spiritual infidelity amounting to a species of adultery against God if they did not obey the dictates of their consciences.[36] Under the pressure of divided loyalties, some marriages suffered spectacular breakdowns, and here the interpretations that John Bale fastened upon Anne Askew's unhappy marital history point to an exploration of the new avenue Bullinger had developed. In his commentary

---

[32] MacCulloch, *Cranmer*, 420–1; Kenneth W. Stevenson, 'Cranmer's marriage vow: its place in the tradition', *Thomas Cranmer: Churchman and Scholar*, ed. Paul Ayris and David Selwyn (Woodbridge, 1993), 189–98.

[33] Bullinger, *Matrimonye*, 54r-56v.

[34] 1 Corinthians 7: 10–17; Bullinger *Matrimonye*, B6r-v.

[35] Bullinger, *Matrimonye*, 6r; Todd, 'Spiritualised household', 29.

[36] Thomas Freeman, '"The Good Ministrye of Godlye and Vertuouse Women": the Elizabethan Martyrologists and the Female Supporters of the Marian Martyrs', *JBS* 39 (2000), 8–33.

upon her second *Examinacyon*, which she recorded not long before she was burned in 1546, Bale related that she had been 'compelled against her will' by her father, Sir William Askew of Lincolnshire, to marry Thomas Kyme. Kyme had been affianced to Anne's elder sister, but the sister had died before the marriage could be solemnised, and in order to save the complicated marriage agreements (for 'lucre', Bale tersely observed), Anne entered the match against 'her free consent'. Bale was careful to say that once the marriage was made, Anne 'demeaned herself like a Christian wife', and bore Kyme two children. But then came the breach: through 'oft reading the sacred bible', she fell away from her husband's traditional religious views, from 'all old superstitions of papistry', to embrace 'a perfect belief in Jesus Christ'. Deeply offended, Kyme 'cruelly' and 'violently' drove her out of his house; Bale conjectures that this was at the suggestion of the local clergy.[37]

It is impossible to know how much of Bale's commentary is an accurate representation of events as they actually occurred (which he could not observe himself from his exile), or how much of his 'elucidation' of her unrevealing references to 'master Kyme' is meant to excuse her unusual independence as well as to attack conservative clergy. Bale said that 'she sought of the law a divorcement from him'. Perhaps on the basis of information supplied by those who were actually acquainted with Askew, Bale wrote that 'she thought herself free from that unseemly kind of coacted marriage', and that her marriage was unlawful from its start. This was based on the same verses from 1 Corinthians 7, that 'if a faithful woman have an unbelieving husband, which will not tarry with her, she may leave him. For a brother or sister is not in subjection to such.'

The fascinating and novel aspect of the Askew example lies in her belief, according to Bale, that Kyme was not 'worthy of her marriage'. She pursued the same loophole that any woman in her predicament had to use: Kyme had 'spitefully hated God, the chief author of marriage', and here we have the same problem that had been elucidated by Vives, but with a startlingly different interpretive outcome: instead of sticking by him, and seeking to preserve her marriage despite her husband's cruelty, Askew felt no compunction to sacrifice herself to save his soul. God came before the earthly husband, and since Kyme had repudiated her, she was free. Nor had Kyme been worthy of her, Bale averred, because in this

[37] *The Examinations of Anne Askew*, ed. Elaine V. Beilin (Oxford, 1996), 92–3; John Bale, *Select Works*, ed. Henry Christmas (PS, 1849), 198–9; Todd, 'Spiritualised household', 30.

case her religious sensibilities, and her understanding of the Bible and the workings of salvation, were closer to the eternal verities than Kyme's could be.[38]

IV

In future years, under Mary Tudor, Protestant women faced the same dilemma again as they had to chose between their obedience to their Catholic husband and their loyalty to God. But now the theories of what it meant to disobey a tyrannical monarch and what it meant to disobey an unreasonable husband developed in parallel, and fed each other. As exile became the preferred response of the godly subject who refused to risk God's wrath by attending the newly reinstated mass, so, too, did the separation of the believing godly wife from her Catholic husband become a legitimate solution. To obey wicked princes against God was rebellion against God, Christopher Goodman argued from the safety of Geneva, where John Knox was at the centre of a circle of supportive women, including Anne Locke and Elizabeth Bowes, who had left husbands behind rather than sacrifice their consciences. To disobey man and obey God was true obedience.[39]

Despairing women managed to communicate with the bishops imprisoned in Oxford and London to ask their advice in solving the most trying conundrums of conflicting allegiances. Their plight was all too real, for Bale maintained that Anne Askew had been reported to the authorities at Kyme's 'labour and suit'; and John Foxe identified other women, including Joyce Lewes and Elizabeth Lawson, who went to the stake upon their husbands' rejection.[40] John Hooper's letter 'for a woman that was troubled with her husband in matters of religion' is one of the most developed articulations of the obligations and limits of wifely duty. The woman must 'remember the counsel' in Paul's first Letter to the Corinthians that the unbelieving spouse may not be forsaken by the 'faithful' partner. Therefore the wife could not desert her husband. But what did her spouse believe? To think that 'the priest can make God',

---

[38] Keith Thomas, 'Women and the Civil War sects', *Crisis in Europe 1560–1660: Essays from Past and Present*, ed. Trevor Aston (1965), 317–40.

[39] Christopher Goodman, *How Svperior powers oght to be obeyd of their subiets: and wherin they may lawfully by Gods Worde be disobeyed and resisted* (Geneva, 1558), 60–1; Patrick Collinson, '"Not sexual in the ordinary sense": women, men and religious transactions', in his *Elizabethan Essays* (1994), 119–50.

[40] Freeman, '"Good Ministrye"', 8–33; Maria Dowling and Joy Shakespeare, 'Religion and politics in mid-Tudor England through the eyes of an English Protestant woman: the recollections of Rose Hickman', *Bulletin of the Institute of Historical Research* 55 (1982), 100.

or to 'honour that which was but very bread yesterday' and mistake it for the true God, is 'very idolatry' that must not be committed by any Christian, upon pain of 'everlasting damnation'. The faithful spouse must open the truth to the partner who was not persuaded. 'How knowest thou O woman, whether thou shalt save thy husband' – in this case, through her efforts to instruct him. But if the husband refused to be 'amended', and continued to offend God, then the wife should 'labour with her companion to be free and at liberty', rather than be compelled to honour a false God against her conscience. In this case she still must not leave her husband. But if he would not improve, and would not permit her 'liberty in the faith of Christ', she should marshal some friends, 'some godly men or women to persuade with her husband'. If still he would not reform ('which God forbid'), or suffer his wife to be excused from the mass, the wife must answer him 'soberly and Christianly' that she is forbidden by the laws of God to commit idolatry, and that 'God's [law] is more to be obeyed then man'. Perhaps now the husband might perceive that his wife's 'love and reverence towards him', plus her constancy, would content him to permit her to use her liberty of conscience. In this case her lowly obedience towards him would actually gain her mastery over the predicament.

However, if her wisdom and 'womanhood' still could not amend her husband's 'foul words' or his 'churlish and cruel' nature, and she perceived that he was about to report her to the authorities, she then had but two 'extreme' courses of action left. If, by prayer, she found herself strong enough to withstand the law, even if she should be executed, she should 'in no case depart from her husband'. Here Christian fortitude and martyrdom marked the ultimate triumph of godly strength over human weakness. Through the grace of God, the wife would be proven to be the superior as a witness for her faith. But if she found herself 'too weak to suffer such extremity', she should respect the marriage that had been made between God and her soul, rather than that between herself and her husband, and convey herself away out of the danger of idolatry. She must always live 'honest, virtuous, and godly', living 'with prayer and soberness to God' in the hope that all wicked laws and wicked religion that created 'debate between God and man, and husband and wife' would be banished.[41]

---

[41] Miles Coverdale [and Henry Bull], *Certain most godly, fruitful, and comfortable letters of such true Saintes and holy Martyrs of God* (1564), 143–5. Professor Collinson reminds us that the Catholic martyr Margaret Clitherow sent her husband her hat as a sign of her loving duty towards him as her head, immediately before she was pressed to death. ' "Not sexual" ', 130–1.

Hooper's reluctance to countenance any breach between husband and wife was self-evident, though in the last extremity the woman could leave if her husband behaved in such an unnatural fashion towards her, and she did not have the courage to die. His emphasis on the value of women's godly instruction and the potential of spiritual fellowship with her husband and other men is one of the most remarkable aspects of our story, one of the great strengths of the early Protestant movement, and an amendment of the harshest implications of the Pauline model for silent womanhood.[42]

For Miles Huggarde, a staunch defender of Queen Mary and traditional religion, the runagate wives he observed were part of the great failings of Protestantism, one indicator among many of the wretched inversions that heresy had wrought. Lustful women who had the names of the apostles always on their lips were 'wandering gillottes', like heretics of old time, who had disguised their evil lives under the 'colour of sticking to the gospel'. And, 'by saint Mary, a number are contented to run from their husbands into Germany'. Far better would it be if women should spend their lives not for any 'fantastical opinion' that was only 'newly crept out of the shell', but for the 'safeguarding of your husbands', the 'defense of your chastity' and the sacramental 'band of matrimony'.[43]

In the most conservative reaches of society, the older model of partners sacrificing themselves spiritually for the benefit of each other, especially in the north of England among recusant families, was a useful strategy to protect a covert Catholicism at home. In her study of *Church Papists*, Alexandra Walsham has identified how the ostensibly Protestant husband, who attended public worship at the parish church, sheltered his traditionalist family. His sacrifice made it possible for domestic devotions to be practised. His public presence at church cloaked his wife's recusancy. Here her invisibility under the law, as a married woman, was a distinct advantage, and allowed her enormous scope in sustaining the threatened community. Her attachment to traditional faith answered for his soul, for her profession sanctified him, no matter what constraints he was forced to acknowledge in his public life. The wife's 'recusancy seems just as often a natural division of labour in the management of dissent'.[44]

---

42 Collinson, ' "Not sexual" ', 119–50; Freeman, ' "Good Ministrye" ', 8–33; Ozment, *When Fathers Ruled*, 80–99; Wabuda, 'Woman with the rock'.
43 Miles Huggarde, *The displaying of the protestantes* (1556), I2r-I8r.
44 Alexandra Walsham, *Church Papists: Catholicism, Conformity and Confessional Polemic in Early Modern England* (Woodbridge, 1993), 35, 77–81; John Bossy, *The English Catholic Community, 1570–1850* (1975), 150–8; Collinson, ' "Not sexual" ', 119–50.

But when no doctrinal debates separated husband and wife, there was no need for the wife to pull away from him. The godly husband served God's interests, and there was no defensible reason for the wife to challenge his authority overtly, any more than it was proper to test God. When Latimer declared that women needed to learn that they were underlings as a 'matter of damnation and salvation', he was identifying what he and other Protestant preachers felt was a distinctive relationship between women and God, bridged by their husbands, which was the basis of the contract between the sexes. The new model for a godly marriage was conveyed in a pair of letters printed by Foxe in his *Actes and Monuments*, sent from the Coventry weaver John Careless (who died in prison during Mary's reign) to Latimer's servant Augustine Bernher, that great maintainer of the covert London church, and his bride, 'my dear and faithful loving Sister' Elizabeth, who was a member of the spiritual kinship that defined the Protestant community. Careless wrote that Elizabeth should be thankful to God for her creation, redemption and preservation. In particular, she should be thankful that she had a good, godly, faithful husband who is not 'an ignorant, froward, churlish, brawling, wasteful, rioting, drunken husband', the very type of husband with which God 'hath plagued many other (as he might also have done you)'. She should serve this good man diligently, but her obedience should be founded upon her gratitude for her husband's true and faithful heart towards her, a recompense for his concern, rather than an obligatory tribute.[45]

Although reform put new stress upon the kindness and care of the husband, the wife still had no recourse if a godly husband was difficult or cruel. Later in the century Edward Dering wrote to the unhappy Mrs Honeywood, 'in her heaviness', prone to religious doubts as well as marital difficulties; his advice was that if her husband had 'been unkind to you, bear it' and resist giving way to 'any inordinate affections to offend God, and hurt yourself'. The best way to please God was to continue to be 'loving and obedient, even unto an unkind husband'. Dering hoped that with her patience she might 'win him at the last', advice which was not much different from Vives's counsel that through lowly obedience she might eventually have her way.[46]

Patrick Collinson and Margo Todd have asked to what extent the new doctrinal positions constituted an indirect challenge to male authority

---

[45] ECL MS 260, 237r-v, 242r-243v; printed in *AM* (1570), 2115–7; Freeman, ' "Good Ministrye" ', 8–33.

[46] Edward Dering, *Godly and comfortable letters* in *M. Derings Workes* (1597), C1v-C3r, A6–B3v; quoted in Collinson, ' "Not sexual" ', 137; Freeman, ' "Good Ministrye" ', 3–33.

during the Reformation. Were women engaging in a covert revolt against patriarchy? If this was a revolt, it was of the most stealthy, humble and self-limiting kind. It did not mark any systemic reversals, or change the deep foundations of marriage, but was rather a subtle readjustment of the roles of women and men inside an ancient frame, sponsored by the Catholic humanists and further developed by Protestant theology.[47] It led to a greater emphasis upon spiritual equality as it was lived through marriage, where the wife's obedience was tempered by a quiet, new endorsement of male friendliness and fellowship. While it may seem that wifely submission was one of the great constants in the social scheme, a firmly fixed point like a solid edifice that stands unchanged while the surrounding town is rebuilt, the standard of obedience inside the marital union went through its own alterations during the English reforms. The edifice was being rebuilt with the rest of the town, even if some of its pillars remained the same.

[47] Collinson, ' "Not sexual" ', 129; Todd, 'Spiritualised household', 18–34.

CHAPTER 6

Dissenters from a dissenting Church: the challenge of the Freewillers, 1550–1558*

Thomas Freeman

I

The great ecclesiastical historian John Strype declared that the Marian Protestants known as the Freewillers were 'the first that made separation from the reformed Church of England, having gathered congregations of their own'.[1] Strype's assumption that the Church of England, as he knew it, existed in the middle of the sixteenth century makes this claim somewhat anachronistic. Nevertheless, Strype put his finger on one major reason why the Freewillers were historically significant: they were the first English Protestants to establish organised congregations which not only repudiated, but also challenged, the authority of the Protestant clerical leadership. What the Freewillers lacked, however, was the permanence of many later separatist groups. If they were the first who made separation from the English Church, they were also the first to be suppressed. Less than a decade after their first recorded appearance, all traces of Freewiller congregations had disappeared.

Yet during the few years of their existence, the Freewillers were organised and prominent dissenters. A. G. Dickens's dismissive comment that the Freewillers 'give the impression of a discussion group rather than that of an integrated sect' is wide of the mark.[2] The Freewillers represented a

* I would like to thank the Master and fellows of Emmanuel College, Cambridge, and the Master and fellows of Gonville and Caius College, Cambridge, for permission to consult manuscripts in their possession. Many of the documents cited or quoted in this article were printed by the Elizabethan martyrologists John Foxe and Henry Bull, or in the Parker Society volumes or elsewhere. However, if a document exists in a manuscript, the printed version or versions will not be cited. I would also like to thank Brett Usher for reading and commenting on an earlier draft of this article.

[1] John Strype, *Ecclesiastical Memorials* (3 vols. in 6, Oxford, 1822), II (i). 369. Strype coined the term 'freewillers' to designate these Marian Protestants. However, one of their chief adversaries, John Careless, referred to his opponents as 'freewill men' (ECL MS 260, 227r), and an informant reported to Bishop Bonner of London that the 'predestinators' called their opponents 'freewill men' (*AM* (1563), 1605).

[2] A. G. Dickens, *The English Reformation* (2nd edition, 1989), 265.

collection of organised, lay-led congregations, united by their opposition
to the predestinarian, clerical leadership of the 'orthodox' Protestant
Church; yet they were distinct from the Family of Love in their anti-
Nicodemism and from the Anabaptists in their affirmation of the
Trinity and the Incarnation.[3] In this article I will endeavour to give the
Freewillers their due, examining their origins; their conflict with pre-
destinarian Protestantism, and how they came to lose; and the English
Church's failure to repeat this early success against later dissidents.

II

Although the exact origins of the Freewillers remain obscure, their first
appearance in contemporary records came in typically controversial circumstances. On 27 January 1551 one 'Upcharde' of Bocking, Essex, was
interrogated by the Privy Council about a conventicle – 'an assembly,
being of 50 persons or more' – held in his house on Christmas Day 1550.[4]
'Upcharde and one Sympson', along with others involved, were committed to prison and questioned. Further information about the meeting
is provided by a series of depositions taken from Kentish people who attended the Bocking conventicle or were affiliated with the conventiclers.
The assembly at Bocking was convened for discussion and debate, not
for worship, and thus was not a congregation, much less a separatist congregation. Yet those linked to it included future Freewiller leaders: John
Simpson, John Barry, George Brodebridge, Robert Cole, John Ledley,
Humphrey Middleton, Nicholas Sheterden and, above all, Henry Hart.[5]

---

3 Christopher Marsh's attempts to argue for close connections between the two groups (*The Family
   of Love in English Society, 1550–1630* (Cambridge, 1994), 59–63) are unconvincing and fail to take
   into account the egregious anti-Nicodemism of the Freewillers, discussed below. Though some
   freewillers seem to have maintained that Jesus Christ was a created being and not fully divine
   (ECL MS 260, 72r, 87r), prominent figures such as John Trew, John Barry and Nicholas Sheterden
   clearly distanced themselves from Anabaptist teaching.
4 It has generally been assumed that the person interrogated by the Privy Council was Thomas
   Upcher, a Marian exile from Bocking who, in Elizabeth's reign, became the rector of Fordham and
   St Leonard's, Colchester. See C. H. Garrett, *The Marian Exiles: A Study in the Origins of Elizabethan
   Puritanism* (Cambridge, 1938), 316–7; Patrick Collinson, *Archbishop Grindal 1519–1563: The Struggle
   for the Reformed Church* (1979), 114, 172–3. But since Thomas Upcher's age was recorded as twenty-
   four years on his ordination as deacon on 24 April 1560 (London Guildhall MS 9535/1, 88v), this
   would make him fourteen or fifteen at the time of the Bocking conventicle. Since 'Upchard' was
   the owner of the house where the conventicle met, he was not Thomas Upcher, unless the clerk
   made an error in recording Upcher's age.
5 *APC* III, 198–9, 206–7; BL Harleian MS 421, 133r–134v. The identification of John Simpson,
   who would be executed for heresy at Rayleigh, Essex, in June 1555, with the 'Sympson' arrested
   in connection with the conventicle is made very probable by his leadership of a congregation with
   members in Suffolk, Norfolk, Essex and Kent. See ECL MS 260, 128r, 252r–253v. Furthermore,
   the will of Robert Cook, a clothier of Bocking who was one of the leaders of the conventicle, was

There was doctrinal continuity as well. Although there were a number of differences and discrepancies in the views of the Bocking conventiclers, there was already considerable opposition to predestinarian teachings. Thomas Cole had declared that children were not born in original sin, while Robert Cole averred that the doctrine of predestination was more suited to devils than Christians. George Brodebridge merely stated that God's predestination was conditional. Although Humphrey Middleton publicly declared that all men were predestined to salvation, numerous witnesses quoted Henry Hart as denying that anyone was predestined to salvation or reprobation.[6]

While predestination does not seem to have been the dominant concern of the Bocking conventiclers, Hart links them conclusively to the Freewillers. He would help initiate the controversy over free will in Mary's reign, but this came towards the end of a long career of religious radicalism. In 1511 the Lollard martyr James Brewster was accused of having associated with Henry Hart, a carpenter of Westminster, who had denounced oblations, images and pilgrimages.[7] Although Hart the Freewiller may or may not have been Brewster's associate, he was certainly the Henry Hart of Pluckley indicted for unlawful assembly in 1538. Ironically, in the light of later developments, Archbishop Cranmer interceded on his behalf, claiming that Hart was being persecuted only because he favoured the new religion.[8] Hart increased his status as a prominent religious radical with three works, written in 1548–9, which argued for free will and the importance of good works in salvation.[9] The depositions taken in the aftermath of Bocking underscore Hart's leadership among the conventiclers; as Martin has observed, Hart was cited and quoted by six deponents while no one else was mentioned more than once.[10] Most importantly, Hart was the leader of a congregation

witnessed by John Simpson (PRO PCC F, 8 Tashe, 52r). A conventicler initially identified as 'John Barrett' in the Privy Council register was subsequently referred to as 'Barrey'. I am assuming that this is John Barry, the Freewiller.

[6] BL Harleian MS 421, 133r–134v.

[7] *AM* (1570), 944. It is impossible definitely to identify this carpenter with the Freewiller. One small piece of corroboration is that the Freewiller may have been an old man in Mary's reign. Hart's adversary John Bradford addressed him as 'Father Hart', a term of respect which can only be explained as having been made in deference to great age (ECL MS 260, 175v). C. J. Clement in his *Religious Radicalism in England, 1535–1565* (Carlisle, 1997), 189–91, has devoted considerable ingenuity to identifying the two Henry Harts with one another; the results are interesting but hardly conclusive.

[8] *The Works of Thomas Cranmer*, ed. J. E. Cox (2 vols., PS, 1844–6), ii. 367.

[9] *A godly newe short treatise* (1548); *A godlie exhortation to all suche as professe the Gospell* (1549); *A consultorie for all Christians* (Worcester, 1549).

[10] J. W. Martin, 'English Protestant Separatism at its Beginnings: Henry Hart and the Free-Will Men', *Sixteenth Century Journal* 7 (1976), 59.

in Kent during Edward VI's reign: in 1551 William Austen, a clothier of Goodhurst, bequeathed £6 13s 4d to 'Harry Hart and to his faithfull brethren'.[11]

Yet there must have been more than one Freewiller, or proto-Freewiller, congregation by the end of 1551. The assembly at Bocking was apparently intended to bring together members of groups scattered across Kent and Essex.[12] One of the witnesses declared that his 'congregation' took up a collection to defray the costs of travel to Essex.[13] These local congregations provided the foundation for the larger and better-organised Freewiller congregations of Mary's reign. John Jeffrey was the brother-in-law of the Freewiller leader John Laurence and worked with Laurence in underground religious activity in Marian London. He would be indicted before the quarter sessions at Colchester, on 25 July 1556, on charges of establishing conventicles of twenty people or more at West Mersea and Dedham.[14] An anonymous letter written in Mary's reign contains greetings to a Freewill congregation in London.[15] An informant reported to Bishop Bonner that Henry Hart led a congregation in London whose members were required to subscribe to thirteen doctrinal articles which he had drawn up.[16] The Edwardine gatherings had evidently blossomed into congregations comparable to their 'orthodox' Protestant rivals in size, geographical distribution and cohesion.

The Edwardine congregations lacked a sense of fully articulated and defiant separation from the Protestant national Church. But they came dangerously close in their insistence on the need for separation in order to maintain doctrinal purity. Several of the Bocking conventiclers believed they should not associate with sinners, a precept applied to their relations with the Church of England; some had refused communion for more than two years.[17] The author of the letter to the London Freewillers mentioned above enjoined his followers to separate themselves completely from unbelievers. Strype interpreted this as an injunction to avoid Catholic services, but the letter does not mention idolatry or the mass,

---

[11] PRO, PCC Prob 11/34/31. I am grateful to Michael Zell for this reference.
[12] J. W. Martin, *Religious Radicals in Tudor England* (1989), 24, 49.
[13] BL, Harleian MS 421, 134v.
[14] Essex Record Office, QSR 2/15. For Jeffrey's activities in London with Laurence, see *AM* (1563), 1605.
[15] Strype, *Memorials*, vol. III (i). 413; III (ii), 321–5.
[16] *AM* (1563), 1605. It is perhaps indicative of rigorous internal discipline that one of Hart's objections to predestination was that it weakened the power of excommunication in Christian congregations. See Bodleian Library MS 53, 60r.
[17] BL Harleian MS 421, 134v; *APC* III, 206.

and attacks the doctrine of predestination at length.[18] It seems clear which unbelievers the Freewillers were being admonished to avoid.

This nascent sense of self-identity as a group apart from the established Church was intensified by further persecution late in Edward VI's reign. In the autumn of 1552 Cranmer headed a commission investigating religious radicals in Kent. On 19 February 1553 the archbishop himself attended a sermon preached by Thomas Cole, who had been imprisoned by the Privy Council in the wake of the assembly at Bocking. Ostensibly an attack on Anabaptism, Cole's sermon seems to have been directed at least partly against his former associates. Many of the 'errors' he denounced – including universal salvation, the belief that a person could keep God's commandments perfectly and the denial of predestination – appear in the Bocking depositions.[19] Despite Cole's denials, it was clearly a recantation: a public break with his radical past which propitiated the authorities and secured him rapid promotion in the Church.[20] Its impact was heightened by the presence of two people forced to stand on a platform in penitential garb while he preached. Judging by Cole's remarks, they were atoning for the belief that Christ died for his own as well as for humanity's sins.[21] It is possible that one of these unfortunates was Humphrey Middleton, who was quoted as denying predestination and affirming universal salvation in the Bocking depositions and who was certainly in Cranmer's custody at this point.[22] It is also possible that Henry Hart was one of the penitents. A few years later Nicholas Ridley would write cryptically that Hart 'hath in times past acknowledged certain of his follies'.[23] Yet they were only two of a number of Freewillers known to have been imprisoned at this time.[24]

By the end of Edward VI's reign, the future Freewillers had already established organised underground congregations and a tradition of *de facto* separation from the established Church. Furthermore, sporadic persecution had intensified their suspicion of and hostility towards the Edwardine

---

[18] Strype, *Memorials*, vol. III (ii). 321–5.

[19] Thomas Cole, *A godly and frutefull sermon, made at Maydstone* (1553), especially B3v, B7v, C8v; cf. BL Harleian MS 421, 133r–134v. On this sermon, see also Diarmaid MacCulloch, *Thomas Cranmer: a Life* (New Haven and London, 1996), 530–1; Clement, *Religious Radicalism*, 145–54.

[20] For Cole's later career, see *Dictionary of National Biography* and Garrett, *Marian Exiles*, 122–3 (although the latter is incorrect in stating that Cole was dean of Sarum).

[21] Cole, *Godly and frutefull sermon*, C1r, C3r, D3v.

[22] BL Harleian MS 421, 134v; John Foxe, *Rerum in ecclesia gestarum . . . Commentarii* (Basle, 1559), 202–3.

[23] ECL MS 260, 271r.

[24] In Mary's reign a former Freewiller writing to his erstwhile associates referred to the imprisonment of a number of Freewillers in the reign of Edward VI. See BL Harley MS 416, 159v.

ecclesiastical establishment. The preconditions for schism existed even before the young king died.

III

Nevertheless, a schism was by no means inevitable. All English Protestants, no matter what their opinions on free will and election, faced intense persecution in Mary Tudor's reign. The time could not have been less propitious for internecine conflict, which threatened to confirm the Catholic charge that Protestantism was inherently factious and divisive. John Bradford, whose treatise on election helped to ignite the controversy, would later protest to Cranmer, Ridley and Hugh Latimer that he had not intended to provoke a quarrel and that he had not distributed copies of his treatise except 'to such as desire to be confirmed in the truth'.[25] Bradford was clearly aware of the dangers of schism and concerned that other leading Protestants would not approve of his treatise. Why then did he write it?

Although he had been incarcerated since the beginning of Mary's reign, Bradford had forged close pastoral relationships with a number of zealous Protestants through a remarkably wide-ranging network of correspondents. He had particularly intimate and intense pastoral relationships with a circle of godly women who consulted him about their doubts of their election and fears for their salvation.[26] During the summer of 1554, Bradford wrote to two of his closest friends, Margery Cook and Joyce Hales, answering their questions about predestination and allaying their doubts about their salvation.[27] Their fears had apparently been stoked by new writings of Henry Hart circulating in manuscript. At about the same time that he wrote to Cook and Hales, Bradford promised Robert Cole and Nicholas Sheterden that he would shortly reply to Hart's writings on election. Bradford also sent a work on predestination, now lost, to an unnamed believer in free will. This individual apparently responded by criticising Bradford for stirring up controversy and also enclosed a letter from Henry Hart rebutting Bradford's predestinarian

---

[25] BL Additional MS 19400, 42r. When Bradford sent a copy of the treatise to Margery Cook, he instructed her not to show it to others, as it would stir up quarrels which he wished to avoid. See ECL MS 260, 136v.

[26] Thomas Freeman, ' "The Good Ministrye of Godlye and Vertuouse Women": The Elizabethan Martyrologists and the Female Supporters of the Marian Martyrs', *JBS* 39 (2000), 8–33.

[27] ECL MS 260, 79r–81v, 136v.

theology. Bradford's reply added further arguments and promised to respond to Hart's 'errors'.[28]

In October 1554 Bradford completed his response to Hart's most substantial work on election, an attack on the 'enormities' of predestinarian doctrine.[29] Bradford answered Hart, despite his considerable fears that he was creating divisions among the godly, because of his pastoral concerns for the spiritual health of his flock, particularly Joyce Hales and Margery Cook. Bradford's treatise on election was dedicated to Hales; and on 14 February 1555, when he believed that his execution was imminent, Bradford wrote to a group of Freewillers, appealing to them not to 'molest' or 'disquiet' Hales or Cook after his death.[30] Bradford and his associates felt obliged to defend predestination at almost any cost: assurance of immutable election was a paramount concern of their followers. When Lady Anne Knevet wrote to John Careless exhorting him to persevere in opposing the Freewillers over election, he replied 'that if every hair of my head was a man's life, I would willingly give them all in the defence thereof'.[31] Another ardent predestinarian, Augustine Bernher, succinctly summarised what was at stake when he claimed that denying predestination undermined 'the glory and majesty of God and the certainty of the salvation of God's chosen and elect children'.[32] When Hart and his associates questioned predestination, it was a challenge that the 'orthodox' Protestant elite could not ignore, even for the sake of unity.

IV

If Bradford expected that his treatise would nip the controversy in the bud, he was doomed to disappointment. Recriminations and criticisms of his work came from Freewillers incarcerated with him in the King's Bench prison. On 1 January 1555 Bradford lost his temper and wrote to these Freewillers that since they were denouncing his teachings on predestination when he visited them, he would break off all personal contact.[33] Two weeks later he urged Cranmer, Ridley and Latimer to

---

[28] ECL MS 260, 144r–145v, 175v; MS 262, 142r–143r.

[29] Hart's work was entitled 'The enormities proceeding of the opinion that predestination, calling and election is absolute'. This treatise has not survived and its contents are known only because Bradford incorporated it completely in his rebuttal of it (Bodleian Library MS 53, 49r–70v). As part of his attempt to dampen the fires of controversy, Bradford did not name Hart as the author of the 'Enormities' in his response. He identified him in a letter to Cranmer, Ridley and Latimer a few months later (BL Additional MS 19400, 42r–v).

[30] BL Additional MS 19400, 33v–34r.   [31] ECL MS 260, 237v.

[32] Bodleian Library MS 53, 126r–v.   [33] *LM*, 682.

write against Hart and his associates, warning that 'more hurt will come of them then ever came by the papists'.[34] The letter was co-signed by other Edwardine Protestant leaders in the King's Bench: Bishop Robert Ferrar, Archdeacon John Philpot and Archdeacon Rowland Taylor. Philpot seems already to have joined Bradford in writing to individual Protestants who questioned predestination.[35] Augustine Bernher was another important ally. Having come to Oxford in 1548 to study theology, Bernher remained in England as Latimer's amanuensis and factotum. During Mary's reign Bernher not only acted as an indefatigable courier between the imprisoned Protestant leaders, he was also the *de facto*, and at times formal, head of the main Protestant congregation in London.[36] After Bradford's death Philpot and Bernher, along with Careless, would lead the struggle against the Freewillers, in part by default, since they failed in their efforts to persuade heavyweight Protestants such as Ridley to lend their names to the cause.

In the meantime, the Freewillers in the King's Bench indignantly returned Bradford's hostile letter. Bradford decided on a more conciliatory approach and wrote again, apologising for giving offence.[37] On 30 January 1555, however, Bradford was transferred to the Counter prison in Bread Street. A second conciliatory letter from there to the Freewillers in the King's Bench was also rebuffed.[38] His departure left the Protestant prisoners in the King's Bench divided into two factions: the predestinarians, led by Philpot and Careless, and the Freewillers, led by the Sussex laymen John Trew and Thomas Avington.

From the Counter prison Bradford continued to try to suture the wounds of intraconfessional conflict. In February he wrote to Hart and other Freewillers, urging them to heed his teachings and promising that if they did so 'all controversies for predestination, original sin, freewill, etc. shall so cease that there shall be no breach of love nor suspicion amongst us'.[39] Repeatedly during the spring of 1555, Bradford wrote to Philpot and Careless, enjoining them to preserve as much unity as possible among the prisoners in the King's Bench, even at the price of tolerating people of unsure doctrines.[40] But this was only a tactical retreat. Bradford was planning another treatise, designed to win Trew, Avington and their followers over to the truth.[41] Careless, he wrote,

---

[34] BL Additional MS 19400, 42r–v.   [35] ECL MS 260, 144v; MS 262, 143r.
[36] Brett Usher, '"In a Time of Persecution": New Light on the Secret Protestant Congregation in Marian London', *John Foxe and the English Reformation*, ed. David Loades (Aldershot, 1997), 233–51.
[37] *LM*, 46–56.   [38] ECL MS 262, 101r.   [39] BL Additional MS 19400, 33v.
[40] ECL MS 260, 204r; cf. MS 262, 141v and BL Additional MS 19400, 49r.
[41] ECL MS 260, 204r.

should maintain amicable relations with the Freewillers, but also pray and work steadily for their conversion: 'a drop maketh the stone hollow, not with once, but with often dropping'.[42]

Bradford's strategy bore some fruit. Robert Cole and John Ledley, alumni of the Bocking conventicle, were converted to predestinarian 'orthodoxy' in the spring of 1555.[43] Bradford also congratulated Careless on the conversion of a Freewiller named Robert Skelthorpe (although this proved ephemeral) and was optimistic about Richard Gibson, a Freewiller imprisoned with him in the Counter.[44] Yet these conversions probably increased the tension between the two groups, even while their leaders were trying to estabish some concord between them.

V

Bradford was executed on 1 July 1555; Philpot was removed from the King's Bench to Bonner's palace on 2 October. John Careless was left as the leader of the predestinarian prisoners in the King's Bench. In many ways, Careless was the odd man out among the predestinarian leaders. The others were university-educated clerics, prominent in the Edwardine Church; Careless was a weaver from Coventry and had no formal education. Nevertheless, he was equal to the responsibility thrust upon him. He continued, and even extended, Bradford's work; his pastoral letters, when published by Foxe and Bull, became classics of Puritan devotional literature. Yet Careless's eloquence was taxed to the limit as the situation in the King's Bench deteriorated throughout 1555. During the first half of the year, Trew and his followers objected to some of the Protestant prisoners playing with dice and cards to pass the time.[45] Bradford, Philpot and Careless defended gaming as spiritually indifferent and harmless in moderation. Trew and his followers (according to Philpot) claimed that their opponents were defenders of 'carnal liberty'; Bradford and his supporters (according to Trew) countered that their adversaries thought they could achieve salvation through abstinence and good works.[46]

---

[42] ECL MS 262, 141v.

[43] BL Harleian MS 416, 160v. Their conversion can be dated approximately from references to them as Freewillers in February 1555 (BL Additional MS 19400, 33r–34r) but as allies of Bradford before his death at the beginning of July 1555 (ECL MS 260, 240r).

[44] ECL MS 262, 141r; MS 260, 204r.

[45] It is interesting to note that Kentish conventiclers associated with the group at Bocking believed as a 'general doctrine' that gambling was sinful. See BL Harleian 421, 134r.

[46] John Philpot, *An apologie for spitting upon an Arian* (Emden, 1556?), B3r–B4r; Bodleian Library MS 53, 116r–v.

This particular dispute was resolved, but Trew's narrative of the disputes over free will in the King's Bench (our main primary source) reveals a pattern of repeated quarrels and temporary reconciliations during 1555. On another occasion the two groups fell out over the question of whether baptisms conducted by a Catholic priest were valid; Trew and his party said no, the predestinarians said yes.[47] But behind all these disputes lay the issue of predestination. Trew claimed that each time there was an agreement, a condition of the truce was that his opponents would not teach predestination or criticise those who refused to believe in it, and that each time the predestinarians broke their word.[48] Increasingly, the two groups took on the character of separate congregations. The Freewillers boasted of the zeal and piety of their worship; Careless responded with a sneering account of their:

> hopping and dancing and wrestling with themselves...howling and crying...gaping and staring and slapping of their breasts....I think was never seen amongst men that were well in their wit. But such shifts must men have to make their prayers seem fervent.[49]

Other events increased the tensions within the King's Bench as 1555 progressed. Bernher's treatise against Hart was circulated. John Clement, a wheelwright and the leader of a Protestant congregation in Surrey, joined the predestinarians in the late autumn.[50] Writing to Careless in October or November, Philpot deplored the 'great trouble' which the freewill 'schismatics' were causing and insisted that Careless defend the gospel 'whatsoever your adversaries may say or do against you'.[51]

The final attempt to unite the two groups began on 18 December 1555, the day of Philpot's execution. Thomas Simpson, Thomas Upcher and Richard Woodman were released from prison and tried to reconcile their feuding fellow prisoners.[52] Although all three were predestinarians, they had connections to the Freewillers. If Upcher was not a participant in the Bocking conventicle, he was from Bocking, as was Simpson, and both may have been related to John Simpson and the Upcher who were leaders of the conventicle. Woodman was a leading Protestant from Trew's and Avington's East Sussex homeland. Thanks to their good offices, a tentative agreement was made in which (according to Trew) the predestinarians might hold their beliefs privately, but were to refrain from propagating them. A series of complex negotiations followed over plans for a

---

[47] Bodleian Library MS 53, 121r–v.   [48] Bodleian Library MS 53, 120v–121r.
[49] BL Additional MS 19400, 62v.   [50] ECL MS 260, 148r.   [51] ECL MS 260, 82r.
[52] Bodleian Library MS 53, 121v–122r. The date is supplied by Foxe: *AM* (1570), 2171.

joint communion service on Christmas Day to celebrate their newfound unity.

Trew, however, had second thoughts about parts of the statement of faith which the predestinarians had drawn up and which he and other Freewillers had signed. His conscience troubled him so severely that he became physically ill. Careless visited him and tried to patch together an agreement, but on the next day, 24 December, the Freewillers repudiated the statement of faith and asked Trew to draft a new one. Careless promptly rejected it as heretical. The reconciliation collapsed amid mutual recriminations and the inability of either side to compromise their beliefs on election.[53]

VI

The disputes in the King's Bench may have been (given the conditions of Tudor prisons) conducted in near darkness, but they were not conducted in obscurity. News of the disputes spread among English Protestants as both sides sought to put their own spin on events or alleviate the doubts stirred up by the protracted controversies. In a confession of faith written in May or June 1555 and sent to the godly in Sussex, Richard Woodman endorsed predestination and the validity of baptisms conducted by Catholic priests.[54] John Philpot was sufficiently concerned that he interrupted a diatribe against Anabaptists to warn his readers against allowing their minds to be 'alienated from the truth' by the rumours circulating over the contentions in the King's Bench. Philpot rebutted charges of antinomianism and 'carnal liberty' and claimed that he was being slandered for maintaining 'that the elect of God cannot finally perish'.[55] John Trew wrote his narrative to demonstrate to Protestants outside the King's Bench that the Freewillers were not responsible for the schism.[56] The controversy crossed the Channel; in January 1556 Joyce Hales reported to Careless that Freewillers in Calais were criticising him for his conduct towards their comrades in the King's Bench and denigrating him as 'a common player for money'.[57]

Outsiders not only followed the prison disputes, they participated in them. At this time Henry Hart lived, with John Kemp, another leading Freewiller, in the house of a cutler named Curl, at the foot of London

---

[53] Bodleian Library MS 53, 122v–123r.
[54] Gonville and Caius College, Cambridge, MS 218, pp. 29, 367.
[55] Philpot, *Apology*, B3r–B4r.   [56] Bodleian Library MS 53, 116r.
[57] BL Additional MS 19400,76v.

Bridge. Kemp and Curl both intervened in the King's Bench disputes. At one point, after the final break with Trew, Careless complained that Kemp and Curl 'hath so baited me of late as I had been a bear at a stake'.[58] And it was reported that the predestinarians Robert Cole and John Ledley 'do resort much unto the King's Bench unto the prisoners about matters of religion'.[59]

Meanwhile, another Freewiller became prominent in the King's Bench controversies. John Jackson had been one of the signatories to Trew's narrative of events within the prison. During the winter and spring of 1556 he engaged in a vigorous epistolary debate with Careless on the subject of predestination.[60] Careless failed to convert Jackson, but he had succeeded with others. In one of his letters Careless prayed that Jackson would repent his errors like 'my dear brother Cornelius and divers other', referring to Cornelius Stevenson, another signatory of Trew's narrative, whose conversion was a propaganda coup.[61]

The importance of such conversions can be seen in the pitched battle waged over six prisoners – William Tyms, Robert Drake, George Ambrose, John Cavell, Richard Spurge and Thomas Spurge – condemned to death on 28 March 1556, and transferred to Newgate.[62] There they came under considerable pressure from Freewillers hoping to reap a propaganda windfall by recruiting these martyrs in waiting. (It is noteworthy that four of the six – Ambrose, Cavell and the two Spurges – came from Bocking.) Henry Hart, John Kemp, Trew's sister-in-law and another female Freewiller visited the six repeatedly, trying to win them over.[63] At Tym's urging, Careless and his ally Thomas Whittle weighed in with letters exhorting the six to remain faithful, while Jackson and Richard Gibson (another imprisoned Freewiller) worked to convert them.[64] Careless then sent a statement of his beliefs (apparently a copy of the articles which Trew had refused to sign a few months earlier) to Newgate. Hart somehow managed to intercept the document and added comments emphasising freewill and the importance of good works in attaining salvation, before forwarding the document to Tyms and his five comrades. Tyms penned a scathing assessment of Hart's

[58] ECL MS 260, 132r; *AM* (1563), 1605. A cryptic remark Joyce Hales made in a letter suggests that Careless wrote a letter on predestination, now lost, to Curl. See BL Additional MS 19400, 78v.

[59] *AM* (1563), 1605.

[60] ECL MS 260, 271, 239r–v; BL Additional MS 19400, 62r–63v.

[61] ECL MS 260, 239r.   [62] *AM* (1563), 1504–6.

[63] An informant of Bonner described Hart and Kemp as sharing a residence at this time. See *AM* (1563), 1605. Careless implied that the two women had worked to reconvert John Clement. See BL, Additional MS 19400, 73v.

[64] ECL MS 260, 271, 69r–v; BL Additional MS 19400, 73v–74r; *AM* (1563), 1530.

'most blasphemous' teachings on the parchment, and similarly terse, caustic comments were added by his five companions. In an impressive display of the power of what might be called the celebrity endorsements of martyrs, copies of this multiply annotated document were made and circulated among Protestants.[65] On 24 April 1556 Tyms and the other five were burned and the hopes the Freewillers had entertained for their conversion went up in smoke.

Worse was to follow. On 25 April Careless identified Richard Gibson as one of the leaders in the attempt to convert Tyms and his companions.[66] Yet on 19 June Gibson was denounced for apostasy by Jackson and a group of Freewillers. In a reply sent the next day, Gibson emphasised the insufficiency of good works in attaining salvation and asserted that God had predestined his elect to salvation.[67] Gibson's conversion was sudden, but it remained permanent; he was a still a predestinarian when he was burned on 18 November 1557. One of the Freewillers who reproached Gibson for changing sides, Stephen Gratwick, later embraced predestinarian teachings himself.[68] And by the late spring of 1556, Roger Newman, the brother of a martyr, and one of the Freewillers to whom Bradford had appealed in February 1555, had joined the predestinarians.[69]

What made the loss of prominent Freewillers especially painful was that their numbers were steadily diminishing overall. Persecution was thinning out the ranks of both factions, particularly in the prisons. Trew's lieutenant Thomas Avington was burned on 6 June 1556; Humphrey Middleton and Nicholas Sheterden had been executed together almost a year earlier.[70] Henry Hart's long and eventful career ended with his death early in 1557. John Trew escaped from prison in late May or early June 1556.[71] On the other side, Bradford, Ridley and Philpot were all

---

[65] Careless's description of how Hart, Tyms and the others edited the document is found in *AM* (1563), 1529–30. A copy of the revised document survives as ECL MS 260, 87r–v.

[66] *AM* (1563), 1630. 'John' Gibson had been one of the Freewillers whom Bradford had addressed in his letter of 14 February 1555. See BL Additional MS 19400, 33r. Because of this there has been a great deal of hesitation in identifying Richard Gibson as a Freewiller. M. T. Pearse has convincingly argued that the two Gibsons were one and the same person in his *Between Known Men and Visible Saints: A Study in Sixteenth-Century English Dissent* (Cranbury, NJ, 1994), 49–50. Neither Pearse, nor apparently anyone else, knows of Richard Gibson's letter responding to charges of backsliding from Freewillers (see note 67).

[67] ECL MS 260, 72r.   [68] BL Additonal MS 19400, 82r.

[69] BL Additional MS 19400, 33r, 78v. See Thomas Freeman, 'Notes on a source for John Foxe's account of the Marian Persecution in Kent and Sussex', *Historical Research* 67 (1994), 203–11.

[70] *AM* (1563), 1217, 1522.

[71] Kent County Record Office, PRC 3/15, 22r; *Archdeacon Harpsfield's Visitation, 1557*, ed. L. E. Whatmore (2 vols., Catholic Record Society, 1950–1), i. 120; BL Additional MS 19400, 67v; *LM*, 615.

executed in 1555, while Careless and John Clement died in the King's
Bench during the summer of 1556.[72] But while both factions suffered
losses from death, the Freewillers were also losing converts to their
opponents, many of whom (Robert Cole, John Ledley, John Clement,
Richard Gibson) then proselytised effectively against their former
associates.

VII

Death succeeded (where Christian charity had not) in abating the controversies within the King's Bench. Nevertheless, the predestinarians were
still faced with the considerable task of restricting the spread of Freewiller
teachings outside the gaols. Unable to apply coercion to their opponents,
the only way the predestinarians could neutralise them was to convert
enough of them or their supporters to isolate those who remained. From
the beginning of Mary's reign, the leading Protestants were tireless in dis-
seminating doctrinal statements, backed by their moral authority, among
their co-religionists.[73] Later the 'orthodox' Protestant leaders shrewdly
sponsored confessions of faith by leaders of local congregations, such
as Richard Woodman and John Clement, which defended predestination explicitly and at length.[74] Endorsements from such respected local
leaders helped the 'orthodox' leadership, which might otherwise have
seemed remote and even autocratic, to have controversial teachings accepted with little resistance.

Of course, there was nothing to stop the Freewillers from circulating
works, such as Hart's 'Enormities' and Trew's narrative of events in the
King's Bench, expounding their own theological views. One Freewiller
work written in response to the King's Bench disputes – 'The confutation
of the errors of the careless by necessity' – reached the English Protestants in Geneva.[75] It alarmed the exiles; Knox declared that he wrote his
rebuttal of it at 'the earnest request of some godly brethren', and the cost
of its printing was entirely financed by two of the English congregation's

---

[72] *AM* (1563), 1523, 1529.
[73] See for example BL Additional MS 19400, 31r–32v, a confession sent from Bradford to Protestants in London; ECL MS 260, 38r–39r, sent by Robert Samuels to a Protestant congregation
in Ipswich. The ability of the Marian Protestants to disseminate their works across a wide
geographical area is demonstrated by the circulation of Bradford's treatise 'The Hurt of Hearing
Mass' in London, Kent and Lancashire. See *LM*, 355; ECL MS 260, 40v, 81v, 171v.
[74] Gonville and Caius College, Cambridge, MS 218, 28–40; Strype, *Ecclesiastical Memorials* III (ii).
434–67.
[75] The 'Confutation' is now known through John Knox's rebuttal of it: *An answer to a great number of
blasphemous cavallations* (Geneva, 1560).

leading members.[76] Yet while individual Freewiller works circulated widely among English Protestants, the Freewillers do not seem to have matched the thorough and systematic penetration of the grassroots which the predestinarians achieved. The dynamo driving the dissemination of predestinarian works was the main London underground congregation. On 26 February 1558 the leadership of the London congregation forwarded a copy of Bradford's treatise on election to an unnamed Protestant congregation outside London, warning against the blandishments of those 'whose minds are corrupt with errors in the matter concerning God's eternal election'.[77]

A glance at the leaders of the London congregation helps to explain their predestinarian activism. Among its deacons was Thomas Simpson, who had attempted to mediate the King's Bench dispute and who was described by Trew as a predestinarian.[78] Robert Cole, who displayed a convert's zeal in promoting predestination, was as influential as he was ubiquitous; in a remarkable passage John Foxe described Thomas Bentham, the titular head of the London congregation, as presiding over it 'with Robert Cole'.[79] But it was Augustine Bernher, the most influential member of the London congregation, who was the guiding spirit in the offensive against the Freewillers. Sometime before the summer of 1556, he arranged what was unmistakably a formal debate with the leading Freewillers John Laurence and John Barry, and followed it up with a treatise, 'Certayne testamonies taken out of Gods boke', which sought to refute the arguments which Laurence and Barry had presented.[80] The two Freewillers responded by protesting that they had not started the controversy and demanded that if Bernher did communicate further with them, he should first answer a work which they had left with his followers.[81] Bernher replied to what he called a 'beastly letter' with a highly rhetorical missive forcefully presenting his predestinarian theology and vehemently denouncing Laurence and Barry.[82] Apparently, he failed

---

[76] Knox, *Answer*, 8. See also Jean-François Gilmont, *Bibliographie des éditions de Jean Crespin 1550–1572* (2 vols., Verviers, 1981), i. 133.

[77] Bodleian Library MS 53, 146v.

[78] Bodleian Library MS 53, 122r. For Simpson's importance in the London congregation, see Usher, 'In a time of persecution', 233–7, 241–3.

[79] *AM* (1563), 1700.

[80] Bodleian Library MS 53, 141r–142r, 126r–137v.

[81] Bodleian Library MS 53, 138r–139v.

[82] Bodleian Library MS 53, 140r–146r. Bernher here stated that he had written his response to Henry Hart eighteen months earlier (141r). This establishes the approximate date of this response and of the entire exchange between Bernher and Laurence and Barry. Bernher's response to Hart refers to Latimer as still living (114v) and was thus written before 16 October 1555. C. J. Clement's

to convert them. But his tactics – staging formal debates, writing open letters designed for a wide Protestant readership – suggest that Bernher was trying to discredit his opponents, confident that he and his allies would be able to crush them in oral or written argument.

With death scything down prominent and learned Protestant prisoners, Bernher may have turned to the Continent for reinforcements in his propaganda war. On Palm Sunday 1556 Robert Cole and John Ledley returned to London from a trip overseas, during which they had consulted Protestant leaders 'about questions of religion'.[83] Given their backgrounds, it is reasonable to assume that they were sent as emissaries of the London congregation and that the problem of the Freewillers was one of the topics discussed. On 10 November 1557 John Rough, an ex-Dominican and celebrated Edwardine preacher, returned to London from Friesland, swiftly taking over the leadership of the London congregation. Brett Usher has cogently argued that Rough was sent by the English Protestants in exile in an effort to impose quasi-episcopal discipline on a congregation which had begun to exhibit alarming particularist tendencies.[84] But if he was sent at the request of the London congregation, this would hardly be the reason why they requested him. It may be that Rough was also despatched to furnish the congregation with a trained theologian, of proven reputation and skilled in debate, to combat the Freewillers.

Rough was quickly captured and executed, but Thomas Bentham, an Oxford-educated theologian who had been working on the Geneva Bible, arrived in London in spring 1558 and assumed leadership of the congregation.[85] It is possible that he, too, was sent to battle the Freewillers as a result of Cole's and Ledley's visit. This is, of course, speculation, but what is beyond doubt is the determination of the London congregation and its leaders to silence anyone who opposed predestination. In response to Laurence's and Barry's demand to be left in peace, Bernher wrote that he would:

study, write and speak against your opinion so long as my life lasts. . . . Although you began not with me (as you say) yet shall I begin with you. I shall make you aweary of writing and printing against the manifest truth of God's most holy word.[86]

suggestion that Bernher's response was written early in 1558 is based on the specious premise that Bernher (a leading figure in the London congregation throughout Mary's reign) must have written it when he was the formal leader of the London congregation. See Clement, *Religious Radicalism*, 132–3.

[83] *AM* (1563), 1605.   [84] Usher, 'In a time of persecution', 241–2.

[85] *AM* (1563), 1700; Garrett, *Marian Exiles*, 86–77.   [86] Bodleian Library MS 53, 146r.

Indeed, it is safe to say that the only reason why the Marian persecution was not followed by an Elizabethan persecution was that, by the time Elizabeth came to the throne, the Freewiller threat had already been largely eliminated.[87]

VIII

After Mary's death some of the leading Protestants returning from exile were alarmed by the prospect of further controversy over predestination. Around May 1559 a group of eminent divines, including Richard Cox, John Jewel and Edwin Sandys, drew up a statement of their doctrines. The document was intended as a justification of their conduct and statements during the recent disputation at Westminster, at which the topics of election and free will were not mentioned; yet, remarkably, one of the articles was a defence of predestination, inserted because 'some even in these our days (who also pretend the name of the Gospel)' denied it.[88] In 1561 Jean Veron wrote against John Champneys, the author of a treatise attacking predestination, and echoed this comment, declaring that advocates of free will were not only to be found among Catholics, 'but also among them that will be counted most perfect Christians and most earnest favourers of the gospel'. Yet although Veron claimed that Champneys was the 'standard-bearer' of the 'freewill men', there is no indication that Champneys had any supporters at all.[89]

In fact, by this time predestinarian divines who attacked the Freewillers were wrestling with ghosts. There were a few advocates of free will, such as Champneys and an anonymous author, dubbed 'Cerberus' by his opponent Robert Crowley, who attacked predestination in a work written in 1563.[90] In 1562 Thomas Walbott, the rector of St Mary Magdalen, Milk Street, addressed a letter to the bishops in which he denied that God predestined any evil, wickedness or sin.[91] But there is no evidence

---

[87] There is a cryptic and fascinating reference in a letter written to a Dutch minister in Emden on 2 May 1559 about a group of (presumably Dutch) prisoners in the Marshalsea who were incarcerated for advocating free will doctrines. See Andrew Pettegree, *Marian Protestantism: Six Studies* (Aldershot, 1996), 198. This reveals not only the readiness of the Elizabethan authorities to persecute those who opposed predestination, but also the disappearance of the Freewillers. Had the Freewiller congregations still existed, the imprisonment of these dissenters would not have been an isolated and obscure incident.

[88] CCCC MS 121, 139.

[89] Jean Veron, *A moste necessary treatise of fre wil* (1561), A2r–v, A5v, E8v, I1r.

[90] Pearse, *Between Known Men*, 111–7; D. Andrew Penny, *Freewill or Predestination: The Battle over Saving Grace in Mid-Tudor England* (Woodbridge, 1990), 198–204.

[91] John Strype, *Annals of the Reformation* (3 vols., Oxford, 1824), I (i) 494–8, mistakenly referring to 'Thomas Talbot'. Thomas Walbott compounded for the first fruits of St Mary Magdalen, Milk Street, on 20 March 1561: PRO E334/7, 111v. I am grateful to Brett Usher for this reference.

to support Walbott's claim to be speaking on behalf of a large number of English Protestants. Nor can any of these writers be linked with the earlier Freewillers; Walbott, indeed, pointedly distanced himself from them.[92]

The Freewillers' disappearance can partly be explained by the death of some of their leaders, particularly Hart and Thomas Avington. But others – John Trew, John Kemp, John Laurence and John Barry – all apparently survived into Elizabeth's reign.[93] It could be argued that the Freewillers were cowed into silence by the fear of persecution, but that had not stopped them in Mary's reign. The elimination of the Freewillers suggests that the predestinarians had succeeded in their project: to retain the loyalty of their own supporters while converting a significant number of their opponents and discrediting the remainder.

Throughout Mary's reign, as we have seen, the Freewillers suffered the loss of defectors, many of whom had been prominent in their ranks: Thomas Cole, Robert Cole, John Ledley, Roger Newman, Richard Gibson, Stephen Gratwick, Richard Proude and Cornelius Stevenson among them. Against this, the Freewillers' efforts at winning converts from the predestinarians seem to have borne meagre fruit. John Knox implied that the author of the 'Confutation of the errors of the careless by necessity' was a convert from predestinarian 'orthodoxy', and Robert Skelthorpe, a prisoner in the King's Bench, seems to have been converted from the free will to the predestinarian camp and then back again.[94] Yet the rarity of such cases emphasises the Freewillers' failure to win significant numbers of converts, despite considerable efforts.

The predestinarians did more than isolate the Freewiller leaders – they also disgraced them. In his letter to the Elizabethan bishops, Thomas Walbott protested that 'because he denied that God predestined any particular sin' he suffered 'daily the shameful reproach and infamy' of being regarded as one of the 'Freewill men, Pelagians, papists, epicures [and] Anabaptists'.[95] Polemicists attacking members of the Family of Love sought to discredit them by associating them (tendentiously) with the Freewillers. John Rogers claimed that the Family of Love originated 'about the latter end of Queen Mary's reign, when many of our brethren were entered into that gulf of free will . . . certain Arians with Pelagians

[92] Strype, *Annals*, I (i) 496.
[93] For Trew under Elizabeth, see *Historical Manuscripts Commission Reports*, VII, 665.
[94] Knox, *Answer*, 167. Knox also implies that he knew the author of the 'Confutation' before Mary's reign (207). On Skelthorpe see ECL MS 262; 141 rv; Gonville and Caius College, Cambridge, MS 218, 30.
[95] Strype, *Annals*, I (i) 146.

joining together'.[96] Indeed, William Wilkinson explicitly linked the origins of the Family of Love to the King's Bench disputes.[97]

The clearest evidence of the aura of infamy surrounding the Freewillers in Elizabeth's reign comes from John Kemp, a minister in the Isle of Wight. Kemp contributed a detailed account of his movements, activities and teachings in the years 1554–5 to the third edition of Foxe's *Actes and Monuments* in order to clear himself of the slander of having denied predestination.[98] (There appear to have been two John Kemps, one of whom was a Freewiller denounced by Careless.[99]) Kemp clearly regarded the suspicion of being a Freewiller as so damaging to his reputation that he took the extraordinary step of writing a narrative of his earlier life to disprove it; and in doing so underlined the extent of the predestinarian triumph. It was a triumph which was unprecedented and unrepeated in early modern England. Not only were the dissenters discredited, they were effectively eliminated – and through persuasion, without coercion or state sanctions. How was this extraordinary victory achieved?

IX

The predestinarians had a major advantage over the Freewillers from the outset. They were led by the cream of English Protestant theologians, whereas only one Freewiller leader, Thomas Cole, even had a university education. This observation is not a reflection on the merits of the Freewillers' doctrines or the validity of their theological insight. However, theological training is excellent preparation for theological argument and, in religious disputation, people are sometimes convinced by argument. One convert from free will wrote that he had rejected predestination because of his understanding of James 2:17, 'till our

---

[96] John Rogers, *The displaying of an horrible sect . . .* (1574), B1 v.

[97] William Wilkinson, *A Confutation of Certaine Articles* (1579), 3r–4r.

[98] *AM* (1576), 1975–7.

[99] In addition to incurring Careless's wrath *AM* (1563), 1530, Kemp was described as a close associate of Henry Hart, active in Kent and London (ibid., 1605). The minister from the Isle of Wight may have been John Kemp the draper, who guaranteed the first fruits of Alexander Wimshurst. See Brett Usher, 'Backing Protestantism: The London Godly, the Exchequer and the Foxe Circle', *John Foxe: An Historical Perspective*, ed. David Loades (Aldershot, 1999), 129. In his narrative of his activities in Mary's reign, John Kemp the minister relates that he bought cloth in Bristol and transported it to London to be sold (*AM* (1576), 1976). If Kemp the minister was formerly a draper who guaranteed Wimshurst's first fruits, this might explain how his narrative came to be in Foxe's book, for Foxe described Wimshurst as 'veteri amico meo'. See *Rerum in ecclesia gestarum*, 637.

good preachers which were my prison fellows' explained the predestinarian exegesis of the verse to him.[100] A particular advantage was the
predestinarian clerics' knowledge of biblical languages. The question of
whether particular scriptural passages had been correctly translated was
a frequent flashpoint in disputes between the Freewillers and their opponents. For example, Bernher often claimed that Laurence and Barry
misunderstood particular biblical verses by reading them too literally and
interpreting the words according to contemporary usage.[101] Stung, they
responded by saying that Bernher was condemning all English translations of the Bible, although they had been made by men as learned
as he was.[102] Bernher riposted that, 'the more you jest at me because
of my Greek tongue, the more I shall study both in Latin and Greek
and Hebrew tongues to confound and throw down your fantastical and
wicked opinions'.[103]

Such exchanges were not without drawbacks for the predestinarians.
Trew repeatedly charged them with believing that only learned men
could truly understand the Bible and observed that 'in affirming that no
simple man without the tongues can truly understand them, it doth not
only agree with the papists, but also it doth cause all such as believe it to
neglect reading of the holy scriptures'.[104] This was rather too accurate
for comfort. Yet the Freewillers' anger at their opponents' erudition in
biblical languages chiefly indicates their frustration and impotence. The
predestinarian monopoly of such knowledge made it difficult for the
Freewillers to interpret scriptural passages (the bedrock of Protestant
religious debate) convincingly in support of their positions.

As a result, the Freewillers became, like many sixteenth-century sec-
tarians, defensive about their relative lack of education and markedly
anti-intellectual, professing contempt for the authority of scholars and
divines. Laurence and Barry, for example, accused Bernher of exalt-
ing 'yourself and your own company, calling some of them most godly
learned, as though neither the prophets nor apostles were to be compared
with them'.[105] Such attacks, however, were self-defeating. They opened
the way for the predestinarians to stereotype the Freewillers as ignorant
and uneducated; Bradford, for example, tersely declared, 'They utterly
condemn all learning.'[106] He and other predestinarians dismissed the

---

[100] BL Harleian MS 416, 160r.   [101] Bodleian Library MS 53, 132v–133r, 135v.
[102] Bodleian Library MS 53, 139r.   [103] Bodleian Library MS 53, 144v.
[104] Bodleian Library MS 53, 120v; also 118r, 120r.   [105] Bodleian Library MS 53, 126r, 139r.
[106] BL Additional MS 19400, 42v. The martyrologist Henry Bull elaborated on this point. See *LM*,
    359.

writings of the Freewillers because they did not use proper theological vocabulary and did not conform to the rhetorical standards expected in learned disputation.[107] It is easy for us in turn to dismiss these criticisms as elitist, but sixteenth-century England was an elitist society, which placed a high value on education. The effectiveness of predestinarian learning as a propaganda weapon can be seen by the way in which Bernher organised his campaign against Laurence and Barry around formal debates and theological arguments, all designed to highlight the 'ignorance' of his adversaries.

It would seem logical for the educational divide between the predestinarians and the Freewillers to have been matched by a social divide, with the former enjoying the support of those Protestants of higher social and economic status, and this does indeed seem to have happened. Most Freewillers appear to have been affluent and educated artisans. There were exceptions: John Laurence was a gentleman, Robert Cole may have been a former baliff of Faversham,[108] and, more strikingly, Richard Gibson's grandfather had been Lord Mayor of London and his father was a royal serjeant at arms, bailiff of Southwark and a Master of the Merchant Taylors.[109] But the predestinarians could muster an impressive array of bishops, senior clerics, minor aristocrats and gentry both in England and among the English exiles. Social status also brought financial advantages. The predestinarians had supporters among London's wealthy mercantile and artisan elites, and among women from aristocratic and gentry families.[110] Convincing, because reluctant, testimony to the generosity of London Protestants came in a letter Careless wrote denouncing them for their outward conformity with the Marian regime. Careless conceded the 'liberal relief' that they had given him, but warned them that it was not enough: for the salvation of their souls they must refuse to attend mass.[111] The money donated by wealthy women to Ridley, Philpot, Bradford, Careless and others is mentioned throughout the correspondence of the Marian martyrs.[112] The Freewillers were not nearly as successful in raising money. Their jealousy is evident in one Freewiller's allegation that Careless gave wealthy Protestants assurances

---

[107] See for example Bodleian Library MS 53, 60r, 61v.

[108] Penny, *Freewill or Predestination*, 57.

[109] S. T. Bindoff, *The House of Commons, 1509–1558* (1982); cf. *The Diary of Henry Machyn*, ed. J. G. Nichols (Camden Society o.s. 42, 1848), 157–8.

[110] For the support of leading London merchants and artisans for the Protestants in Mary's reign, see Usher, 'Backing Protestantism', 105–34; for the female supporters of the Marian martyrs see Freeman, 'Good Ministrye'.

[111] ECL MS 260, 208v.   [112] See Freeman, 'Good Ministrye', 10 note 6.

of their salvation, 'though they be drowned in many vices', as long as they gave generously to the predestinarians.[113]

Securing money was not a matter of avarice, but of survival. The many members of both groups who were in prison needed money to bribe their gaolers. With money, prisoners could obtain good food, decent quarters, visitors, books and even temporary release from prison; without it, their lives would be miserable and, very probably, of short duration. John Hooper wrote that he would have starved in prison, were it not for 'the benevolence and charity of godly people'.[114] Gaolers could be paid to allow prisoners pen, ink and paper; warders could be remunerated for turning a blind eye as manuscripts were smuggled in and out of prison. (It is worth remembering that many of the major works in the controversy over predestination – among them Bradford's treatise on election and Trew's narrative of the disputes in the King's Bench – were written in prison, smuggled out and circulated among Protestants.) Money may not have been the lifeblood of the competing Protestant factions, but it was their muscle and sinew. They could not move, much less fight, without it; and this gave a potentially decisive edge to the predestinarians.

X

If the predestinarians had educational, social and financial advantages over their opponents, recent scholarship might lead us to expect the Freewillers to have had the more appealing doctrines. As studies such as Paul Seaver's portrait of Nehemiah Wallington have reminded us, the doctrine of predestination placed heavy emotional burdens on believers. Religious despair among the godly was not uncommon.[115] Christopher Haigh has argued that the doctrine not only caused considerable suffering but was also consistently unpopular with Elizabethan and Jacobean believers.[116] If predestination was so burdensome and rebarbative, why did the Marian Protestants so thoroughly repudiate the Freewillers? The charge that predestination led to despair was certainly made by the

---

[113] Knox, *Answer*, 191.   [114] BL Additional MS 19400, 25r.

[115] Paul Seaver, *Wallington's World: A Puritan Artisan in Seventeenth-Century London* (1985). See also John Stachniewski, *The Persecutory Imagination: English Puritanism and the Literature Of Religious Literature* (Oxford, 1991), especially 27–61; Peter Iver Kaufman, *Prayer, Despair and Drama: Elizabethan Introspection* (Champaign, IL, 1996).

[116] Christopher Haigh, 'The taming of the Reformation: preachers, pastors and parishioners in Elizabethan and early Stuart England', *History* 85 (2000), 577–83.

Freewillers, and hotly denied by their opponents.[117] Trew charged that predestination 'destroyeth the certainty of our election and is enough to drive all such as believe it to despair for lack of knowledge, whether Christ died for them or not'.[118] Yet this appeal failed. An important clue as to why is found in the Freewiller accusation that Careless had promised salvation to wealthy Protestants, no matter how great their sins had been.

This was a caricature of the close pastoral relations between Bradford, Philpot and Careless and their 'sustainers', but like most caricatures, it is based on reality. Many Marian Protestants certainly feared for their salvation. It was in trying to alleviate Joyce Hales's anxieties on the subject that Bradford was first drawn into the controversy over free will. Indeed, the predestinarians leaders' most sustained and intense discussions of these issues were written for wealthy and godly women – a key constituency among whom the Freewillers signally failed to make any converts.[119] Bradford, Philpot and Careless pioneered the practice of 'practical divinity'; in doing so they also created a heartland of Marian Protestants, including, but not limited to, wealthy and influential female 'sustainers', who would remain profoundly committed to the doctrine of predestination. With a surefooted guide to lead one dextrously over the theological crags and emotional precipices of predestination, the doctrine could prove extremely comforting. The denial of any efficacy for good works or individual merit in attaining salvation reassured those whose consciences were gnawed by guilt. Joyce Hales maintained that the Freewillers, in emphasising the importance of good works, taught 'fear of the law . . . which is the next way to drive a man to despair'.[120] By stressing God's transcendence and the inevitability of his grace, the doctrine of predestination provided particular reassurance in a time of persecution. Bradford used the doctrine to emphasise to Hales the immutability of God's love,[121] and he and Bernher both argued that belief in free will engendered the worse despair of 'doubting of God's favour'.[122] By contrast, Stephen Gratwick, a convert from free will, wrote that predestination was a doctrine 'which so cheereth our hearts and quickeneth our spirits that no trouble or tyranny executed against us can dull or

[117] BL Additional MS 19400, 33r.   [118] Bodleian Library MS 53, 120r.
[119] On this pattern of spiritual guidance for godly women, see Patrick Collinson, *The Birthpangs of Protestant England: Religious and Cultural change in the Sixteenth and Seventeenth Centuries* (Basingstoke,1988), 75–6; Freeman, 'Good Ministrye', 17–20.
[120] BL Additional MS 19400, 76v.   [121] ECL MS 260, 80v.
[122] Bodleian Library MS 53, 49r, 129r.

discomfort the same'.[123] In a time of persecution, the certainties of predestination had their attractions.

XI

Bradford, Ridley, Philpot, Careless, Tyms and other predestinarian leaders were formidable opponents while they were alive: but they were far
more formidable after their deaths. The stake and prison had transformed them from servants of God into martyrs and confessors. As
such, they were, at least to those of their own confession, both logically and emotionally beyond criticism. If they were martyrs, they were
by definition orthodox in their beliefs; perhaps more importantly, they
were figures of devotion, even veneration, to the Protestants. 'Orthodox'
Protestants ceaselessly exploited the celebrated, high-profile martyrdoms
of their leaders. John Clement and Richard Woodman, in confessions
of faith intended to counter Freewillers, Anabaptists and other religious
radicals, insisted that the doctrines they were championing were held
by Bradford, John Rogers, John Hooper and other martyrs 'who sealed
the same with their blood'.[124] Such invocations were repeated throughout the writings of 'orthodox' Marian Protestants.[125] John Knox enumerated the predestinarians who were martyrs to demonstrate that the
Freewillers must be heretics.[126] Similarly, Bernher cited the belief of
Latimer, Cranmer, Ridley, Bradford, Careless and Philpot in predestination against Laurence and Barry.[127] The moral authority of martyrdom
was irrefutable.

The Freewillers also extolled martyrdom. Both Jackson and Trew
boasted to Careless that the Freewillers' willingness to die for the gospel
proved they were members of the true church.[128] It was their misfortune
that they did not succeed in associating any of the martyrs with their beliefs. Hart, Kemp, Laurence, Barry and Jeffrey all avoided incarceration.
In late May or early June 1556, Trew escaped from prison by breaking a
promise to return to his gaolers, who released him temporarily. Careless
regarded this 'beguiling' of his keeper with scorn: 'Thus you may see
the fruits of our Free will men, that made so much boast of their own

---

[123] BL Additional MS 19400, 82r.
[124] Gonville and Caius College, Cambridge, MS 218, 38; Strype, *Memorials*, III (ii) 457.
[125] Nicholas Ridley, *A pituous lamentacion . . . whereunto are annexed certayne letters of Iohn Careless* (1556),
     F7r; Bodleian Library MS 53, 145r.
[126] Knox, *Answer*, 195.   [127] Bodleian Library MS 53, 146r.
[128] BL Additional MS 19400, 62v–63r, 67r–v.

strength.'[129] It was a gift for predestinarian propaganda. Indeed, John Foxe was so taken with this episode that he broke his ironclad rule of deleting all references to the Freewillers and printed Careless's derisive remarks about Trew's escape.[130]

There were Marian martyrs who died as Freewillers. Thomas Avington and Thomas Read maintained their belief in free will to the end.[131] It is not coincidental that in a letter written within a week of the joint execution of Avington, Read, Harland and Osward at Lewes on 6 June 1556, Careless praised the martyrdom of the latter two and did not even mention the others.[132] Humphrey Middleton and Nicholas Sheterden, who were executed together at Canterbury on 12 July 1555, had both been associated with the Bocking conventicle and were among the Freewillers whom Bradford addressed in a letter of 14 February 1555.[133] George Brodebridge, who had declared in 1550 that God's predestination was conditional, does not seem to have changed his convictions before he was burned on 6 September 1555.[134] William Morant, executed in late May 1557, had been one of a group of Freewillers in the King's Bench led by John Jackson.[135] There may have been one or two others. Yet it is not a very extensive list, and none of those on it came close to matching the fame of Ridley, Bradford or other predestinarian martyrs. During Mary's reign the predestinarians were able to point out that the most eminent of the martyrs of God endorsed their doctrine. Under Elizabeth, John Foxe's *Actes and Monuments* – to Protestants, the authoritative history of the Marian persecution – concealed the fact that there had been any martyrs who were not predestinarians.

The Freewillers were a polemical liability to Protestants in general because a schism within English Protestantism over a major doctrinal issue confirmed a fundamental Catholic accusation: that Catholics were united in common faith, practices and doctrines, but Protestants were fragmented into quarrelling sects. This point did not elude Marian Protestants. Thomas Whittle wrote to Careless deploring 'these ungodly contentions and controversies which do now too much reign' as a means 'to speak evil of the gospel ministered to our adversaries'.[136] Indeed, the

---

[129] *LM*, 615.   [130] *AM* (1570), 2111.

[131] Avington was Trew's right-hand man in the King's Bench. Read ('Thomas Arede') was one of the signatories of Trew's account of the dispute in the King's Bench. See Bodleian Library MS 53, 125r; Pearse, *Between Known Men*, 76.

[132] *LM*, 615.

[133] BL Harleian MS 421, 134v; *APC* III, 199 and 206–7; BL Additional MS 19400, 33r.

[134] BL Harleian MS 421, 134r; *AM* (1563), 1273.

[135] ECL MS 260, 72r; *AM* (1563), 1570.   [136] BL Additional MS 19400, 58r–v.

dispute over free will did not escape the notice of the regime. Copies of the documents circulating as a result of the Freewiller attempt to convert Tyms and his companions in Newgate fell into the hands of the authorities, provoking the Privy Council to order an investigation of the dispute in the King's Bench. Jackson, Trew and Careless were interrogated; Careless, despite inner anguish, felt obliged to lie in an attempt to conceal the schism from the Catholics.[137] It may even be that the authorities attempted to prolong the dispute. This would help to explain why Careless and Trew survived so long in prison without being executed; and why Hart, Kemp, Laurence, Barry, Cole and Ledley were never arrested, although Bonner was informed of their activities and even knew where they lived.[138]

If Catholic attempts to perpetuate the controversy over predestination saved leading Freewillers from martyrdom, then the Catholics did the Freewiller cause substantial harm. Catholic attacks on Protestant disunity in Elizabeth's reign further harmed the Freewillers by provoking Foxe to airbrush them from history. Nicholas Harpsfield made Protestant factiousness a major part of his scathing and systematic criticism of the first edition of the *Actes and Monuments*.[139] In response, Foxe deleted almost all references to the Freewillers, or indeed to any religious divisions among the Marian Protestants.[140] Most particularly, he strove to conceal Freewiller or other 'heterodox' beliefs held by any of the Marian martyrs. He did such a thorough job that it is a matter of some guesswork to establish which martyrs died Freewillers. It is certainly suspicious that when describing the martyrdoms of Harland, Osward, Avington and Read, Foxe printed Harland's and Osward's answers to the charges against them, but omitted the answers of Avington and Read.[141] The zeal and cunning of Foxe's obfuscation is exemplified by his comment, after printing the examination of John Jackson, that 'no more' material from Jackson 'as yet came into our hands'.[142] This was probably literally true:

---

[137] *AM* (1563), 1529–34, 1612.

[138] *AM* (1563), 1605. Canterbury diocesan officials did order Hart's arrest, probably unaware of the strategic advantages in keeping him at liberty; but death removed Hart to a different jurisdiction before the arrest could be made. See *Archdeacon Harpsfield's Visitation*, i. 120.

[139] Nicholas Harpsfield, *Dialogi sex contra summi pontificatus, monasticae vitae, sanctorum sacrarum imaginum oppugnatores et pseudomartyres* (Antwerp, 1566), 802–17.

[140] Among the material printed only in the 1563 edition was the invaluable letter to Bonner describing the activities of leading Freewillers and predestinarians (1605); Careless's account, when interrogated, of his disputes with Trew and Hart (1529–34); and a description of the harassment of Protestants in East Anglia, Essex and Kent, which, *inter alia*, supplied a good deal of information about individual Freewillers (1676–80).

[141] *AM* (1570), 2095.   [142] *AM* (1563), 1611–12.

nothing written by Jackson survives and his eventual fate is unknown. But Foxe's remark was profoundly disingenuous. Surviving among his papers are several letters *to* Jackson which reveal Jackson's opposition to predestination and other opinions which Foxe would have considered heretical.[143]

Foxe's text lies over the landscape of Edwardine and Marian Protestantism like a blanket of snow, imposing frozen, pristine uniformity upon a variegated landscape. Nevertheless, he did not completely obliterate the memory of the Freewillers. A few mentions of them remain in the later editions of the *Actes and Monuments*; there were more extensive references in Foxe's first edition and in Henry Bull's *Letters of the Martyrs*. What Foxe did effectively obliterate was the fact that there were martyrs and confessors who were Freewillers. When the Freewillers were remembered at all, it was as the opponents of the blessed martyrs of God. Thanks to Foxe, few people in early modern England knew that some Freewillers had sealed *their* doctrine with their blood.

XII

The Freewillers had real weaknesses: their lack of theological training; their comparatively poor social and financial position; their failure to duplicate the intimate spiritual relationships which bound the predestinarian martyrs to their lay supporters; their lack of famous martyrs. But the Freewillers were also eliminated because the predestinarians were willing to go to a great deal of trouble, even to risk schism and a propaganda coup for the Catholics, in order to destroy them. Paradoxically, the greater strength of the Freewillers, at least in comparison to other dissenters, was a fatal weakness in that it spurred their enemies on to strenuous efforts against them.

A key source of Freewiller strength was their organization, based on congregations and conventicles established in Edward VI's reign, if not earlier. In fact, because the 'orthodox' Protestant church was weakened and outlawed in Mary's reign, the Freewillers were closer to parity with the Protestant leadership than any subsequent dissenters. Yet much the same could be said of the Family of Love, who were also active in Mary's reign and were also well organised. The difference was that the Familists, even when they did not dissemble their beliefs, avoided confrontation with both the Marian authorities and 'orthodox' Protestants.

---

[143] BL Additional MS 19400, 62r–63r; ECL MS 260, 27r, 239r–v.

The Freewillers openly and consistently defied both. John Trew was placed in the pillory and had his ears cut off after publicly exhorting people not to attend Catholic services; while Richard Harmon, who signed Trew's account of the dispute in the King's Bench, had been committed to the prison on 27 May 1554 for 'his lewd and seditious behaviour in Sussex'.[144] But the Freewillers were even more aggressive in combating their co-religionists. They threatened the predestinarians' very survival by actively proselytising against them, as in the attempt to convert Tyms and his companions while they awaited execution in Newgate. Although in hindsight their aggressive zeal might have doomed the Freewillers, it also made them a real and very serious threat. If they had succeeded in converting a few high-profile martyrs; if some of their own leaders had been martyred; if they had attracted a few more prominent supporters, then Elizabeth's reign might have begun with the returning exiles facing a full-blown schism.

Instead, by 1559 the Freewillers were merely a memory, with their congregations dispersed and their surviving leaders vanished into obscurity. Apart from a handful of works, which would be unread for centuries, the Freewillers left virtually no traces of their existence. Attempts to link them to seventeenth-century Arminianism are wishful thinking: there was no anti-predestinarian tradition in Elizabethan England and Freewiller writings – indeed, the very existence of most of the Freewillers – remained unknown to the Arminians.

Yet the failure of the Freewillers reveals a great deal about mid-Tudor Protestantism. The achievements of the Marian Protestants were not limited to enduring persecution passively, albeit heroically; they also established a hierarchy with a leadership consisting largely of clerics from the Edwardine Church who imposed a measure of unity and control on the scattered Protestant congregations. In the process of establishing this hierarchy and central control, the Protestant leadership successfully suppressed dissent, even the organised dissent of the Freewillers. Outlawed, proscribed and, in many cases, imprisoned, the Marian Protestant leaders nonetheless succeeded in maintaining, even extending, clerical domination of the English Protestant Church. Indeed, such a thorough victory could perhaps only have been won in a time of persecution, when they could wrest the moral authority of martyrdom from their opponents. It was the ill-fortune of the Freewillers to be facing opponents who, while persecuted themselves, were tirelessly dedicated to the elimination of dissent.

---

[144] *AM* (1563), 1682; *Historical Manuscripts Commission Reports*, VII, 665; *APC* V, 28.

CHAPTER 7

Printing and the Reformation: the English exception

Andrew Pettegree

I

It is a fundamental weakness of literature on European Protestantism that the printed book is considered almost exclusively as text and far too little as an industrial process. The printed book was one means by which the core messages of the reformers were brought to the reading public; in this it functioned alongside the sermons preached by Luther and his supporters and the wider amorphous categories of aural communication. The part played by the book in this process was undoubtedly considerable. But it could play this part only because medieval craft society had perfected an industrial process that seventy years before had been no more than experimental. In the first days of the printed book, fortunes were wasted and hopes cruelly dashed, but within a remarkably short time the technical skills and associated industrial processes (typecasting, papermaking) were embedded in European urban society. By 1520 the book was a mature artefact and the book industry one of the fastest-growing craft processes in Europe.

The impact of the book was not, however, even throughout Europe. In rural societies, somewhat distant from the centre of Europe's largest economies, print took a much smaller part in the craft world. For the purposes of printing, England must be regarded as part of this outer circle, the outer ring of a two-speed Europe, for at least the first century of the book's existence. This is not always recognised by historians of the English Reformation, nor indeed by book historians. Partly this is because English bibliographers have done such a remarkable job in reconstructing the story of early English printing. Early English printed books are among the best documented, and most fully studied of all European print cultures. In celebrations of the art and artistry of Caxton and his heirs, it is easy to overlook the fact that the thoroughness of this research has been largely made possible by the fact that the industry

This chapter is © Andrew Pettegree

157

in question was so small, and thus comparatively easy to reconstruct.[1]
English print culture was both relatively modest and relatively simple,
being overwhelmingly concentrated in London and Westminster – a
contrast to the dispersed culture of print that was the pattern in most
major Continental societies.

It is my belief that the exceptional nature of English print culture has
not always been fully recognised by students of the Reformation, who
understandably read books mostly for their contents. Understanding is
also not advanced by adopting for England broad-brush generalisations
about the importance of print normally based on the German experience (which is not in fact normative for other European cultures, such as
France, never mind England). Reflections on the size, capacities and organisation of the English printing industry in fact encourage some rather
different perspectives on how the first generation of English Protestants
responded to the opportunities raised by the Continental evangelical
movement.

                                    II

Let us begin by reviewing the process by which a sixteenth-century book
is made. An understanding of what is involved in these processes is important if we are to appreciate the technical constraints that governed the
growth of an English printing industry. To begin the process of creation,
a text is brought into a printshop by an author, a bookseller or another
interested party who is prepared to bear the cost (he would be the publisher). The manuscript is marked up in blocks that will correspond to
pages of type, and the compositor then begins to set up the text pages
of one side of a sheet. The individual metal types are composed line by
line, and then transferred into the 'form', the metal frame on to which
the paper will be impressed. Remember that for a book in octavo (i.e.
eight leaves to a sheet), the most popular size for small vernacular books,
the first plate (the obverse of the sheet) will have the text of pages 4, 13,
16 and 1 facing (the other way up) pages 5, 7, 9 and 8. The second page
of the gathering will be on the second form, for printing the reverse of
the sheet. It is for this reason that accuracy in blocking out the body of
text for each sheet is essential. Once the compositor has completed this

---

[1] One should add to this the peculiarity of English book collecting, especially the dominance of the
three major libraries, the British Library, the Bodleian and Cambridge University Library. This
made possible the compilation of the first edition of the *Short-Title Catalogue* at a remarkably early
date (1926); all subsequent bibliographical work rests on this solid foundation.

work, the plate of the completed text will be fixed to the press, inked, and a sheet of paper, dampened to improve the evenness of the impression, will be pressed down with a pull of the press. Once a first proof has been hurriedly checked, the process will be repeated as many times as necessary for the required edition size. The printed sheets will be set aside to dry, possibly until the next day, when the pages of text on the reverse will be printed. The plates of type will then be broken up for the compositor to set the next sheet, and so on until the end of the book.

The mechanics of the process bring in their train certain technical limitations not always fully acknowledged. The speed at which an edition could be published was not particularly dependent on the size of the edition. Pressmen could work remarkably fast. The printshop ordinances of Geneva assume production of 1,300 copies of a single sheet, front and back, as the normal daily rate of operation for a single press.[2] This is an astonishing rate of production, implying that in a ten-hour day the pressmen could operate a press at the rate of four pulls a minute, all day, without a break. But it also implied that the size of an edition was roughly determined by the shape of the day. There would be no great advantage of small runs (except a saving of paper), and certainly no time saving, since the reverse of each sheet could not be printed until the front side was dry. Editions therefore tend to be calculated in multiples of 700 or 1,300 – a half day or full day's work for the pressmen.

Large projects would take a long time to finish. A Bible or large folio of 400 sheets might be months at the press, with very significant outlays before any money could be recouped: on wages, ink and paper (an extremely expensive element of the whole project). There was very little that could be done to accelerate the process. With large books it was possible to share out the book between different teams of compositors and pressmen working on two or more presses, but this added greatly to the complexity, and worked best when the book naturally separated into parts, permitting a smooth division of the text. Bibles were frequently published in this way. But adopting this strategy would tie up all the printshop's presses, and so prevented the printer undertaking smaller jobs to maintain cashflow while the bigger projects were in progress.

The economics were daunting, and yet paradoxically the larger and more expensive the book, the larger was likely to be the size of the initial edition: all the really large edition sizes we know of (3,000 or 4,000 copies) tend to be of larger books. This was simply because the larger

[2] Jean-François Gilmont, 'Printers by the Rules', *The Library* 6th series, 2 (1980), 129–55.

the book, the greater the cost of time and money in organising a reprint. It was impossible – except perhaps with broadsheet proclamations and the like – to save composed sheets of type for any length of time; in most cases, the type would be needed to continue to set up further reaches of the book. For a new edition this whole laborious, time-consuming and highly skilled job would have to be done from scratch. Thus, whereas for a popular pamphlet of one or two sheets – the German *Flugschriften* in quarto, or octavos in most other cultures – repeat editions were very feasible, this was not so for larger books.

These technical factors had certain consequences for the organisation of the industry. Firstly, the largest, most expensive books (and size and expense were directly related) tended to be the preserve of the largest, best-capitalised printshops. These bigger businesses also secured a large share in the market for the most profitable small books. In all European countries the privilege of printing proclamations and other official publications was eagerly sought, since works such as these offered a very steady return, and helped cashflow while more ambitious projects were in progress. The larger shops also dominated the market in illustrated books, particularly the important market in Books of Hours. Such books, while popular, required an unusually high initial investment for building up the necessary stock of illustrative woodcut blocks, and this would have deterred the smallest operators.

Further, larger books, particularly Latin works, tended both to be kept in stock for longer, and to be distributed over a wider area. To a great extent the market in Latin books was one European market, with books distributed throughout the cities of Europe rather than reprinted locally. The sole possible exception among sizeable books was the Bible, where demand was so steady and the market so vast that it was possible to contemplate repeat editions.

Finally, and particularly with respect to large books, printers were likely to be the originators of publication projects far less often than is commonly assumed. Printers could – and did – dip speculatively into the market for small books, where the gap between the outlay and sale might be a matter of days or at most a few weeks. But big books needed very careful financing. This is why so many key figures in the printing industry in the incunabula age were prosperous merchants, used to relatively long-term capital investments, and familiar with the principles of spreading risk. It also suggests that historians of the book should give more attention than is customary to those who initiated and financed such projects – the publishers. This is an area where confusion is rife, since it was often the publisher, rather than the printer, who was named on the title page. Sometimes the relationship was precisely expressed ('Printed by John Day for Edward Whitchurch') but more often not.[3] In general it seems that book-industry figures often combined two of the three essential functions of printer, bookseller and publisher, but seldom all three.

III

Let us apply some of the lessons of this brief technical review to the study of the English and European book markets. One can immediately sense striking differences, both between the Latin and vernacular markets, and between the book cultures of different parts of Europe. The Latin market was immense because, as has been stated, it was essentially one European market. Only the commonest school texts were likely to be reprinted locally. The most prized Latin books, the major editions of the classics and Church Fathers which featured so strongly in the first age of print, together with many medical and scientific texts, could only be undertaken in the largest centres of Latin printing. In the first age of print, Paris and Venice established an easy and enduring supremacy in this Latin book world; later in the sixteenth century they would be joined by Antwerp, Basle and Lyons. Their products were distributed throughout Europe by a sophisticated and efficient network of book wholesalers and bookshops.

On the whole this was a situation that continued for much of the sixteenth century: as the market in vernacular books expanded, the Latin market remained fairly stable; a lower proportion of the whole, but still a considerable volume of books. Thus when English readers pursued fine Latin books, they inevitably looked abroad; as the market grew, booksellers simply imported more from the major centres of Latin print abroad.[4] This was a situation that had hardly changed by the end of the sixteenth century, when the English book world was robust and well established. The extent to which English readers continued to rely on

---

[3] In French books the publisher/bookseller was often named on the title page ('Imprimé pour . . . ') and the printer only in the colophon (that is, the details of printer and date of completion sometimes added at the end of the text). As colophons fell out of fashion in the second quarter of the sixteenth century the identity of the printer, as opposed to the publisher who commissioned the project, therefore sometimes became more difficult to fathom.

[4] For import of foreign books in the first century of print, see Lotte Hellinga, 'Importation of Books Printed on the Continent into England and Scotland before c. 1520', *Printing the Written Word. The Social History of Books, circa 1450–1520*, ed. Sandra Hindman (Ithaca, 1991), 205–24; Elizabeth Armstrong, 'English purchases of printed books from the Continent, 1465–1526', *EHR* 94 (1979), 268–90.

foreign publishers for their Latin books can be clearly documented from surviving library catalogues, whether the first catalogues of the Oxford and Cambridge colleges, or the recently published list of foreign books in English cathedral libraries.[5] The sorts of books that would form the backbone of scholarly collections were almost all imported. The most recent and complete survey of early English book collections for the period before 1550 suggests that books printed in England (at London and Westminster) account for only 4 per cent of titles known from surviving collections and library lists.[6]

The Latin book world was a special case, though an important one, for the Latin book market was, and remained, the cornerstone of the industries in the larger European centres of print. The greatest and best-known names in the international print world – Estienne in Paris, Froben and Oporinus in Basle, the Aldine press in Venice – were usually major figures in the world of Latin print before they became purveyors of vernacular books. But even among vernacular markets there were very stark differences in book culture. Here it is probably best not to think in terms of political boundaries but in language groups. In these terms, the three largest vernacular markets were the German, the French and the Italian. In secondary position one finds the Spanish and Dutch: the Spanish with a well-developed urban culture and some eight million native speakers were an obviously important market; the Dutch was smaller, but pulled into the second rank by an exceptional degree of urbanisation and high literacy rates. The English market forms part of a third group, with the Portuguese, Polish and Czech. There were fewer than four million native English speakers, and a low rate of urbanisation implied an undistinguished level of literacy. London provided the only market of any size. England had only two universities, both of which would be adequately supplied with Latin books from the Continent.

IV

All these structural factors pointed to a relatively slow growth for English printing – and so it proved. In the third quarter of the fifteenth century, the English nobility, in common with other European elites, certainly

---

[5] David J. Shaw, *Books printed on the Continent in the Anglican Cathedral Libraries of England and Wales* (1998).

[6] Margaret Lane Ford, 'Importation of Printed Books into England and Scotland', *The Cambridge History of the Book in Britain. Vol. III: 1400–1557*, ed. Lotte Hellinga and J. B. Trapp (Cambridge, 1999), 183.

began to manifest curiosity about the new technology, but the first books to reach England were imported foreign works. That England was represented at all in the first incunabula age owed much to the curiosity of Caxton, a gentleman merchant with time on his hands as a successful business and diplomatic career stalled in the vicissitudes of the Wars of the Roses.[7] As Caxton spread the word, it became a matter of pride that there should be an English press – like printers elsewhere in Europe, Caxton relied heavily on royal patronage – but the market remained select. And early English printing was heavily dependent on the Continent in all respects. Caxton, who had observed the craft of printing while a merchant in Bruges, brought with him from Flanders everything necessary for running his own press: the typefaces, woodblocks and ornaments, and, most important of all, skilled technicians. This continued throughout his long and successful career. When types wore out he reordered from his reliable partner Veldener in Louvain, and other Continental craftsmen cut his woodcuts and distinctive print insignia. Even after the printed book caught on in England, the pattern established by Caxton did not much change. Caxton's principal rival in London, Richard Pynson, was a Frenchman from Normandy, and the pioneering presses in Oxford and St Albans were also run by foreigners. The anti-alien statute of Richard III specifically excluded the book industry from its provisions. It would have been throttled at birth otherwise.

Caxton's work has a revered place in the folklore of English bibliophiles, but overall the English contribution to the print culture of the incunabula age was extraordinarily modest. The new electronic version of the *English Short-Title Catalogue (E-STC)* lists 422 items for the period 1468–99.[8] But of these books more than fifty were works in fact printed abroad for sale in England (mostly Books of Hours and other small devotional works printed for English booksellers and publishers at Paris, Rouen or Antwerp). Of the remainder, some thirty items at least were single-page broadsheets. This leaves a little over 300 books (i.e. printed works of more than one sheet) printed in England during the incunabula age (before 1500). If, as is now reckoned, the total number of printed works published throughout Europe before 1500 is around 10,000, then printers in England contributed only about 3 per cent to this

---

[7] For Caxton see George G. Painter, *A Quincentenary Biography of England's First Printer* (1975); N. F. Blake, *Caxton and his World* (1969).

[8] This is my own calculation; for earlier data, based on the published print version, see Maureen Bell and John Barnard, 'Provisional Count of *STC* Titles 1475–1640', *Publishing History* 31 (1992), 48–64.

total. One single Continental city – Venice – published ten times as many incunabula as were published in England.[9]

The first years of the sixteenth century did little to alter this situation. With the help of the *E-STC* I have attempted a relatively full analysis of the output of a single year in the decade before the Reformation: 1514. There were thirty-seven works that the *E-STC* allocates to this year, but of these seven were printed abroad, in Paris or Rouen. These were mostly Books of Hours and missals printed for the Cologne-based printer Arnold Birckman, who had established a profitable bookshop in London; that he should have looked to Paris for these editions is no surprise, since Paris was the acknowledged centre of high-quality work in this field. Of the remaining thirty books, five were broadsheets and seventeen books were in Latin (mostly grammars and schoolbooks, though with one edition of Virgil's *Bucolia*). There was one legal text in Law French and one book of English statutes. Of the remaining vernacular books, five were small devotional works, all from the shop of Wynkyn de Worde, the German artisan who had managed Caxton's printshop and taken it over after his death. He was also responsible for a proportion of the Latin works. The proclamations and law books were handled by Richard Pynson.

These two printshops dominated the output of English books in 1514. Yet neither seems to have been especially busy. To underline this point I recalculated the output of English printing for the year, this time calculating the length of each book in sheets (in an octavo, either a gathering of eight leaves or sixteen pages). If one assumes that each sheet would have been a single day's work for an individual press, then the surviving books account for some hundred days' work in de Worde's shop, and only thirty days in Pynson's.

In other words, the entire output of the English printing industry for the year 1514 could have been handled by two shops, each possessing just one press, working at much less than full capacity. Not surprisingly in the circumstances, the competition between the two men was not very intense. Both had their established areas of specialisation, Pynson through his appointment as king's printer, de Worde through his mastery of the business since its introduction in England. Their domination of London printing was remarkably enduring. De Worde, who had moved Caxton's shop from Westminster to London in 1501, had by the time of his death in 1535 issued some 800 books. Pynson's contribution, before he

---

[9] The estimate of 3,000 pre-1500 editions for Venice is in Ford, 'Importation of Printed Books', 184, citing data from the ongoing *Incunabula Short-Title Catalogue*.

succumbed to old age and the growing competition of his rival Richard Redman in 1529, was a scarcely less considerable 500 editions.

V

It is now time to investigate how these established patterns were affected by the onset of the Reformation. On the Continent, of course, the controversies unleashed by the German monk Martin Luther stimulated a torrent of printed books.[10] More especially, the particular nature of the books published during the German debates had a profound impact on the publishing industry. The German *Flugschriften*, short books, quick to produce and selling massively, generated quick profits, and this in turn provided the capital for new projects. Thus the profits from Luther's smaller vernacular writings helped underwrite the publication of his German Bible, the most ambitious book of the Reformation, but ultimately the most profitable of all.

In the process there were fortunes to be made. In the 1520s Luther's hometown of Wittenberg boomed, essentially as a one-industry town.[11] The same effect was evident later in the century in Calvin's adopted home of Geneva, which grew rich on the publication of his prolific writings.[12] Frankfurt, meanwhile, established itself as Europe's major distribution centre, as readers across Europe sought to follow the new debates, and booksellers responded by improving their networks of distribution to meet this demand.

In England the initial impact of this veritable flood of print was comparatively slight. Luther's criticisms of the Church attracted some attention; we know that copies of the second Latin edition of Luther's collected writings, a venture of the sharp-eyed Basle entrepreneur Johannes Froben, sold in England.[13] But the official condemnation of his teachings came before interest could broaden sufficiently to develop a real

[10] Data on German Reformation printing is summarised helpfully in Mark U. Edwards, *Printing, Propaganda and Martin Luther* (Berkeley, 1994) and John L. Flood, 'The Book in Reformation Germany', *The Reformation and the Book*, ed. Jean-François Gilmont (Aldershot, 1998), 21–103. See also *Flugschriften als Massenmedium der Reformationszeit*, ed. Hans-Joachim Köhler (Stuttgart, 1981).

[11] There is no good modern study of Wittenberg printing, but see Andrew Pettegree, 'Books, pamphlets and polemic', *The Reformation World*, ed. Pettegree (2000), 109–26. For the education industry in Wittenberg, see Maria Grossman, *Humanism in Wittenberg, 1485–1517* (Nieuwkoop, 1975).

[12] Jean-François Gilmont, *Jean Calvin et le Livre Imprimé* (Geneva, 1997); H. J. Bremme, *Buchdrucker und Buchhändler zur Zeit der Glaubenskämpfe* (Geneva, 1969).

[13] Froben to Luther, February 1519. *D. Martin Luthers Werke: Kritische Gesammtausgabe, Briefwechsel*, (18 vols., Weimar, 1930–85) i. 331–5 (letter 146).

vernacular market in evangelical books. For those without a command of Latin, Luther remained an unknown quantity. None of his works was rendered into English before 1535, and even then those chosen for translation tended to be relatively uncontroversial devotional works and sermons, rather than the great milestones of Reformation controversy. Significantly, none of these early translations identified Luther as the author, preferring weak circumlocutions – 'a book made by a certain great clerk' – or simple anonymity.[14]

This tendency to publish Luther's works only with his role as author disguised was one shared with a number of European lands where the condemnation of Luther's writings was upheld.[15] Large amounts of disguised Luther works came out in French, Dutch and Italian; in some cases, the disguise was so effective that the work has only recently been revealed as a translation of Luther.[16] But in other respects all three of these countries diverged sharply from the English model. Readers in France, Italy and the Netherlands found their way to Luther's writings and those of other early evangelical authors far more easily than did English readers. In France the tight control exercised by the conservative Paris authorities led quickly to the establishment of centres of publication within the French-language zone, but outside the jurisdiction of the Parlement of Paris: first at Antwerp and Neuchâtel, later, and most famously, at Geneva.[17] In Italy the sheer volume of publishing allowed a large number of works sympathetic to the Reformation to slip through the net. The fact, too, that printing was divided between several urban centres, all of which jealously guarded an independent jurisdiction, made the job of the censors far more difficult. This seems to have been the crucial factor also in the Netherlands, where evangelical print flourished in the period of doctrinal uncertainty before 1544. Finally, and most crucially (and in contrast to France), in the Netherlands the publication of vernacular scripture was not forbidden, and this provided an opening for evangelical influence. Consequently, readers in the Netherlands could take advantage of a torrent of evangelical publishing in Dutch – some

[14] *A Book made by a certain great clerk, against the new idol and the old devil* (1534); *A very excellent and sweet exposition upon the 23ʳᵈ psalm* (Southwark, 1537).

[15] Bernd Moeller, 'Luther in Europe: his works in translation, 1517–1546', *Politics and Society in Reformation Europe*, ed. E. I. Kouri and Tom Scott (1987), 235–51; Gilmont, *Reformation and the Book*.

[16] Francis Higman, 'Les traductions françaises de Luther, 1524–1550', in his *Lire et découvrir: La circulation des idées au temps de la Réforme* (Geneva, 1998), 201–32.

[17] Francis Higman, *Piety and the People. Religious Printing in French, 1511–1551* (Aldershot, 1996); Bettye Chambers, *Bibliography of the French Bible: Fifteenth- and Sixteenth-century French-language editions of the Scriptures* (Geneva, 1993).

eighty editions of Luther's works and another sixty editions of scripture in the years before 1546 – and this despite some of the most savage punitive legislation in the whole of Europe.[18] The figures for France are scarcely less impressive. A recent survey conducted as part of my own researches into European Protestant print has enumerated some 484 editions of Protestant or evangelical works published in French by 1546.

If the results for England are far less awesome, this is partly because the structural underpinnings of the publishing enterprise were so very different. English print had in any case a small market, and the industry was overwhelmingly concentrated in one city, London, which happened to be the capital and was therefore most easily regulated. The industry was so small that it was virtually impossible for one of the established printers to publish disapproved works without being immediately identified as the culprit. Nor would they want to, given that the cornerstone of their prosperity was the publication of official and quasi-official publications, patronage that would be speedily withdrawn if they strayed into disapproved areas. It is therefore no accident that the publication of Protestant works in English largely awaited the more favourable atmosphere that came with the break with Rome in the 1530s. Even then, the larger and more established firms tended to steer clear of polemical and controversial works that carried with them any element of risk.

Many of the same structural and economic barriers would also face any potential evangelical entrepreneur interested in following the Continental trend for the publication of the vernacular Bible. Given the size of the undertaking with a text of this length, and the level of investment required, a Bible was hardly a suitable text for clandestine publication. With a work of this size, the length of time for which the partly completed sheets would be hanging around the printshop, exciting comment in the small and gossipy English print world, and inevitably liable to inspection and confiscation, meant that such a project could be contemplated only with official support. This is precisely how William Tyndale first attempted to proceed, applying initially to Cuthbert Tunstall, bishop of London, in the hope that he would sponsor publication of his own new translation.[19] It was only when this hope was dashed that Tyndale decided to pursue his ventures abroad, first in Cologne, the German city where Caxton had first observed the printer's art, then later in Worms and Antwerp. Tyndale's task, pursued with astonishing zeal and

---

[18] C. Ch. G Visser, *Luther's geschriften in de nederlanden tot 1546* (Assen, 1969); A. A. Den Hollander, *De Nederlandse Bijbelvertalingen, 1522–1545* (Nieuwkoop, 1997).
[19] David Daniell, *William Tyndale* (New Haven and London, 1994), 83–107.

perseverance, was far from straightforward. To the normal obstacles to finding capital were added problems particular to the publication of early English printing abroad: compositors and proof-readers working outside their native language, and type alphabets designed for German rather than English orthography. Nor was Cologne an especially happy choice for Tyndale's venture. Although a major centre of the typographic art, it was also a loyal Catholic city. Halfway through the planned print run, the Catholic theologian Cochlaeus intervened to have the venture terminated, and Tyndale could save himself and the precious sheets only by carrying them off for finishing in Worms. Here an edition of the New Testament was finally seen through to completion, but Worms was no print capital, and Tyndale soon moved on: by 1528 he was in Antwerp.

Tyndale's arrival in Antwerp, though largely fortuitous, was the salvation of English Protestant print. At last he had fixed upon a location that provided both the chance of high-quality publishing in English and easy access to the English market. Antwerp was the home of the English cloth staple, with a large resident community of English merchants and artisans; by the 1530s it was fast becoming the hub of the intense and varied trade between England (principally London) and the Netherlands. The resident English community included a number sympathetic to or interested in the new evangelical doctrines, and would provide easier access to capital and native English proof-readers. Most important of all, Antwerp had both a large and well-capitalised publishing industry and an established tradition of vernacular Bible publication.[20] Although the printing industry was theoretically subject to tight controls to cut down the flow of evangelical print, Bibles were not included in the prohibition. This was important, because it meant that not only were the major Antwerp printers experienced in the particular demands of Bible printing, they had also had time to build the stock of illustrative material which could turn a relatively rudimentary text into a fine edition.[21]

Tyndale made good use of his time in Antwerp. His translation of the Pentateuch was completed in 1531, and an improved revision of the Cologne/Worms New Testament appeared in 1534. Meanwhile, he used the intervals of leisure afforded by his translation work to publish several more polemical works: the *Parable of the Wicked Mammon*, *The Obedience of a Christen Man* (both 1528), and the bitingly satirical *Practyse of Prelates* (1530).

---

[20] W. Nijhoff and M. E. Kronenberg, *Nederlandse bibliographie van 1500 tot 1540* (The Hague, 1923–71); Den Hollander, *Nederlandse Bijbelvertalingen*.

[21] Bart A. Rosier, *The Bible in Print: Netherlandish Bible Illustration in the Sixteenth Century* (2 vols., Leiden, 1997).

Thanks to Tyndale and Antwerp, English Protestantism had been able to make a first original contribution to the European polemical debate of the Reformation.[22] The wave of imported Protestant works that were imported infuriated the English authorities, particularly Thomas More, who replied with a vigour and lack of restraint that has consistently troubled admirers of a more delicate disposition. From that point Tyndale was a marked man, though his Bible project continued to flourish, reaching completion finally in 1535 with the publication of the Coverdale translation, incorporating much of Tyndale's work. Coverdale was working in Cologne, but all the internal typographical evidence points to Antwerp as the place of printing of the first Coverdale Bible. This is indeed the conclusion of the most recent scholar to subject the text to detailed scientific investigation.[23]

By this stage the climate for Protestant works in England was beginning to change. Shortly after Tyndale's arrest and execution in the Low Countries, Henry VIII licensed an English translation of the Bible, and Protestants viewed, for the first time, the prospect of legal publication and distribution of the text of English scripture. But the London printing industry was not yet in a position to take advantage of this official encouragement. To carry out such a prestige project, the London book industry continued to rely on tried and tested Continental friends. The Bible edition published with this royal favour – the so-called Matthew Bible of 1537 – was produced in Antwerp on the presses of Mattheus Crom, a man fast emerging as a crucial figure in the English Protestant book world.[24] Crom provided the Bible with a fine version of the 'Law and the Gospel' title-page developed in Wittenberg for the first generation of Luther Bibles and popularised for western Europe by the Antwerp printers.[25] Even more surprising than this Antwerp enterprise, when the English authorities took in hand their own semi-official translation (the so-called Great Bible of 1538–9), it, too, was printed abroad, though on this occasion in Paris. This is all the more astonishing in that Paris printers had since 1526 been forbidden from publishing any vernacular French editions of scripture, and the printer involved in the project,

[22] David Daniell, *Antwerp: Dissident Typographical Centre. The Role of Antwerp Printers in the Religious Conflicts in England (16th century)* (Antwerp, 1994), and *Tyndale*, 155–280.

[23] Guido Latré, 'The 1535 Coverdale Bible and its Antwerp Origins', *The Bible as Book: The Reformation*, ed. Orlaith O'Sullivan (2000), 89–102.

[24] Willem Heijting, 'Early Reformation Literature from the Printing Shop of Mattheus Crom and Steven Mierdman', *Nederlands Archief voor Kerkgeschiedenis* 74 (1994), 143–61.

[25] Andrew Pettegree, 'The Law and the Gospel: The Evolution of an Evangelical Pictorial Theme in the Bibles of the Reformation', *The Bible as Book*, ed. O'Sullivan, 123–36.

François Regnault, was an established and respected Catholic member of the local trade fraternity.[26] One can only surmise that on this occasion industry considerations – the sheer incapacity of the London printers to meet the sudden demand for printed scripture in this 'Prague Spring' of the English Reformation – took precedence over politics. Certainly, Paris printers would have been delighted to be offered the work, since many still had stocks of biblical woodcuts from the early 1520s for which they now had little use.[27]

However, the venture ended badly. The publishers, Grafton and Whitchurch, had taken the precaution of obtaining a licence from the French king allowing them to print the Bible with any French printer they chose, but the long months of work required meant that the agreement with Regnault inevitably attracted attention locally. The local ecclesiastical authorities were probably goaded into action by Regnault's outraged industry competitors, who queried why he should publish vernacular Bibles when they could not. In any case, in December the publication was banned and the completed sheets were confiscated. It was only after tortured diplomatic negotiations that the project was rescued, and even then the printers were forced to buy back a portion of the completed sheets from a haberdasher who had purchased them for wastepaper – the rest had already been destroyed. In due course the project was finished in London, with type, printers and paper transferred from the Paris shop. The result, not surprisingly, fell some way short of the prestige edition that had initially been envisaged.[28]

The evangelical moment of the late 1530s proved of short duration. By 1540, with the execution of Thomas Cromwell and the Act of Six Articles (1539), the tide had turned, and soon legislation would be published imposing new restrictions on the reading of the vernacular Bible. But this conservative turn in the royal mind was ultimately far less of a disaster for English Protestantism than it is sometimes portrayed. Most evangelical sympathisers at the heart of the regime – Cranmer and his lay sympathisers on the Privy Council – remained entrenched, and there were few negative consequences for English Protestant print. At first

[26] For the ban on vernacular scripture in France, see Francis Higman, *Censorship and the Sorbonne* (Geneva, 1979), 26 ff.

[27] The displacement of these redundant Bible illustrations into other sorts of illustrated books has not yet been systematically studied, but see Max Engemarre, 'Les représentations de l'Ecriture dans les Bibles illustrées du XVIe siècle: Pour une herméneutique de l'image imprimée dans le texte biblique', *Revue Française d'Histoire du Livre* 86–87 (1995), 118–89.

[28] This story, reconstructed from the State Papers, is told in Colin Clair, *A History of Printing in Britain* (1965), 61–4.

Protestant publishing continued in London largely undisturbed, and it was only with the conservative assault of 1543 (the maximum point of danger for Cranmer also) that the publication of openly Protestant works in England became more hazardous.[29] A number of clergy authors who had identified themselves most conspicuously with the evangelical cause through their writings or actions now took refuge abroad. But once again the Antwerp connection served English evangelicals well. During the last six years of Henry's reign, Antwerp printers produced for the English market a considerable number of Protestant texts, including the works of leading lights of the emerging generation of English Protestant authors, George Joye, John Bale and William Turner. These were fine-looking books, published in a clean and easy black-letter type; undoubtedly they were of finer quality than would have been achieved had they been published in England. The smooth and rapid trading connections between the ports of Antwerp and London meant that there were no obstacles to distribution in London; the city's Protestant community remained well supplied with books even while conservatives in Henry's Privy Council believed they were winning the battle for control of English policy.

Many of these books were the work of the emerging Antwerp firm of Mattheus Crom and Steven Mierdman. Crom, the printer of the Matthew Bible, was a committed evangelical, and he was happy to add to his established Dutch evangelical work a series of commissions from English authors abroad. From 1544 he was joined in the business by his son-in-law Steven Mierdman, and between 1537 and 1546 they turned out no fewer than thirty English language Protestant works.[30] Eventually their evangelical connections were too obvious to be ignored. In 1546 the firm was caught in Charles V's determined clampdown on evangelical activity in Antwerp and forced to close. Crom retired from business and Mierdman transferred to London, joining the growing number of Antwerp refugees active in the London publishing industry.

Mierdman was thus among a number of foreign immigrant printers well positioned to take advantage of the sudden change of climate upon the death of Henry VIII in January 1547. When the old king expired, it was the connections of his favourite wife, Jane Seymour, who were

---

[29] For the chronology and events of these years, see especially Diarmaid MacCulloch, *Thomas Cranmer: A Life* (New Haven and London, 1996); Alec Ryrie, 'English evangelical reformers in the last years of Henry VIII', D.Phil thesis, University of Oxford (2000), 282–5; Ryrie, 'The Strange Death of Lutheran England', *JEH* 53 (2002).

[30] Heijting, 'Crom and Mierdman'.

positioned to take advantage; and they, led by Edward Seymour, soon to be duke of Somerset, were closely associated with the evangelical sympathisers who had carefully bided their time since the execution of Thomas Cromwell in 1540. For those able to read the runes, the prospects for the future were clear, and evangelical authors seized their chance. The first years of the new reign witnessed an explosion of Protestant print – all the more remarkable when one considers how few Protestant works had been printed in England in the first two decades of the Reformation. This revolution in the London printing industry took advantage of – and in turn helped to stimulate – a much wider public discussion of evangelical issues. This was deliberately encouraged by the new regime: indeed, one of the first and most crucial acts of the new regime was to pass through Parliament a statute that removed previous restrictions on the publication of unauthorised religious works. The consequences were striking. From an average of around 100 editions (of all types of works) for the first half of the 1540s, the industry expanded dramatically, with 192 published in 1547 and an astonishing 268 in 1548. The figures declined somewhat in 1549 (after the reimposition of censorship restrictions), but climbed back to 249 in 1550. Furthermore, these publications were dominated by works of a religious character – Bibles, catechisms, and works of exegesis and polemic – almost all of them Protestant.

Further analysis confirms this impression of a revolution in English print culture. With the exception of what might be called official print (proclamations and liturgies), the new Protestant print fell mostly into three categories. There were reprints of the classics of the early English Reformation – Tyndale enjoyed a new vogue – and multiple editions of scripture. There were numerous translations of the works of Continental authors: for the first time English readers had access to a full range of the thought of Protestant Continental divines. The Swiss Reformation was represented by Zwingli and Bullinger (a very popular author), the Germans by Bucer, Brenz, Musculus and Melanchthon. French evangelical writing was present in translations of Calvin, Marcourt and Veron, and the wider international movement by Bernardino Ochino and Peter Martyr Vermigli – both, of course, like Bucer, by this time enjoying Cranmer's hospitality in England. The reputation of the dead Luther was upheld by William Lynne's translation of a series of pastoral sermons, though curiously the milestones of Luther's theological writing were not rendered into English. Apart from texts by these major Continental figures, English readers were exposed to a range of writings by returning or emerging leaders of the English Church: Becon, Crowley, Latimer, Hooper, Joye and Ridley, along with Cranmer, were all heavily published. The principal focus of these writings was the Catholic mass, and the construction of the new Church; for this reason English translations of major contemporaneous Continental church orders, such as that of Hermann von Wied, archbishop of Cologne, were also published.

At the end of this brief survey of the new English Protestant print, two points need to be stressed. Firstly, it is now increasingly clear that this Protestant publishing offensive was deliberately fostered by those at the very heart of the Edwardine regime. It was once fashionable (though always inherently implausible) to argue that the Edwardine Privy Council presided over the construction of a Protestant polity without fully realising what was afoot. If it is stretching credulity too far to suggest that Somerset blundered into reform almost by mistake,[31] it has certainly been thought that the reform of the Church was far from Somerset's first policy priority.[32] Against this school of argument, always perverse and counterintuitive, recent research has demonstrated very convincingly the centrality and full radicalism of the Edwardine project.[33]

Examination of the way in which Protestant works were brought into the public domain only increases this sense of clarity of purpose. Here what has been said about industry constraints becomes very relevant. There is a real question, in a period in which the constraints on the articulation of evangelical opinions had only barely been loosened, and when the audience for evangelical publishing could hardly be assumed, of how such a mass of printed work could have been financed. What can now be demonstrated, thanks to painstaking work by Diarmaid MacCulloch, John King and Christopher Bradshaw, among others, is that leading figures in the Protestant regime and London society actively promoted Protestant projects.[34] Printers, authors and members of the Privy Council operated within a tightly knit circle of friendship, patronage and personal connection. Somerset, Cranmer and their key allies

---

[31] Although this, bizarrely, is precisely what is suggested by Christopher Haigh. 'Somerset had blundered into a total ban on images, and he had got away with it.' See Haigh, *English Reformations: Religion, Politics and Society under the Tudors* (Oxford, 1993), 170.

[32] M. L. Bush, *The Government Policy of Protector Somerset* (Manchester, 1975).

[33] Diarmaid MacCulloch, *Tudor Church Militant: Edward VI and the Protestant Reformation* (1999), and *Cranmer*.

[34] For what follows, see MacCulloch, *Cranmer*; John N. King, *English Reformation Literature: The Tudor Origins of the Protestant Tradition* (Princeton, 1982).

all put work the way of sympathetic printers; authors and publishers responded with fulsome dedicatory letters. After the fall of Somerset, the principal role at the centre of this network was increasingly filled by William Cecil. Printers who did the regime's work were rewarded by valuable monopolies on the printing of popular liturgical handbooks and schoolbooks. The patent granted to John Day in 1553 to publish the works of Becon and Ponet became the cornerstone of Day's later prosperity when Ponet's *A Short Catechisme* was appended to the *ABC*.

The will and the resources were clearly present; but the London industry was still very deficient in terms of technical expertise. Many of the books published in the first years of Edward's reign were short polemical works; but others were of considerable length and complexity. The demand for editions of scripture alone would have stretched the rather conservative and somnolent London print culture of the early 1540s.

The London industry was forced to expand, and at very great speed. The extent to which this expansion depended on Dutch technical expertise has hitherto been scarcely acknowledged. Just as English evangelical authors relied heavily on Antwerp for the first stage of their engagement with the Henrician Reformation, and the opposition campaign of the 1540s, so now Antwerp provided the means to meet the new demands and opportunities of the reign of Edward VI. It is not much of an exaggeration to say that the London industry in this period became an effective satellite of the print world of the Scheldt entrepôt. Many of the new sets of type supplied to the new and expanding London printshops came from Antwerp. Thanks to these clean types, and improving technical skill, there is a marked improvement in the appearance of English books printed during the six years of Edward's reign. Design also shows a marked improvement: London printers begin during these years to show a far greater facility and assurance in handling type of different sizes and styles on the same page.

This improvement also owed a great deal to Dutch expertise. By the middle years of Edward's reign, and thanks in part to Charles V's crackdown on evangelicals in the Netherlands, there were a large number of Dutch printworkers employed in London – both independent master printers like Mierdman, and ordinary pressmen and compositors. All were able to take advantage of the mass enrolments of new denizens (i.e. legally authorised alien residents) associated with the foundation of the London stranger churches, of which many of the print artisans were members.

We can illustrate some of the effects of these developments in the early career of the well-known London printer John Day.[35] Although Day was a member of the Stationers' Company as early as 1550, the first books bearing his name date only from 1546. But from these tentative beginnings, he quickly emerged as one of the leading purveyors of Protestant print during the reign of Edward VI. Day worked first mainly in partnership with William Seres, a bookseller and also leading printer with close connections to the new regime. Among Seres's publications were books by some of the most prominent authors: John Hooper, Hugh Latimer, John Ponet and William Turner of the new evangelical establishment, John Calvin of the major Continental theologians. Day and his partner were deeply involved in the most controversial issues of the day. Ten of the twenty books they published in 1548 were contributions to the debate over eucharistic doctrine, including works by Luke Shepherd, Robert Crowley and William Turner. Day's partnership with Seres was dissolved in 1550, but his career went from strength to strength. All in all, some 130 works can be attributed to his press for the six years of Edward's reign, including a substantial and elaborate folio Bible. Day's work was also characterised by a notable technical assurance. This may be attributed partly to the extensive use Day made of foreign workmen in his printshop. The 1549 census of immigrants recorded four Dutchmen (presumably journeymen) living in the house at Aldersgate which also housed his printing works; for Day this connection extended to a close relationship with leading members of the Protestant refugee community in London. This link established a professional reliance on foreign expertise that would last for the whole of Day's career. As his publishing expanded in range and sophistication, Day inevitably looked abroad, or to foreigners settled in London, for the new typefaces, woodcut artists or proficiencies required. Much later in his career, at a moment of crisis in the production of the second edition of Foxe's *Actes and Monuments*, Day would petition William Cecil for relief from the order prohibiting the employment of more than four foreign journeymen.

Day was far from unique in his reliance on foreign expertise, and for their own part foreign printers settled in London (Mierdman, Lynne, Nicolas Hill, Gilles van der Erve) made a substantial contribution to the output of English Protestant print. All in all, by the end of Edward's reign the London publishing industry, stimulated by growth in demand, investment and availability of skilled workmen, was finally

---

[35] On Day see also John King's essay in this volume.

beginning to make up some ground on the major centres of Continental publishing.

VI

We are almost ready to say that English printing, after a century in the shadows, had come of age; but there was one further trial still to be undergone. The accession of Mary Tudor occasioned a sharp recession in the London printing industry. With the death of Edward VI and the restoration of traditional forms of Catholic worship, demand for religious books was now once again sharply circumscribed and closely regulated; many of those London publishers who had been most closely associated with the old regime had few prospects with the new.

It is often said that the attitudes of the new Marian regime to the printed word were deeply ambiguous, and it is true that with the restoration of Catholicism timeless truths and forms of worship called for a different sort of religious literature. It is not true, though, to say that the Marian regime was not alive to the need to justify its religious policies in print. It is now recognised that the new government could mount a very effective press campaign in the right circumstances – as, for instance, was the case with its efforts to convince European opinion of the legitimacy of the Marian succession.[36] But for this purpose it employed Continental presses. The recession in domestic printing had at least as much to do with the fact that relatively few of the printers who had flourished under Edward VI were ready and willing to print the sort of books the new regime required.

Of the best-capitalised London publishers, those who had flourished through official patronage under Edward either sharply cut back their operations, or left England altogether. This is worthy of emphasis, not least because it has become customary to regard printers as motivated, in the main, more by profit than conviction. During Edward's reign there had certainly been profits to be made, but the fact that so many of the leading figures in the industry made no effort to accommodate to the change of regime suggests that for many their commitment to the Protestant religion was heartfelt rather than tactical. Some, like Day, simply disappeared from view;[37] others went abroad. This was not an easy decision for a printer. Vacating a London printshop often meant

---

[36] Jennifer Loach, 'The Marian establishment and the printing press', *EHR* 101 (1986), 135–48.
[37] For suggestions regarding what Day was up to in this period, see John King's essay in this volume.

leaving equipment behind or selling up – and with the industry in recession, this was hardly a propitious time to be putting print equipment on the market. Even if a printer hoped to set up abroad, there was no guarantee of being able to make a living. Continental towns guarded the privileges of their trade guilds as jealously as did London, and a London printer going abroad would have to exchange the privileged status of a free tradesman for the marginal existence of the interloper. That so many of London's Protestant printers chose these uncertain prospects speaks strongly for the depth of their commitment to the now-defunct Edwardine regime.

Once abroad, some did ultimately succeed in making a living. They profited at least from their position as part of a larger exile community, for the dispossessed leaders of the Edwardine Church hierarchy had little intention of accepting in silence the destruction of their work and hopes for a Protestant England. Settled in safe havens in Germany and Switzerland, they quickly returned to the fray, sending out a steady stream of writings denouncing the new Marian regime and calling on those who had stayed behind to remain true to shared values.[38] They also put such resources as they had salvaged from England into the polemical struggle; several English and Dutch emigré printers were able to reequip, and with this help to establish reputable new printshops.[39] It says a great deal for the commitment of the exile communities that even in these cramped and difficult conditions, English Protestants succeeded in at least matching the Marian regime in their output of polemical literature. This was despite the fact that the English government controlled what remained of the London industry, and bent every sinew to prevent Protestant literature from the Continent from reaching its intended readership.

The new English Catholic hierarchy did not ignore the battle for hearts and minds. The defence of the Catholic faith was important for morale and self-esteem, and the leading authors of the Marian Church published some important and effective works of controversy and theology. But this was hardly the first priority. The re-creation of a Catholic church required a different sort of literature: missals and breviaries for the mass, Books of Hours for private devotion. Some could be restored from the churches

---

[38] Edward J. Baskerville, *A Chronological Bibliography of Propaganda and Polemic published in English between 1553 and 1558* (Philadelphia, 1979).

[39] Especially at Wesel and Emden. On Wesel see Robin A Leaver, *'Goostley Psalmes and Spirituall Songes': English and Dutch Metrical Psalms from Coverdale to Utenhove, 1535–1566* (Oxford, 1991), ch. 6. On Emden see Andrew Pettegree, *Emden and the Dutch Revolt* (Oxford, 1992), ch. 4.

where they had been kept in safety against this very day; but much had been lost, and needed to be replaced.

This, however, was precisely the sort of religious literature with which the English print industry lacked experience. Missals and breviaries were traditionally printed in two colours (inked in red and black), which required a complicated and delicate system of double impression. Before the Reformation the usual practice had been to import such books from the established publishing centres where such techniques had been fully mastered, most notably in France; Paris, in particular, was the established European centre of fine-quality liturgical printing. With the heavy demand at the beginning of Mary's reign, these patterns of trade were quickly restored. Even when editions were printed ostensibly for an English publisher, a French press was often used.

Books of Hours constituted a rather different case. With a text that was frequently largely in Latin, often rubricated (printed in red and black), these were complex and lavish books, purchased not simply to be read. Often the text was encased in an elaborate border, and accompanied by numerous woodcut illustrations. Few English printers had the necessary stock of woodcut blocks to hand; there had been no call for them in the previous reign, when the English book industry had been making steady profits, and before that the English book trade had been still relatively small. Even when Books of Hours had been published in England, the illustrative material would have been bought abroad. In the first half of the century, the pictorial arts in England lagged so far behind the Continent that English printers would send abroad even to have their monograph symbols cut, never mind woodcuts of complex figures and devotional scenes.[40] In short, the obstacles to the development of a strong vernacular tradition of publishing Catholic devotional literature within England during Mary's reign were formidable; and during the short time available little progress was made in this regard. England became, once again, a major importer of religious books.

Thus the Elizabethan inheritance, in this as in so much else, was very mixed. The Marian government had not been unaware of the importance of printing in the moulding of religious opinion. The Privy Council actively promoted the Catholic viewpoint in religious controversy, both at home and abroad. And in common with all Continental regimes, the regulation of the flow of printed books was seen as fundamental

---

[40] For the comparatively undeveloped state of English woodcut art, see Ruth Samson Luborsky and Elizabeth Morley Ingram, *A Guide to English Illustrated Books, 1536–1603* (Tempe, AZ, 1998), especially the illustrations in vol. 2.

to good religious order. Under Mary this extended beyond attempts to prevent the infiltration of hostile Protestant propaganda to the reorganisation of the London Stationers' Company (1557). But the price paid for the restoration of control over the industry was a heavy one. The flight abroad of expertise and capital, English and foreign, meant that the English industry lost much of the ground it had gained during the reign of Edward VI. The turn back to traditional liturgical literature, away from scripture and polemic, meant that carefully nurtured expertise was now redundant, and skills (as in the printing of Catholic liturgical manuals) now urgently necessary were not available.

The accession of Elizabeth I would permit the re-creation of the basic features of the industry as it had developed under Edward VI, both in personnel and in the categories of books in demand. This would be a major source of its success, and a major boost to the London economy in the first decade of the new reign. Studies of the Elizabethan settlement now acknowledge the large elements of continuity with the interrupted Edwardine establishment, be it in terms of church order, or in the leading personnel and policies of the new regime. Much the same point could be made for the London printing trade, as is demonstrated in the resurrected career of John Day, whose great new printing venture, the *Actes and Monuments*, would be one of the seminal creations of early English print. In so many respects this book built on the Edwardine tradition, both in the materials garnered by leading figures of the Church, and in the production process, underpinned by Dutch expertise (evident in the typographical material used, the workshop personnel and the style of the illustrations). Considered purely as a physical artefact, this milestone in the formation of an independent English Protestant identity epitomised (not without a certain irony) the English Reformation's extensive dependence on the Continental movement of which it formed a sometimes reluctant part.

CHAPTER 8

John Day: master printer of the English Reformation[1]

John N. King

John Day's printing career exemplifies a lifelong commitment to the dissemination of Protestant books and pamphlets. He eventually became one of the most prominent and wealthy members of the London book world not only because of his technical expertise and sound business principles, but also because of patronage that he received from powerful members of the establishments of Edwardine and Elizabethan England. Publication of ephemera and affordable copies of small-format books – such as *ABC*s, sermons and metrical translations of the Psalms – afforded the foundation for his prosperity, but he won renown as publisher of Foxe's *Actes and Monuments of These Latter and Perilous Days*, which constituted the most physically imposing, complicated and technically demanding English book of the Shakespearean age.[2]

The focus of the present essay lies not on Day's technical expertise as a printer and illustrator of books,[3] although he produced some of the finest examples of Tudor printing, but on the formative stages in the career of this ideologically motivated publisher. His pre-Elizabethan imprints included many important books published in defence of the Edwardine settlement of religion. Recognition of the centrality of this printer in the development of English book culture takes on great significance at the present moment, as revisionist historians interpret early English

[1] I thank Andrew Pettegree for permitting me to read an advance copy of his entry on John Day for the *New Dictionary of National Biography*, in progress. I am also indebted to helpful suggestions offered by James Bracken; and to Kathleen Kennedy's unpublished handlist of imprints by John Day and her bibliography of publications by Day preserved at the Rare Book and Manuscript Library of University Libraries at The Ohio State University, Columbus, Ohio. I thank Justin Pepperney for his assistance in research. I am grateful to the College of Humanities at The Ohio State University for research support.
[2] Published by Day in four ever-expanding editions (1563–83).
[3] See C. L. Oastler, *John Day, the Elizabethan Printer*, Oxford Bibliographical Society Occasional Publications, no. 10 (Oxford, 1975); Bryan P. Davis, 'John Day', *British Literary Booktrade, 1475–1700*, ed. James K. Bracken and Joel Silver; *Dictionary of Literary Biography*, vol. 170 (Detroit, 1996), 78–93.

Protestantism as a relentlessly destructive, if not malevolent, force.[4] In focusing on the smashing of saints' images, shattering of stained-glass windows, dismantling of altars and despoliation of shrines, these scholars maintain an embarrassing silence about the contribution of the printing press to the production of richly diverse publications grounded upon William Tyndale's scriptural translations and geared to readers (and hearers) at all social levels.

Day's origins are obscure. Born in 1522, he maintained close ties to Suffolk throughout his life. According to tradition, he was born in Dunwich, a once-prominent port on the North Sea that had gone into decline because of severe erosion of the coastline.[5] A printer's most formative stage is his apprenticeship, but the identity of Day's master is unknown. Day's use of a device once employed by Thomas Gibson affords a flimsy basis for belief that he was apprenticed to that printer. Publication of two octavo editions of Antoine Marcourt's *A Declaration of the Mass* in 1547 indicates that Day embarked upon his printing career close to the end of the reign of Henry VIII, before he became a member of the Stationers' Company in 1550.[6] Identified by its false colophon ('Wittenberg, H[ans]. Luft') as a surreptitious translation, this book fell under a prohibition on publication of Protestant controversial literature that remained in effect until Henry VIII's death on 28 January 1547. Despite earlier attribution of this book to a German printer of Lutheran tracts, typography reveals that the two editions represent the first publications attributable with certainty to John Day.[7] This book exemplifies from the outset Day's long-term interest in publishing Protestant propaganda and translations of writings by Continental reformers, his tendency to produce affordable small-format editions of popular vernacular publications, and his recourse to pseudonyms to conceal facts of publication during periods of religio-political uncertainty.

Day's career began in earnest after the accession of Edward VI (1547–53). The nine-year-old boy was legally incapable of governing, and his taste for courtly entertainment and hunting did not measure up to his mythic representation as a pious boy in Protestant sermons, pamphlets

---

[4] Eamon Duffy, *The Stripping of the Altars: Traditional Religion in England 1400–1580* (New Haven and London, 1992), 377–477; Christopher Haigh, *English Reformations: Religion, Politics and Society under the Tudors* (Oxford, 1993), 1–21, et seq.
[5] Oastler, *John Day*, 4.   [6] Davis, 'John Day', 79.
[7] *STC* 17314–17314a. The 1548 publication of a 3rd edition by John Oswen at Ipswich is in keeping with Day's Suffolk connection. Attribution to Day's press of two 1546 editions of an influential Lollard treatise, *Wyclif's Wicket*, whose colophons falsely identify Nuremberg as the place of publication, lacks certainty. See *STC* 25590–25590.5.

and chronicles including Foxe's *Actes and Monuments*. Although King Edward lacked theological sophistication, he embraced anti-Catholic views and endorsed efforts to impose a Protestant settlement of religion by leaders of his regime, notably his imperious uncle, Edward Seymour, who governed in a monarchical manner as Duke of Somerset and Protector of the Realm, and John Dudley, earl of Warwick, who deposed Seymour on 11 October 1549 and was created Duke of Northumberland on 11 October 1551. It must be acknowledged that Seymour and Dudley were military leaders and men of affairs who delegated religious leadership to Archbishop Thomas Cranmer.[8] Nevertheless, they and other high-ranking members of the Edwardine establishment did patronise Protestant ideologues whose publications had been banned under Henry VIII. Their commitment to ecclesiastical reform appears to have been genuine, despite Dudley's recantation during the reign of Mary I.

Edward's accession opened the way to renunciation of prior censorship and licensing regulations imposed during his late father's reign. Parliamentary abrogation of all treason and heresy statutes passed since the reign of Edward I, including the prohibition on expression of unauthorised religious opinion that had been enforced by the notorious Act of Six Articles (1539), allowed Protestant printers including John Day to flood bookstalls in London and provincial towns with Protestant propaganda. The historical fact of the explosion of Protestant propaganda under Edward VI, a time when religious publication dominated the book trade, is undeniable. It concurred with outbursts of popular iconoclasm, free circulation of the vernacular Bible, and Cranmer's introduction of a Protestant worship service in the vernacular.[9]

Day played a central role in the Edwardine printing explosion, despite his youth and recent entry into the book trade. That he was about twenty-five when he became a master printer means that he must have possessed capital, but its source is unknown. Although it seems doubtful that he commissioned most writings that came his way, it is clear that he attracted manuscripts addressed to an audience of avid Protestant readers. London printers produced books at the highest rate since Caxton established England's first printing press in 1476. The average Edwardine output

---

[8] Jennifer Loach, *Edward VI* (New Haven, 1999), 42–7, 116–35, 130–4, 152–8.
[9] John N. King, 'The Book Trade under Edward VI and Mary I', *The Cambridge History of the Book in Britain. Vol. III: 1400–1557*, ed. Lotte Hellinga and J. B. Trapp (Cambridge, 1999), 164–9. In a letter of 6 June 1547 to Protector Somerset, Stephen Gardiner protested against the open sale of Protestant propaganda at Winchester market. See *AM*, 1347a.

of 171 books per year was almost double that during Henry VIII's final decade. Not until midway during the reign of Elizabeth I did London printers exceed the output of the peak years of 1548 and 1550, when London presses produced about 260 books per year.

John Day's output of about 35 books in each of those years accounted for approximately 13 per cent of English imprints.[10] Of course, counting titles affords only a crude measure of printing output. Printing many books in small formats of the kind that Day specialised in at the outset of his career is not equivalent in investment of resources or time to the printing of a single massive folio book like the *Actes and Monuments*. The work and capital required for the production of a few large-format books would have exceeded Day's investment of time and money in the production of pamphlets. Some printers never printed folios, for example, and had a great number of titles; others printed folios and as a result printed fewer titles, but were just as busy and probably made more money in the long run. Nevertheless, it took a longer time for expensive folio volumes to go out of print than most inexpensive octavos. The sale of pamphlets and tracts might have been quite lucrative in the short run.

Uncertainty clouds our knowledge of Day's activity during 1547 because his responsibility for one-third of the twenty publications attributed to him in the *Short-Title Catalogue* remains doubtful.[11] The colophon of *A Simple and Religious Consultation by What Mean a Christian Reformation May Be Begun* by Hermann von Wied, the evangelical elector-archbishop of Cologne, does indicate that Day established his printing establishment at the sign of the Resurrection near Holborn Conduit in Sepulchre's parish by 30 October.[12] (His printing devices incorporated Resurrection symbolism throughout his career.[13]) Compiled by leading reformers, Martin Bucer and Philip Melanchthon, the liturgical services in this book were appropriate to a time when Thomas Cranmer began to move towards promulgation of an English worship service. Its scripturalism is compatible with another Day octavo published in the same year, *Of the Sum of the*

---

[10] King, 'Book Trade', 164–9. For an overview of Edwardine patronage and publication, see John N. King, *English Reformation Literature: The Tudor Origins of the Protestant Tradition* (Princeton, 1982), 76–113.

[11] Dates of publication for books printed by Day and other early printers are often absent or problematic. Queries (?) mark inferred dates that fall within 'two or three years on either side' of the date indicated; c. indicates 'a broader range, of approximately five years on either side' (*STC* I.xxxviii).

[12] *STC* 13213.

[13] See R. B. McKerrow, *Printers' and Publishers' Devices in England and Scotland 1485–1640* (1913), nos. 116, 124, 128, 208.

Holy Scripture and Ordinary of the Christian Teaching. According to tradition, Simon Fish produced this translation of a French tract.[14]

Day's publication in 1547 of newly permissible writings by prominent Protestant authors identifies book production and sale at the sign of the Resurrection with the evangelical ideology of the Edwardine regime. Indeed, Thomas Becon composed *A New Dialogue between the Angel of God and the Shepherds in the Field* during his service as a chaplain in the household of Protector Somerset, at a time when he also preached at Whitehall Palace.[15] Henrician regulations had banned writings that Becon composed under the pseudonym of Theodore Basille. The catechetical manner, twin choruses and stage directions of this nativity play suggest that he composed it for production in a church or chapel, possibly for Christmastide performance before Seymour or at the royal court.[16] Day also republished William Tyndale's *Parable of the Wicked Mammon,* a seminal exposition of the Lutheran doctrine of *sola fide.*[17]

Little explicit documentation exists concerning the source of Day's capital and the organisation of his business. His ownership of expensive type fonts and ability to commission the carving of costly woodblocks, which required long-term investment of capital, suggest that he enjoyed the support of powerful backers able to provide financial support or otherwise underwrite his enterprise. Without a significant source of capital, it is unlikely that he could have taken such a large share of the London book trade so soon after starting his business. In some cases he functioned as publisher rather than printer when he advertised books on sale at his shop in colophons of publications printed by job printers such as Steven Mierdman, a Dutch immigrant, with whom Day had a close association. In the case of his 1551 folio Bible, edited by Edmund Becke, at least three printers executed the printing job on Day's behalf.[18]

Day's publication of tracts by Becon indicates a possible connection to Protector Somerset, who was the great literary patron of Edwardine England. Seymour often extended patronage through the offices of his private secretary, William Cecil, later Lord Burghley.[19] Day also printed books by John Hooper, a radical Protestant who joined Becon as a chaplain to Seymour upon return from exile in Zürich.[20] Seymour's personal

---

[14] *STC* 3039. For other evangelical tracts, see *STC* 96–7 and 1034.7.   [15] *STC* 1733.5 (1547?).
[16] King, *English Reformation Literature,* 290–4. See also Paul Whitfield White, *Theatre and Reformation: Protestantism, Patronage and Playing in Tudor England* (Cambridge, 1993), 149.
[17] *STC* 24457.   [18] Oastler, *John Day,* 7.
[19] King, *English Reformation Literature,* 106–12, 274–5, 291.
[20] *STC* 13763–4, 13757–8 (1550–52). Hooper received appointment as bishop of Gloucester (1550) and Worcester (1552).

physician, William Turner, was another member of Day's circle of reformist zealots. Turner dedicated *The Names of Herbs in Greek, Latin, English Dutch & French* to Seymour 'from your grace's house at Syon'.[21]

Even more suggestive is Day's publication of *A Godly Meditation upon Twenty Select Psalms of David* by Anthony Cope, Katherine Parr's principal chamberlain, who was knighted by Edward VI. It indicates a possible avenue of support from an important patron of evangelical writing. The dedication of this collection of 'prayer[s] and contemplative meditations' as a New Year gift to the widow of Henry VIII and stepmother of King Edward indicates that it originated as a courtly manuscript. A prominent woodcut of the royal coat of arms and the text's status as Day's first quarto, a more expensive format than that of his octavo pamphlets, further mark this book as an elite text whose pietism is in keeping with the evangelical temper of England's dowager queen.[22]

John Day came into his own as a printer during the great flood of Edwardine printing (1548–50), when he produced more than thirty books per year in his own right or in partnership with a bookseller, William Seres.[23] By entering into partnership Day and Seres shared the risks and rewards of book publication and sale. Either partner or both may have contributed money to their enterprise. Whatever the case, it seems likely that Day was the senior partner. Only he functioned as a printer-publisher, and he commissioned woodblocks that he retained after the breakup of the partnership.[24] It was Day, rather than Seres, who maintained career-long relationships with powerful Protestant patrons and received monopolies on the publication of *ABCs* and books such as the collected sermons of Hugh Latimer. For this reason, this essay draws no distinction between books published by Day alone and by the Day-Seres partnership unless otherwise noted.

Readers purchased books printed by Day at five shops operated by him, Seres or Seres's second partner, Anthony Scoloker, in addition to

---

[21] *STC* 24359 (1548), A3v. See also Turner's *New Dialogue Wherein is Contained the Examination of the Mass* (*STC* 24361.5–62, 1548?).

[22] *STC* 5717, *3r, *4r.

[23] Despite the claim that the partnership of Day and Seres began in 1548 (Davis, 'John Day', 79), it may have begun in 1547 with the production of a broadside ballad on behalf of John Turk, a bookseller on Paternoster Row (*STC* 13089). Their association may even date to the 1546 publication of a combined edition of *A Supplication of the Poor Commons*, attributed to Henry Brinklow (or Robert Crowley), and Simon Fish's *Supplication of Beggars* (*STC* 10884.8). The social gospel propounded by these texts is in keeping with the ideas of proponents of commonwealth reform during the reign of Edward VI, such as Robert Crowley, Hugh Latimer and Thomas Lever.

[24] See *Seven Sermons Made upon the Lord's Prayer and Preached before the Duchess of Suffolk* (1572).

the premises of other booksellers. During 1548 Seres established shops at two locations: Ely Rents and Peter College. The first was a commercial property facing Holborn at the front of Ely Place, the residence of John Dudley, which was only 300 metres away from Day's premises at the sign of the Resurrection. At the western end of St Paul's Churchyard, the second was close to the centre of London's bookselling quarter. Not only did Seres sell books in concert with Scoloker at Ely Rents, he also shared shops that Scoloker established in 1548 in St Botolph's parish without Aldersgate and Savoy Rents without Temple Bar. Books imprinted by Day and Seres went on sale at the Savoy Rents bookshop, which differed from the other shops in its greater distance from the City of London, with its audience of bourgeois readers. This shop presumably catered both to law students at the Temple to the east and to aristocrats resident at Thameside manors that backed on to the Strand to the west.

The thick network of associations that links these bookmen to Suffolk has direct bearing upon likely sources of Day's capital investment. Like Day, Seres hailed from Suffolk. For a brief interval in 1548, Scoloker maintained a printing house in Ipswich prior to moving to London. Another Ipswich printer republished Day's first known imprint.[25] During the same year an Ipswichman named John Overton published John Bale's *Illustrium maioris Britanniae scriptorum summarium*, a discursive catalogue of British writers throughout the centuries.[26] A fierce Protestant partisan and one-time protégé of Thomas Cromwell, Bale compiled this book after fleeing England following passage of the Act of Six Articles in 1539. Bale oversaw its production at the printing house of Derick van der Straten at Wesel, a Rhineland port in the County of Cleves that was an ideal location for the export of English books forbidden by Henrician regulations. Despite the book's status as an exile publication, Bale proudly announces his identity as a Suffolkman on the title page. When Bale returned to England upon the Edwardine relaxation of restraints on Protestant publication, Day published one of his books. Not only was Bale a Suffolkman, he was born in Day's hometown of Dunwich.

The inclusion of the coat of arms of the dowager duchess of Suffolk in four books printed in 1548 indicates that John Day operated under her patronage (figure 1). (Miles Coverdale was another protégé.) Day's ownership of the woodblock with which he printed her heraldic device shows that he rather than his partner was her client.[27] A notable sponsor

---

[25] Oastler, *John Day*, 4.   [26] *STC* 1295.   [27] See *Seven Sermons*.

Figure 1. Coat of arms of Catherine Brandon, duchess of Suffolk. From Hermann von Wied, *A Simple and Religious Consultation by What Mean a Christian Reformation May Be Begun* (1548).

of Protestant publicists, Catherine Brandon (née Willoughby) lived at Suffolk Place to the immediate west of the Savoy Rents bookshop.[28] Day's inclusion of her coat of arms in Tyndale's *Exposition upon the Fifth, Sixth, and Seventh Chapters of Matthew* and Pierre Viret's *Very Familiar Exposition of the Apostles Creed*, translated from French, should come as no surprise given the evangelical piety that the duchess shared with Katherine Parr and the coterie of pious women to which they belonged.[29] William Cecil attested that he 'set forth and put in print' an edition of Parr's *The Lamentation of a Sinner* (1547), published by Edward Whitchurch, 'at the instant desire of the right gracious Lady Catherine, duchess of Suffolk'. In all likelihood she provided Cecil with a copy of a manuscript that members of the Parr circle had used in private devotions. Publication of this book marks a clear effort to disseminate among members of the reading public at large pietistic ideas that originated within a feminine coterie. Its affirmation of the doctrine of justification by faith alone lends a Protestant tenor to the text.[30]

Even more significant is the presence of the duchess's device in Day's edition of Hugh Latimer's *Sermon on the Plough*.[31] Latimer had served as chaplain in Katherine Parr's household before her marriage to Henry VIII, and he functioned as a spiritual adviser to the circle of devout women that surrounded her as queen. As a protégé of Catherine Brandon, Latimer emerged from disfavour under Henry VIII to become the most influential preacher of Edward VI's reign. Delivered in the Shrouds at St Paul's Cathedral, an enclosure where clerics preached as an alternative to the outdoor pulpit of Paul's Cross during inclement weather, Latimer's 18 January 1548 appeal for clerical reform was deservedly popular.

The duchess's insignia also appeared in Thomas Some's collection of seven Lenten sermons that Latimer preached at Whitehall Palace in 1549. Because the Chapel Royal could not accommodate the courtiers who flocked to his addresses, a wooden pulpit was erected for the occasion in the privy gardens.[32] The editor dedicated this transcription to Catherine Brandon not only because of her reputation for piety and patronage of

---

[28] When the male line of the dukedom of Suffolk became extinct at the 1551 death of the duchess's sons, Henry and Charles, Edward VI conferred the dukedom on Henry Grey, father of Lady Jane Grey.

[29] *STC* 24441a, 24784.

[30] James K. McConica, *English Humanists and Reformation Politics Under Henry VIII and Edward VI* (Oxford, 1965), 229–30; John N. King, 'Patronage and Piety: The Influence of Catherine Parr', *Silent But for the Word: Tudor Women as Patrons, Translators, and Writers of Religious Works*, ed. Margaret P. Hannay (Kent, OH, 1985), 50.

[31] *STC* 15291.   [32] *AM*, 1739.

Christian learning, but 'chiefly for the profit which shall ensue through them unto the ignorant'. The colophon advertises the sale of these sermons at Day's 'new shop by the Little Conduit Cheapside', a location at the north-east corner of St Paul's Churchyard. Because individual editions usually numbered about 1,500 copies, Day printed an exceedingly large print run of about 6,000 copies of this two-part collection during 1549.[33] It exemplifies the homiletic spirit of the Edwardine court. After leaving the royal court Latimer resided at Catherine Brandon's manor of Grimsthorpe in Lincolnshire, where he preached a series of private sermons before her in 1552.[34]

Over and beyond these books, John Day acknowledged Catherine Brandon's patronage of the dissemination of the Bible in the vernacular, a project embraced by the Protestant intelligentsia, by printing her coat of arms in an octavo edition of Tyndale's translation of the New Testament.[35] As a publisher of vernacular translations of the Bible, Day acted as an entrepreneur who engaged the services of an editor, Edmund Becke, and actively involved himself in production of vernacular scriptural texts. Day's work as a technically innovative populariser of the English Bible is in keeping with praise of the duchess, in another one of his publications, because of 'the ardent love and desire that your grace doth bear to the holy word of God, but especially for the diligent promoting and setting forth to your great charges'.[36] In the preface to Day's 1548 New Testament, the printer explains his innovation of moving annotations from the margins to the end of each chapter so that the reader 'mayest the better find the things noted'. Use of this location also permits an editor to tailor his commentary to the requirements of the text. Day often refers the reader to his original source in notes such as 'Look more of this in the Image of both the churches, gathered by John Bale'. Piety mingles with profit, because this note also serves as an advertisement for the octavo edition of Bale's *Image of Both Churches*, the first full-length printed commentary on the Book of Revelation in English, which Day republished at about this time.[37]

Day could afford to tie up capital in the 1551 folio Bible edited by Becke, in contrast to six booksellers who collaborated in publishing a competing folio Bible during the same year.[38] Becke's acknowledgement

---

[33] *STC* 15270.7, A2v. See also *STC* 15270.5–74.7.
[34] *Seven Sermons*, ¶2r, A4v.   [35] *STC* 2853 (1548).
[36] Dedication by Nicholas Lesse, translator of Joannes Aepinus's *A Very Fruitful and Godly Exposition upon the Fifteenth Psalm* (*STC* 166.5, 1548?), A5r, A6r.
[37] *STC* 1298 (c. 1550).   [38] *STC* 2083–86.5.

that high book prices reduced Bible circulation because ordinary people had been discouraged by 'the price of late time . . . from buying of the same' helps to explain the caution of that syndicate at the same time that it emphasises Day's relative freedom from financial constraint.[39]

Day's publication of the Bible in large and small formats indicates that he cultivated a mixed clientele that ranged from poor to well-to-do readers. His own words provide a rationale for his publication of translations of the Bible, 'in which all men ought to delight and exercise themselves both day and night, to the amendment of their own lives and to the edifying of their neighbours'.[40] The opportunity to expand his market and maximise the output of his presses by printing in smaller formats must have appealed to so shrewd a businessman. He demonstrates particular concern for low-born readers in his innovative project of publishing the Bible in six octavo editions, including the Apocrypha (1549–51). His preface to the Pentateuch, which also bears the coat of arms of the duchess of Suffolk, addresses 'the commodity of these poor' by enabling them to purchase part or all of the Bible, and explains that folio Bibles are too costly for poor readers (and hearers), 'to whose chief comfort and consolation the Holy Ghost hath caused them to be written'.[41]

The great majority of the books published during Day's active partnership with Seres (1548–50) contributed to the flood of Protestant treatises opposed to the doctrine of transubstantiation and Roman-rite mass and in favour of Thomas Cranmer's step-by-step introduction of a new English service, which culminated in the institution of the first *Book of Common Prayer* on Whitsunday 1549. In addition to writings by Hugh Latimer, Thomas Becon, John Hooper and William Turner, Day printed anti-Catholic propaganda composed by William Tyndale, John Frith, Robert Crowley and others. He also printed some of the earliest English translations of writings by Jean Calvin. Published under the initials A. G., *An Answer to the Devilish Detection of Stephen Gardiner* was written by Anthony Gilby, who would lead the congregation of English exiles in Geneva under Mary I and underwent prosecution for nonconformity under Elizabeth I.[42] Day printed sermons by Thomas Lever, a popular cleric who received invitations to preach in the Shrouds at St Paul's Cathedral and at the royal court.[43] Not only did Edmund Becke edit

---

39 *STC* 2088, *3v. In 1549 Becke edited Day's first folio edition of the English Bible, a revision of the 'Matthew' version (*STC* 2077).
40 *STC* 14018 (1560), A3v.
41 *STC* 2087 (1551). Day printed this book after the breakup of his partnership with Seres.
42 *STC* 11884 (1548?).   43 *STC* 15543–3a, 15547–8 (1550).

Day's editions of the English Bible, he also composed a versified tract against Anabaptism and in favour of the recent execution of Joan Bucher on 2 May 1550: *A Brief Confutation of this Anabaptistical Opinion, That Christ Did Not Take His Flesh of the Virgin Mary.*[44] One of the more enigmatic books published by Day is *A Godly Exhortation to All Such as Profess the Gospel* by Henry Hart. A radical advocate of free will against predestination, Hart was an early proponent of separatism.[45]

Day's publication of books attributed to Luke Shepherd, a mysterious figure who wrote a spate of anti-Catholic satires c. 1548, attests to the printer's high standing within evangelical circles at the royal court. Although the poet's name suggests that it may be a pseudonym made up of elements suggesting Christ, the Good Shepherd, and the evangelist Luke, in all likelihood he was the physician whom Edward Underhill, a gentleman pensioner at the court of Edward VI, referred to as 'Master Luke, my very friend, of Coleman Street' in the City of London. Underhill credits his friend with many 'proper books against the papists', for which he was jailed in Fleet Prison. Satires published by Day included *The Upcheering of the Mass* and *Pathos, or An Inward passion of the Pope for the Loss of His Daughter the Mass.* These scurrilous allegorical attacks on the mass personified as a harlot, Mistress Missa, overflow with obscene invective against the Church of Rome as the Whore of Babylon.[46]

Pressure from the royal court allowed Day to resist local efforts to curtail his publication of polemics by Shepherd. When the Lord Mayor of London, Sir John Gresham, and conservative aldermen harassed Day for printing Shepherd's *John Bon and Mast Person*, a satire on transubstantiation and the mass, Underhill speedily intervened by handing the mayor a copy and informing him that it accorded with courtly taste: 'there is many of them at court'.[47] Gresham's agreement, on reading it, that 'it was both pithy and merry' suggests that Shepherd's polemics established a standard of Reformation wit that could appeal to both elite

---

[44] *STC* 1709 (1550).

[45] *STC* 12887.3–87.7 (1549, 1549?). See J. W. Martin, 'English Protestant Separatism at its Beginnings: Henry Hart and the Free-Will Men', *Sixteenth Century Journal* 7 (1976), 55–74. See also Thomas Freeman's essay in this volume.

[46] *STC* 17630 and 19463. Day and Seres also published *The Comparison between the Antipus and the Antigraph*, an interlocking set of controversial poems composed largely by Shepherd, and *A Poor Help, The Buckler and Defense of Mother Holy Kirk*, an ironic defence of the Church of Rome (*STC* 5605a, 13052). See Janice Devereux's edition of Shepherd's complete works, forthcoming from the Renaissance English Text Society.

[47] *STC* 3258.5 (1548?). See John N. King, ed., 'Luke Shepherd's *John Bon and Mast Person*', *ANQ: A Quarterly Journal of Short Articles, Notes, and Reviews* 5 (1992), 87–91.

and popular readers.[48] According to John Strype, this 'book took much at the court, and the courtiers wore it in their pockets'.[49]

Day published as well books by Robert Crowley, a prolific publicist whose pamphlets outline a gospel ethic favourable to social reform. It seems likely that Day produced Crowley's earliest publications: *A Dialogue between Lent and Liberty* and *The Opening of the Words of Prophet Joel*.[50] The first tract opposes fasting during Lent, whereas the latter employs densely scriptural language to lodge an apocalyptic attack on religious and social abuses. Crowley also contributed a polemical preface to editions of Tyndale's *Supper of the Lord* probably printed by Day, which constitute an opening salvo in the pamphlet attack on the Catholic mass that would intensify during 1548–9.[51] Crowley's *Confutation of the Misshapen Answer to the Ballad, called the Abuse of the Blessed sacrament of the Altar* contains an anonymous anti-mass ballad in addition to a versified response by Miles Huggarde, a Catholic artisan poet, which survives only because Crowley quotes it in its entirety during the course of his confutation.[52] Furthermore, Day published Crowley's *Information and Petition against the Oppressors of the Poor Commons of this Realm*, an appeal to Parliament for reform of the commonwealth through prohibition of abuses such as hoarding, exaction of undue price increases and rack renting.[53]

Crowley's *Confutation of Thirteen Articles, Whereunto Nicholas Shaxton Subscribed* kept alive the furore roused by the heresy examinations and execution of Anne Askew at the end of Henry VIII's reign.[54] Crowley attacks Shaxton, at one time the reformist bishop of Salisbury, for recanting prior to Askew's burning with three men on 16 July 1546. He not only recanted after being condemned to die in the company of Askew, but also counselled her to follow his example and abjure heresy. Unlike Shaxton, Askew and her companions refused to accept the doctrine of transubstantiation, the Roman-rite mass and other Catholic beliefs.

By attributing Shaxton's recantation sermon to Stephen Gardiner, bishop of Winchester, Crowley's edition articulates a potent attack on Gardiner, the leader of the Catholic opposition. Indeed, the editor claims that, 'I think them [Shaxton's words] to be Winchester's workmanship,

---

[48] *Reformation Narratives*, 171–2.
[49] John Strype, *Ecclesiastical Memorials* (3 vols., Oxford, 1721), vol. 2, 116.
[50] *STC* 6084.5, 6088.9 (1547?).   [51] *STC* 24470–1 (1547?).   [52] *STC* 6082 (1548).
[53] *STC* 6086 (1548).
[54] *STC* 6083 (1548). Shaxton's recantation is preserved in Bishop Bonner's register (Guildhall Library, London, MS 9531/12, 108r–109r).

because they agree so well with his doctrine.'[55] It is worthy of note that Askew's *Examinations* claims that the conservative faction led by Gardiner attempted to implicate Catherine Brandon, Anne Stanhope (wife of Edward Seymour), Katherine Parr and other members of the queen's circle for aiding the Lincolnshire gentlewoman during her imprisonment.[56]

John Day enlivens Crowley's point-by-point refutation of Shaxton's views by inserting a separately printed foldout frontispiece of 'the burning of Anne Askew' (figure 2).[57] This picture is virtually without precedent as an outsize, tailormade illustration for an inexpensive English octavo. Not only did the printer go to great expense in order to embellish this tract, he retained ownership of the costly woodblock for fifteen years before using it for a second time as an illustration for the version of Anne Askew's *Examinations* that John Foxe incorporated into the *Actes and Monuments*. The woodcutter followed the description of the scene that John Bale inserted into his original publication of Askew's examinations. As Shaxton preaches from a portable pulpit, the councillors who participated in her interrogation sit on a dais in front of the church of St Bartholomew the Great. A bolt of lightning alludes to Bale's commentary.

Day published no books by Crowley after 1548, when the latter established a bookshop at Ely Rents in Holborn at about the time that William Seres closed the one he had maintained at the same location.[58] Day continued to print many polemical and devotional books composed by figures patronised by high-ranking members of the Edwardine establishment. For example, he published many enduring favourites by Thomas Becon that went into edition after edition under both Edward VI and Elizabeth I, such as *The Flower of Godly Prayers* and *The Principles of Christian Religion*.[59]

---

[55] Crowley, *Confutation*, A2r.

[56] *The Examinations of Anne Askew*, ed. Elaine V. Beilin (Oxford, 1996), 122, 125–6. In refusing to recant, Askew told Shaxton that 'it had been good for him never to have been born' (119). Foxe is our only source for a courtly conspiracy led by the bishop of Winchester against Katherine Parr, as noted by Glyn Redworth, *In Defence of the Church Catholic: The Life of Stephen Gardiner* (Oxford, 1990), 231–4.

[57] Reproduced from a reuse in *AM* (1563).

[58] Like John Day, Robert Crowley received patronage from a high-ranking woman, Lady Elizabeth Fane (or Vane), whose versifications of scripture appeared under his imprint: *Certain Psalms in Number 21, with 102 Proverbs* (1550). She was the wife of Sir Ralph Fane (or Vane), a retainer who was executed with Edward Seymour in 1552. John Foxe later described her as a 'special nurse, and a great supporter . . . of the godly saints, which were imprisoned in queen Mary's time'. See *AM*, 1642a.

[59] *STC* 1719.5–20.3 (c. 1550, 1551, c. 1551); 1751–2.5 (1550, 1553?).

Figure 2. The execution of Anne Askew. From John Foxe, *Actes and Monuments of These Latter and Perilous Days* (1563).

Day also continued to publish devotional texts that circulated among aristocratic women. Examples include an octavo edition of *Fourteen Sermons Concerning the Predestination and Election of God* by Bernardino Ochino, a religious reformer who emigrated from Italy and lived at Lambeth Palace under the patronage of Thomas Cranmer. The translator of the text 'out of Italian into our native tongue' was Anne Cooke, one of three daughters of Sir Anthony Cooke (tutor in classical languages to Edward VI). Renowned for her learning, she would become the second wife of Sir Nicholas Bacon, the eminent jurist and statesman, and sister-in-law of William Cecil. Cooke's dedication of the text to her mother, who had a taste for 'godly exhortations', suggests that this translation originally circulated in manuscript within a circle of pious women. The address 'To the Christian Reader' by the editor, G. B., indicates that the translator's 'shamefastness would rather have suppressed them, had not I to whose hands they were committed half against their will put them forth'.[60] It may be that G. B. stood for Gulielmus Baldwinus (William Baldwin), who employed the same initials to sign his fanciful satire on the concealed survival of Catholic ritual practices, *A Marvellous History Entitled Beware the Cat*.[61]

In 1549 Day moved his printing presses from Holborn to Aldersgate. During the following year he shifted book sales from his 'new shop' to the sign of the Resurrection near the Little Conduit in Cheapside and established his printing house above Aldersgate. By this time he had begun to serve in his own right as a patron to figures such as Edmund Becke and, possibly, William Baldwin. We know that Baldwin had an intimate acquaintance with Day's premises from a vignette in *Beware the Cat*, which affords a unique account of a Tudor printing house. At this time Baldwin worked on Fleet Street as an assistant to the prominent Protestant printer Edward Whitchurch, for whom he corrected books in press. As 'servant to Edward Whitchurch', Baldwin published two books printed at his master's establishment.[62]

In *Beware the Cat* the narrator recounts a time when he lodged at Day's premises, 'which, more roomish within than garish without, standeth at Saint Martin's Lane end and hangeth partly upon the town wall that is called Aldersgate'. This stay took place soon after the hanging, drawing and quartering of traitors in 1549 or 1550, when 'dead men's quarters'

---

[60] *STC* 18767 (1551?), A2r–3r.
[61] *STC* 1244 (composed c. 1553, published 1570). [62] *STC* 1253, 2768.

were displayed on pikes at gateways into London as a warning to potential malefactors:

I was lodged in a chamber hard by the printing house, which had a fair bay window opening into the garden ... At the other end of the printing house, as you enter in, is a side door and three or four steps which go up to the leads [i.e. roof] of the gate, whereas sometime quarters of men, which is a loathely and abominable sight, so stand up upon poles.[63]

John Stow's description of Aldersgate corroborates this description in a passage that states: 'John Day, stationer, a late famous printer of many good books, in our time dwelt in this gate, and built much upon the wall of the city towards the parish church of St. Anne.'[64]

The number of imprints produced by Day decreased sharply during the years after he moved to the printing house above Aldersgate, when he published about fifteen extant books. It is worthy of note that publication rates fell generally after the Privy Council reinstituted prior censorship following the deposition of Edward Seymour as Lord Protector. Nevertheless, Day's 7 per cent share of London imprints during 1551–2 was decidedly less than his 13 per cent share during 1548–50. If Day had received patronage from Seymour, either directly or indirectly, the Protector's disgrace might have contributed to this shift. Seymour was imprisoned in the Tower of London from 11 October 1549 until 6 February 1550. After his second fall he was imprisoned from 16 October 1551 until his execution on 22 January 1552.

It was during these years that Day published several books by John Bale, newly returned from Continental exile under the patronage of yet another pious woman (Mary Fitzroy, duchess of Richmond). *The Apology of Johan Bale Against a Rank Papist* inveighs against Catholic images, clerical vows and ritual practices. A vehement personal narrative, *An Expostulation or Complaint Against the Blasphemies of a Frantic Papist of Hampshire*, decries resistance to ecclesiastical change within the parish at Bishopstoke, to which John Ponet, bishop of Winchester, had appointed Bale, his chaplain, as vicar.[65] This book begins with a dedication to John Dudley, duke of Northumberland, who extended ecclesiastical reforms

---

[63] *'Beware the Cat' by William Baldwin: The First English Novel*, ed. William A. Ringler, Jr. and Michael Flachmann (San Marino, CA, 1988), 10 and note 23.

[64] John Stow, *The Survey of London*, ed. H. B. Wheatley (1987), 33. For detailed discussion of writings by Baldwin, Bale, Crowley, Shepherd and others, see King, *English Reformation Literature*; Andrew Hadfield, *Literature, Politics and National Identity: Reformation to Renaissance* (Cambridge, 1994); Thomas Betteridge, *Tudor Histories of the English Reformations, 1530–1583* (Aldershot, 1999).

[65] *STC* 1275 (1550?), 1294 (1552?).

begun under Edward Seymour. Day also published Bale's translation of the ninth eclogue of Baptista Mantuanus Spagnuoli, which attacks clerical corruption.[66]

During the final years of Edward VI's reign, Day continued to publish sermons by Thomas Lever and Bernardino Ochino, scriptural commentaries by Anthony Gilby, and miscellaneous Protestant devotional writings. Publication of Ponet's *A Short Catechisme* afforded a foundation for Day's prosperity later in life, because letters patent of Edward VI (25 March 1553) granted the publisher a monopoly on this staple grammar-school text and the *ABC* published in the same volume. Raynold Wolfe disputed Day's patent, however, because he held a monopoly on the printing of books in Latin, the language in which Ponet wrote his *Brevis Catechismus*, the original version of *A Short Catechisme*. Settlement of the suit resulted in an agreement whereby Day published the English version and Wolfe retained a monopoly on the Latin text. Day's patent also gave him exclusive rights to treatises by Thomas Becon.[67]

The death of Edward VI on 6 July 1553 triggered a sea change in Day's career, for his royal patents underwent cancellation because of his religious views. A sequence of proclamations, injunctions and other measures forbade the printing and sale of works of religious controversy. Public burnings destroyed many Protestant books. Nevertheless, the Marian regime had limited success, especially at the outset, in controlling the book trade. Indeed, two extant leaves from the ledgers of a Marian stationer demonstrate that the purchase and sale of forbidden books proceeded unchecked during the first year of the reign of Mary I. In the light of their recovery from the contemporary binding of a book published by Day, these leaves might survive from his own commercial records.[68]

Knowledge of Day's activity under Mary I is limited because many of his printing attributions are conjectural. Like some other ideologically motivated Protestant printers and publishers, Day resorted to anonymity and false imprints in order to mask surreptitious publication, confuse the authorities and mock them with sardonic imprints. It may be that he printed Lady Jane Grey's *Epistle to a Learned Man of late Fallen From the Truth of God's Word With the Words She Spake upon the Scaffold*. If Day was the printer, he turned writings that circulated in manuscript after Lady Jane's

---

[66] *STC* 22992 (1551?).   [67] *STC* 4812 (1553). See also Davis, 'John Day', 81.
[68] John N. King, 'The Account Book of a Marian Bookseller, 1553–1554', *British Library Journal* 13 (1987), 33–57.

execution into a powerful anti-Marian pamphlet. An anonymous attack on Edmund Bonner, *A Commission Sent to the Bloody Butcher Bishop of London, and to All Convents of Friars, by Satan the Devil of Hell*, is another inflammatory pamphlet possibly printed by Day.[69]

Corroboration is absent for the view that Day printed books under the pseudonym of N. Dorcaster of Wittenberg, but the printer's responsibility for ten books that bear the false imprint of Michael Wood of Rouen is now well established. These anonymous pamphlets include *Whether Christian Faith May be Kept Secret in the Heart* (attributed to John Hooper), *A Dialogue between Two Neighbours Concerning Ceremonies Now Set Up Again* (possibly by John Bale), and *A Sovereign Cordial for a Christian Conscience* (attributed to Bale or Hooper). These books offer advice and consolation to the beleaguered Protestant believers unwilling or unable to join the small minority of co-religionists who fled into exile. Other Michael Wood imprints include *A Letter Sent From a Banished Minister unto All Such as be Burdened with Persecution* and *An Excellent and Learned Meditation to be Used in These Dangerous Days of Affliction*. Of particular interest are two anonymous tracts that attack Bishop Stephen Gardiner, who served as Lord Chancellor after the accession of Mary I: *The Communication Between My Lord Chancellor and Judge Hales* and *An Admonition to the Bishops of Winchester, London, and Others*.[70]

John Foxe confirms that Day operated under the pseudonym of Michael Wood when he attests that Sir William Cooke was 'committed to vile prison, for that he suffered this our printer to print the book of Winchester *De vera obedientia*' at Stamford in Lincolnshire. Typography supports Foxe's identification of Day as 'our printer'.[71] Cooke was the brother-in-law of William Cecil, who underwrote a secret press that Day operated at Stamford according to recently discovered archival evidence.[72] (Latimer had preached at this town when he resided ten miles away at the manor of the duchess of Suffolk at Grimsthorpe.) Not only does this evidence corroborate the theory that Day produced books attributed to the press of Michael Wood in 1553–4, it also shows that Day

---

[69] *STC* 3286 (1557?), 7279. See Leslie Fairfield, 'The Mysterious Press of "Michael Wood" (1553–1554)', *Library* 5th series, 27 (1972), 226.

[70] *STC* 5160.3, 10383, 5157, 10016, 17773, 11583, 11593.

[71] *AM* (1563), 1681b. See Fairfield, 'Mysterious Press', 222–4. Two editions of *De vera obedientia* printed by Day bear the date 26 October 1553 (*STC* 11585–6). On behalf of Hugh Singleton, Joos Lambrecht appears to have printed the third edition of the translation at Wesel with an impudent colophon that locates printing at the seat of papal authority: 'Rome, before the castle of Sant' Angelo'. See *STC* 11587, 1553.

[72] Elizabeth Evenden, unpublished D.Phil. research, University of York.

continued to receive patronage from a central member of the Edwardine establishment at a time when nonconformists suffered great peril.[73]

William Cooke clearly intended to embarrass the Marian regime by enlisting Day to print this English translation of *De vera obedientia* by Stephen Gardiner, 'now Lord Chancellor and common cut-throat of England' (A3^r). A one-time supporter of the Henrician Reformation, the bishop of Winchester wrote this defence of the royal supremacy in Latin at the time of Henry VIII's schism from the Church of Rome. Republication of this text with a preface, a conclusion and ironic marginalia possibly composed by John Bale could only serve to embarrass its author as 'a slanderous traitor to the Queen and her mother', Catherine of Aragon (A6^v). In orchestrating England's return to the Church of Rome, Mary I abrogated the royal supremacy and all other changes in religion undertaken during her late father's reign. John Foxe recounts many other instances when Marian martyrs scoffed at Gardiner by citing *De vera obedientia* ironically as an authority. For example, John Bradford insulted the Lord Chancellor by declaring that he would not violate oaths sworn 'according to God's word, as you yourself have well affirmed in your book, *De vera obedientia*'. Before being burned at the stake for heresy, William Tyms goaded his interrogator, Edmund Bonner, bishop of London, by reminding him that he contributed a preface to the book, 'inveighing largely against the Bishop of Rome, reproving his tyranny and falsehood, calling his power false and pretensed. The book is extant, and you cannot deny it.'[74]

Day himself ran afoul of the Marian authorities, presumably for the printing of Michael Wood books. The exact circumstances of his arrest are unclear, but Henry Machyn attests that the government consigned Day to the Tower of London on 16 October 1554 for having printed 'naughty' books.[75] Referring to a face-to-face encounter between Day and John Rogers, Foxe confirms that 'the printer of this present book' (i.e. the *Actes and Monuments*) later underwent imprisonment at Newgate Prison, for 'like cause of religion', shortly before Rogers's execution as a heretic in February 1555.[76] Day remained in the prison until sometime in the spring of that year.[77]

---

[73] Fairfield, 'Mysterious Press', 231–2.   [74] *AM*, 1606a, 1897a.

[75] *The Diary of Henry Machyn, Citizen and Merchant-taylor of London, from A.D. 1550 to A.D. 1563*, ed. John Gough Nichols, (Camden Society o. s. 42, 1848), 72.

[76] *AM*, 1492a. Foxe also records the arrest of individuals engaged in the sale of forbidden books 'about the fifth day of October', that is, when Day was imprisoned (1473b).

[77] See Oastler, *John Day*, 9–10.

Day provided an informative retrospective account of the imposition of Marian prohibitions in the prefatory epistle, 'The Printer to the Reader', of Roger Hutchinson's *A Faithful Declaration of Christ's Holy Supper* (1560), a set of three sermons preached at Eton College in 1552. Day's explanation of why he did not publish this book before the accession of Elizabeth I applies to other titles as well:

> I have therefore taken upon me . . . to set forth and bring to light these sermons, which were given unto me by Master Roger Hutchinson, to put into print, and that a little before the death of the most godly king, King Edward the Sixth, and because immediately after his death God's true religion was overthrown and trodden most shamefully under foot by the bloody papists. I was enforced and compelled not only to surcease from printing of these sermons, but also of diverse other godly men's works.[78]

After his release from prison in 1555, Day was unable to reestablish his career as a printer-publisher in his own right for the remainder of Mary I's reign. Working for the most part as a job printer, he produced books on behalf of publishers such as Thomas Gemini, Thomas Petyt and Abraham Veale. These jobs included at least one Catholic liturgical text, *The Primer in Latin*, which Day produced for the assigns of the printer John Wayland.[79]

It appears that John Day retained ownership, or knew the location, of some of the woodblocks that he commissioned for the illustration of Edwardine books. This broke with standard practice, whereby woodblocks moved from one printing house to another. One example is the large woodcut of the execution of Anne Askew inserted as a foldout illustration for Robert Crowley's *Confutation of Thirteen Articles* (figure 2). Another is an historiated initial capital E used at the head of the dedication to Edward VI in Day's 1551 Folio Bible (figure 3). It portrays Edmund Becke, the editor, kneeling before the king in a standard dedication portrait. The polemical content or Edwardine associations of these blocks rendered them unusable under Mary I, but Day employed them after her death to illustrate Foxe's *Actes and Monuments* (1563). Day either knew where the blocks were preserved, or went to the effort of recovering them, at the outset of the Elizabethan regime.

A woodcut device and title-page border commissioned by Day were, unlike these woodcuts, used by other printers. He regained them after the accession of Elizabeth I. A single-sheet ornament bearing the arms

---

[78] *STC* 14018 (1560), A3v–4r.   [79] *STC* 16079.

Figure 3. Initial E: Edmund Becke giving his revision to Edward VI. From John Day's Folio Bible (1551), edited by Edmund Becke.

of Edward VI between a pair of pillars, at the base of which are the initials of John Day (I. D.), originally appeared in 1549.[80] Day inserted it as an additional leaf into texts such as his 1551 folio Bible. John Kingston and Henry Sutton then included an altered version of it on the title page of *Missale ad usum Sarisburiensis* (1557).[81] A woodcutter altered the initials *E.R.* (Edwardus Rex) to *M.R.* (Maria Regina) and *Rex* to *Re[gina]*. Restoration of *E.R.* rendered the device suitable to the reign of Elizabeth I, when Day inserted the device into some copies of Foxe's *Actes and Monuments* (figure 4).

[80] *STC* 7507 (McKerrow, *Devices*, no. 115).   [81] *STC* 16219.

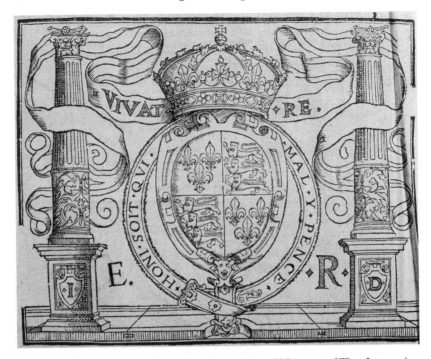

Figure 4. The Royal arms. From John Foxe, *Actes and Monuments of These Latter and Perilous Days* (1570).

Even more important is the title-page border that Day commissioned for his 1551 folio Bible (figure 5).[82] In addition to the royal arms in the compartment at the top, this border contains a trio of resurrection scenes that symbolise Day and the trade he pursued at the sign of the Resurrection. The royal arms are flanked by small images of the raising of Lazarus and of Christ's emergence from the tomb. At the bottom Day's motto 'ARISE, FOR IT IS DAY' flanks a device that depicts one man waking another at dawn. The punning allusion is to 1 Thessalonians 5: 5: 'For you are all sons of light and sons of the day; we are not of the night or of darkness.'

We do not know how John Wayland obtained this compartment, but he used it during the reign of Mary I in printing Giovanni Boccaccio's *The Fall of Princes . . . Whereunto is Added the Fall of All Such as Since that Time Were Notable in England* (1554?). As the title indicates, Wayland planned to add

[82] Reproduced from a reuse in Foxe's edition of *The Whole Works of William Tyndale, John Frith and Doctor Barnes* (1573).

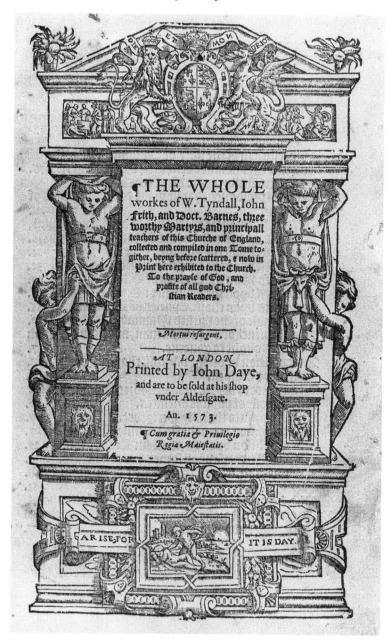

Figure 5. 'ARISE, FOR IT IS DAY.' Title-page border from John Day's *Whole Works of William Tyndale, John Frith and Doctor Barnes*, edited by John Foxe (1573).

a second part containing *A Memorial of Such Princes, as Since the Time of King Richard the Second, Have Been Unfortunate in the Realm of England* (1554?).[83] Its editor, William Baldwin, may have served as an intermediary between Wayland and Day, with whose printing house he had an intimate acquaintance. Stephen Gardiner suppressed publication of the first edition of the *Mirror for Magistrates*, of which only fragments survive, in all likelihood because he wished to block publication of *de casibus* tragedies that were overtly or covertly sympathetic to prominent members of the Edwardine establishment such as Edward Seymour.[84] Baldwin's close association with Edward Whitchurch and John Day suggests that Wayland's printing house may have served as a front that enabled prominent Protestant printers to remain active in the book trade. Despite Wayland's lowly status as a scrivener and minor printer, who had printed no books since 1539, he acquired Whitchurch's printing equipment and occupied his premises at the sign of the Sun on Fleet Street soon after Edward VI's death. The source of his capital investment and the circumstances of his acquisition are mysterious.

After the accession of Elizabeth I on 17 November 1558 led to Day's restoration to favour and reemergence as a preeminent member of the London book trade, the basis for his newfound prosperity rested upon his pre-1558 accomplishments. He resumed operations at his printing house above Aldersgate and opened a bookshop on the ground floor. He succeeded in regaining his Edwardine patent on publication of *The ABC with Little Catechism* thanks to the ascendancy of patrons such as William Cecil, principal secretary to Elizabeth, and Robert Dudley, son of the late John Dudley, who were among the most powerful members of the new regime. Through Dudley's intervention the printer received a *per septennium* privilege that granted exclusive rights to publishing one of the best-illustrated books of its age, William Cuningham's *The Cosmographical Glass*, and any other books 'compiled at Day's expense', for a period of seven years.

This vague phrase enabled Day to monopolise publication of any book that he rushed into print so long as it was not subject to another patent. When the *per septennium* privilege expired, new patents extended his monopolies on specific books to which he had claimed rights. These

---

[83] *STC* 3177.5 and 1246 (McKerrow, *Devices*, no. 116). Under Elizabeth I Day continued to use this woodcut compartment on the title pages of folio editions of religious books such as *STC* 1710, 2434 and 2462. See also R. B. McKerrow and F. S. Ferguson, *Title-page Borders in England and Scotland, 1485–1640* (Oxford, 1932), no. 76.

[84] On the politics of the *Mirror for Magistrates*, see Scott C. Lucas, 'The Suppressed Edition and the Creation of the "Orthodox" *Mirror for Magistrates*', *Renaissance Papers* (1994), 31–54.

royal patents meant he could monopolise publication of books including *The Metrical Psalter* compiled by Thomas Sternhold, John Hopkins and others. Based upon popular pre-Elizabethan precursors, this highly lucrative collection went into at least seventy-three editions published by Day.[85] Not only did these metrical translations of Psalms exemplify Edwardine court taste, the anthology also became popular as a Puritan hymnbook.

Three major collections that rest upon pre-Elizabethan precedents exerted a powerful influence upon the emergence of Elizabethan book culture. At the outset of the reign, Day published *The Works of Thomas Becon, Which He Hath Hitherto Made and Published, With Diverse Other New Books* (1560–4) in three large folio volumes.[86] In addition, he published octavo editions of individual books by Becon, including a very popular consolatory work composed, but never published, during Edward VI's reign: *The Sick Man's Salve* (1561). It went into a dozen editions before Day's death in 1584. It is worthy of note that Day stood as Becon's patron by guaranteeing surety for his first fruits at the Exchequer when the cleric received the living of the church of St Dionis, London, in 1563.[87] Day confirms that it was his custom to function as a patron who commissioned manuscripts for publication in 'John Day to the Christian Reader', the preface to Peter Morwyng's translation of Conrad Gesner's *The Treasure of Euonymus, Containing the Secrets of Nature to Distil Medicines* (1559): 'I thought it my part, by this my travail and expenses, somewhat to serve herein thy necessity. Wherefore I have caused this precious treasure to be translated into our usual and native language.'[88]

Publication of a two-part quarto edition of the sermons of Hugh Latimer, like that of *The Works of Thomas Becon*, exemplifies Day's habit of publishing expensive large-format collections of texts that had proven their profitability before Elizabeth's accession by selling well in more affordable small-format editions. It went into five editions before Day's death. Edited by Augustine Bernher, *Twenty-seven Sermons Preached by Master Hugh Latimer* consists almost wholly of sermons given during the reign of Edward VI. The second part of the collection, *Certain Godly Sermons Upon the Lord's Prayer*, is bound first in some copies. A one-time servant of Latimer, Bernher attended his master during his imprisonment in the Tower of London and in Oxford's Bocardo Prison before Latimer was burned alive for heresy on 16 October 1555.

---

[85] Davis, 'John Day', 84–5.   [86] *STC* 1710.
[87] Brett Usher, 'Backing Protestantism: The London Godly, the Exchequer and the Foxe Circle', *John Foxe: An Historical Perspective*, ed. David Loades (Aldershot, 1999), 115, 133.
[88] *STC* 11800, ✠2r.

We may note the influence of Catherine Brandon as a patron of Protestant publication, yet again, in Bernher's dedication to the duchess. He had lived at her manor at Grimsthorpe during Latimer's residence there in 1551–3. Defining the collection as a monumental summation of Edwardine religious principles that underwent reversal during the Marian reaction, Bernher attributes the project to the demand of zealous Protestant readers: 'I thought it good, at the instant request of the godly learned, to put forth these sermons here following into print, which were preached in King Edward's time, before the right honourable Lady Catherine, Duchess of Suffolk, her grace.' Bernher abbreviates his account of Latimer's martyrdom 'because these things be at large described in the Book of Martyrs'. This reference serves to advertise Foxe's martyrology. Bernher's dedicatory epistle rises to a climax in which he attributes the 'preservation of the Queen's Majesty that now is', for which Latimer tearfully prayed, and the duchess's own avoidance of execution through 'exile for Christ and his Gospel's sake' to providential intervention.[89]

In publishing the *Actes and Monuments*, Day collaborated with Foxe on their joint enterprise of collecting and republishing seminal Protestant texts composed before the accession of Elizabeth I. In some cases, they absorbed tracts that Day may have printed surreptitiously during the reign of Mary I, such as *The Communication Between My Lord Chancellor and Judge Hales* and Lady Jane Grey's *Epistle to a Learned Man With the Words She Spake upon the Scaffold*. At the outset of the reign, Day published Foxe's own edition of a text that they later absorbed into the Ridley martyrology in the *Actes and Monuments*: *A Friendly Farewell, Which Master Doctor Ridley Did Write Unto All His True Friends a Little Before He Suffered*.[90] They also included Foxe's expansion of a Marian heresy interrogation that Day published separately under his *per septennium* privilege: *The First and Second Examination of Thomas Hawkes Before Edmund Bonner, Bishop of London*.[91]

The most important set of precursors is *Certain Comfortable Letters of Such True Saints as in the Late Bloody Persecution Gave Their Lives* (1564), published by Day with a preface by Miles Coverdale.[92] Compiled anonymously by Henry Bull, it contains transcriptions of manuscript letters and documents written by imprisoned Protestant leaders such as Hugh Latimer, Nicholas Ridley, Thomas Cranmer and John Bradford as they awaited execution by being burned at the stake. Bull compiled the collection in

[89] *STC* 15276 (1562), *5v, 6v–7v. See Davis, 'John Day', 81.
[90] *STC* 21051 (1559).   [91] *STC* 12955a (1562?).   [92] *STC* 5886.

Figure 6. Portrait device of John Day. From *The Works of Thomas Becon*, vol. 1 (1564).

collaboration with John Foxe, who absorbed almost all of its transcriptions into the second edition of the *Actes and Monuments* (1570). *Certain Comfortable Letters* also incorporates Foxe's edition of Ridley's *Friendly Farewell* and fugitive texts published under Mary. They include two Michael Wood imprints that Bull and Foxe attribute to John Hooper – *Whether Christian Faith May be Kept Secret in the Heart* and *A Sovereign Cordial for a Christian Conscience* – and letters printed abroad at locations such as Wesel and Emden.[93]

John Day collaborated with Foxe in compiling the *Actes and Monuments* from a conglomeration of documents, in manuscript and print. It would never have seen the light of day without the publisher's active involvement in every phase of book construction. Published close to the outset of the reign of Elizabeth I, the collection constituted a wellspring of Elizabethan culture. Not only was it the most significant book produced by John Day as the master printer of the English Reformation, it built upon his achievement as a young printer supported by powerful patrons under Edward VI and a committed ideologue who continued to produce Protestant propaganda at risk of death under Mary I. Publication and sale of the *Actes and Monuments* at Day's Aldersgate shop was as much a summation as a new beginning for the printer. Published with a bold woodcut portrait of the printer at the very end (figure 6),[94] this book celebrates his contribution to a process of religious and social transformation with a long history before 1558.

[93] See *STC* 3480, 5999, 21051.
[94] Reproduced from an earlier use in *The Works of Thomas Becon*, vol. 1 (1564).

CHAPTER 9

Night schools, conventicles and churches: continuities and discontinuities in early Protestant ecclesiology

Patrick Collinson

I

In October 1588, as the straggling ships of the Spanish Armada were beating a north-west passage around the Scottish and Irish coasts, one Thomas Turton, a London tradesman, sat down in Nuremberg to write a letter home, addressing himself to a cobbler and peddler of illicit books, one Humphrey Newman: 'Brother Newman, I salute you in the Lord . . . I should not be unmindful of you and the rest of our brethren that fear God.' Germany had proved a sad disappointment. 'Truly I may say, London for religion is an earthly paradise to this place.' Oh for news of 'the state of our church', and of 'the rest of our brethren'!

But what was 'our church'? Not the Church of England by law established, and not one of London's many parish churches; rather a haphazard collection of 'brethren' only partly known to one another, loosely connected by a shared 'godliness', and by the peculiar religious language which they employed in signalling to each other. 'I pray you', Turton asked Newman, 'do my commendation to all our brethren that fear God.' There were particular greetings for 'William the tailor that dwelleth over Alderman Starkey's house', and for 'the young man that I bought my hat off'. John Wilkins, who could supply Newman with a certain pamphlet, could be found in the lane between Paternoster Row and the turning to Mr Archer's house, 'unto whom if you go that way do my commendations, and to his servant John'.[1]

This resembles any catalogue of London's religious dissenters which might have been compiled at any point in the sixteenth or seventeenth centuries: the same scatter of locations, the same trades, the same

---

[1] BL Additional MS 28571, 165v–166r. Turton's letter fell into the hands of those investigating the publication of the Marprelate Tracts and bears an endorsement by the future Archbishop Richard Bancroft. For the role in the Marprelate affair of Tufton's correspondent, Humphrey Newman, see Leland H. Carlson, *Martin Marprelate, Gentleman: Master Job Throkmorton Laid Open in his Colors* (San Marino, CA, 1981), 50–2, 79–80.

occasional hesitations over identity. When a spy betrayed the Protestant underground congregation in Marian London, he listed 'one James, a cobbler, dwelling in Budge Row in Well [*recte* Bell] Alley, having also a shop at St Austin's gate in Paul's churchyard. Item, a young fellow, a butcher, dwelling in Shoreditch, whose name he knoweth not. Item, one William Ellerby, tailor, dwelling in St Clement's Lane, by Lombard Street, in St Edmund's parish. Item, one John Osborne, dwelling at Lambeth town, a silk dyer.'[2] (In 1528 a Lollard had identified 'Thomas Tyllesworth, tailor, dwelling in Bugg Row' as 'of his sect'.[3]) In the 1630s an account of the sect which called itself the Family of Love would name 'one Edward Hill, a tailor and his wife in Seething Lane', 'one James Bagg, a heelmaker in Little All Hallows in Thames Street', and 'two leather sellers in one house in Paul's churchyard, one his name is Richard – as you go into Cheapside, the next shop to the gate'.[4]

It may be that Turton's 'brethren', or some of them, already belonged to the separated and 'gathered' church which was about to be galvanised by the leadership of Thomas Barrow, and, after him, Francis Johnson. London's prisons were places for the godly to become better acquainted, schools of intransigent separatism from the Church of England.[5] This, too, was a replay of scenes enacted in Mary's reign, when it was said that 'all the prisons in England were become right Christian schools and churches'.[6] The memory of the Marian persecution retained by a group of imprisoned London separatists in the 1560s was graphic and points forward to the experience of the 'Brownists' of the 1590s: 'That

---

[2] 'The information of Roger Sergeant', *AM* (1563), 1632. Sergeant's 'information', together with the evidence given to Bishop Bonner by other members of the London congregation, was omitted from subsequent editions of the *Actes and Monuments*. According to another witness 'the said multitude called one another "brother"'. For some plausible reasons why Foxe became cautious in what he published about the history of the secret congregation in Marian London, see Brett Usher, '"In a Time of Persecution": New Light on the Secret Protestant Congregation in Marian London', *John Foxe and the English Reformation*, ed. David Loades (Aldershot, 1997), 233–51.

[3] BL Harleian MS 421, 13v.   [4] PRO SP 16/520/85.

[5] *The Writings of Henry Barrow, 1587–1590*, ed. L. H. Carson, Elizabethan Nonconformist Texts, iii (1962); *The Writings of John Greenwood 1587–1590*, ed. L. H. Carson, Elizabethan Nonconformist Texts, iv (1962); B. R. White, *The English Separatist Tradition* (Oxford, 1971), 67–115; Champlin Burrage, *The Early English Dissenters in the Light of Recent Research (1550–1641)* (2 vols., Cambridge, 1912); Patrick Collinson, 'Separating In and Out of the Church: The Consistency of Barrow and Greenwood', *The Journal of the United Reformed Church History Society*, 5 (1994), 239–58.

[6] *AM*, 1531. The Sussex brewer Dirick Carver, no longer a young man, spent his time in prison learning to read, with the result that, by the time of his death, he 'could read perfectly any printed English'. (Ibid., 1682.) The 1563 edition of *Actes and Monuments* has on p. 1260 'A Picture describing the manner and place of them which were in bonds for the testimony of the truth, conferring together among themselves'.

persecution grew so fast as that it brought many a hundred to know one another that never knew before.'[7]

What was it to 'know one another', to know and be known? Back in the mid-fifteenth century, Bishop Reginald Pecocke had reported of an earlier group of London dissenters: 'They give a name proper to themselves and call themselves *"known men"*, as though all other than them be unknown.'[8] In 1511 in Coventry, where the Lollards had a 'secretum vocabulum inter eos' (a secret language among themselves), Alice Rowley, the widow of a former mayor, was said to be 'a known man'.[9] In the Chiltern Hills of Buckinghamshire, a few years later, the expression 'known men' and also 'just fast men', was again recorded, while a Lollard who fell into the bishop's clutches was, his wife bewailed, 'an undone man'.[10] Presently, one Colchester man said of another that he 'hath been taken and reputed totally by the space of a twelve month last past as a known man and a brother in Christ amongst them that be called brethren and known men'.[11] (And here we detect a possibly significant shift in the 'secretum vocabulum', from 'known man' to 'brother in Christ'.)

We can discover in the often fugitive evidence of dissent further cultural continuities, linking the years before and after the Reformation. Rychard Wyche was burned on Tower Hill in 1440, the last of those founding fathers who had distilled the doctrine of John Wyclif into a popular heresy. His ashes, supposedly sweet-smelling (an amateur apothecary

---

7 Peter Lorimer, *John Knox and the Church of England* (1875), 300.

8 Reginald Pecock, *The Repression of Over Much Blaming of the Clergy*, ed. C. Babington, Rolls Series 19, I, II (1860), i. 53–4.

9 Staffordshire Record Office, Lichfield Episcopal Archives BC 13. See J. H. Fines, 'Heresy Trials in the Diocese of Coventry and Lichfield, 1511–12', *JEH* 13 (1962), 160–74; Imogen Luxton, 'The Lichfield Court Book: A Postscript', *Bulletin of the Institute of Historical Research* 44 (1971), 120–5. The most authoritative account of the 'vocabulum secretum' is Anne Hudson, 'A Lollard Sect Vocabulary?', in her *Lollards And Their Books* (London and Ronceverte, WV, 1985), 165–80. It is also a very cautious account, since Hudson is not wholly convinced that there *was* a distinctive Lollard vocabulary or idiom. Hudson reports (167–8) that Bishop Pecock thought the origin of the term 'known man' was in 1 Corinthians 14: 38, but suggests that the more likely source was 2 Corinthians 6: 8, 'sicut qui ignoti, et cogniti', a phrase translated and explained in the Lollard sermon-cycle as 'unknown and known men to God and saints'.

10 *AM*, 818, 820, 821.

11 BL Harleian MS 421, 21. William Raynard deposed that Robert Best had been taken 'as a known man and of the brotherhood'. See ibid., 25v. In earlier heresy trials in the diocese of London, we come across the variant 'privy man'. See Trinity College Dublin, MS 775, 123v–24r; I owe this reference to Susan Brigden. The Norwich heresy trials of 1428–31 contain no mention of 'known men'. The Norfolk Lollards appear to have identified themselves with 'Christ's people', 'God's people', 'Christian people', 'true Christ's people' and 'every good Christian man'. See *Heresy Trials in the Diocese of Norwich, 1428–1431*, ed. Norman Tanner, Camden Society 4th series 20 (1977), 111–2, 115–6, 147, 153, 165–6. These records contain striking examples of the Lollard 'secretum vocabulum', including some clever word games, such as 'shakelment' for sacrament. See ibid., 81.

had seen to that), were no sooner cold than they became an object of devotion and Wyche a 'saint', an instant cult instantly suppressed by turning the site into a dunghill.[12] More than a century later, there was a similar popular response to the Marian burnings, the Catholic polemicist Miles Huggarde describing how the common people of London coveted as relics the bones of 'these stinking martyrs', wallowing in the very ashes in their efforts 'to scrape in that heretical dunghill for the said bones', and even grating them into a powder for medicinal purposes.[13] In Suffolk in 1555 a search was made for two men who were carrying about the bones of a martyr and showing them to the people. At the burning of John Hullier on Jesus Green in Cambridge, 'the people' competed for what 'they could get of him, as pieces of bones. One had his heart, the which was distributed so far as it would go. One took the scalp and looked for the tongue, but it was consumed except the very root.'[14] Neatly bisecting these events of the 1440s and 1550s was the execution in Smithfield in April 1494 of the octogenarian Joan Boughton. The night after her burning, the ashes were removed to be 'kept for a precious relic in an earthen pot'.[15] Four years later, in faraway Florence, there would be a similar scramble for the remains of Savonarola.[16] John Foxe wrote in his preface to the *Actes and Monuments*, 'The utility and profit of this history': 'Full well did the zeal of ancient Christians declare this thing, which flocked together with fervent desire unto the ashes of the Martyrs, and kissed even the very chains wherewith they were tied.'[17] Lollard and Marian martyrs alike were encouraged with cries that if their breakfast was sharp, their supper would be merry.[18]

---

[12] *Chronicles of London*, ed. C. L. Kingsford (Oxford, 1905), 147, 153–4; *The Historical Collections of a Citizen of London in the Fifteenth Century*, ed. James Gairdner, Camden Society 2nd series 17 (1876), 183; *An English Chronicle of the Reigns of Richard II, Henry IV, Henry V and Henry VI*, ed. J. S. Davies, Camden Society o.s. 44 (1856), 56; John A. F. Thomson, *The Later Lollards 1414–1520* (Oxford, 1965), 148–51.

[13] Miles Huggarde, *The displaying of the protestantes* (1556), 54.

[14] BL Harleian MS 419, 133; *AM*, 2004.

[15] Thomson, *Later Lollards*, 156. It is not clear on what grounds Shannon McSheffrey thought this act 'contrary to the usual behaviour of Lollards'. See her *Gender & Heresy: Women and Men in Lollard Communities 1420–1530* (Philadelphia, 1995), 148. But it was not, of course, 'usual behaviour' for Lollards to be burned in the first place. Most preferred abjuration.

[16] Luca Landucci, *Diario fiorentino dal 1450 a 1516*, ed. I. del Badia (Florence, 1883), 178, 125. For other examples, Europe-wide and across confessional divides, of heretic martyr 'saints' and their cults, see B. Gregory, *Salvation at Stake: Christian Martyrdom in Early Modern Europe* (Cambridge, MA, 1999), especially 175–6, 298–301.

[17] *AM* (1563), B6r. Foxe modified this passage in subsequent editions: 'with what admiration, and almost superstition, not only the memory but also the relics of those good Martyrs were received and kept amongst the ancient Christians.' See *AM*, *5r; Tom Freeman helped me with this point.

[18] Thomson, *Later Lollards*, 73; *AM*, 2005.

So far we have proceeded not by argument but by a series of resonances and correspondences. These have little explanatory power, but they do suggest and illustrate some of the continuities of religious dissent: not continuities in doctrine or organisation, the concern of ecclesiastical historians and religious sociologists, but in those areas of popular culture which seem to have been instinctive, inherited and even if learnt none the less spontaneous; people knowing, in certain circumstances, what to do and how to behave – as with that (to us mysterious) shaming ritual, the street theatre known as a 'skimmington'.[19] A. G. Dickens and his pupil, Kenneth Powell, have argued that many new Protestants were but old Lollards writ large, and that some Marian martyrs died for holding essentially Wycliffite beliefs.[20] That may well have been so, although the evidence is clouded by the old-fashioned formularies used by judges of heresy to process the evidence.[21] But whether or not they believed the same things, these people *did* the same things, the martyrs and sympathetic spectators of their sufferings acting out a theatre of martyrdom with a traditional, inherited and probably internalised script. This is the stuff of a kind of historical anthropology, uncovering fundamental infrastructures of religious experience and expression. And it enables and liberates the historian of dissent in the *longue durée* of the fourteenth to eighteenth centuries, who no longer has to prove consistency and strict succession in doctrine.

The case for a more overt dissenting continuity has been made, from very different standpoints and with different methodologies, by Christopher Hill and Margaret Spufford. Hill, in his essay 'From Lollards to Levellers', posited two kinds of linkage between fifteenth-century and seventeenth-century 'radicals': one geographical and, as it were, ecological, certain localities having a persistent tendency to breed dissent; the other mental. 'I think that we can trace direct links in ideas from Lollards, through Familists and Anabaptists, to the radical sectaries, the Levellers, Diggers, Ranters and Quakers of the mid-seventeenth century'; 'a continuing underground tradition', a 'radical

---

[19] Martin Ingram, 'Ridings, Rough Music and the "Reform of Popular Culture" in Early Modern England', *Past & Present* 105 (1984), 79–113.

[20] A. G. Dickens, *Lollards and Protestants in the Diocese of York 1509–1558* (Oxford, 1959); A. G. Dickens, 'Heresy and the Origins of English Protestantism', in his *Reformation Studies* (1982), 363–82; K. G. Powell, 'The beginnings of Protestantism in Gloucestershire', *Transactions of the Bristol and Gloucester Archaeological Society* 90 (1971), 141–57; K. G. Powell, *The Marian martyrs and the Reformation in Bristol*, Historical Association Bristol Pamphlets 31 (1972).

[21] The surest guide to the problem of formulaic and prompted confessions of belief is Hudson, 'The Examination of Lollards', *Lollards And Their Books*, 125–40.

heritage'.[22] Spufford, who for rather different reasons would like to believe in a kind of sectarian genealogy directly linking Lollards with Baptists and Quakers, shares Hill's interest in particular localities, the Buckinghamshire Chilterns especially, but with the aid of her gifted pupils it is more sharply focused and better documented. And she hopes to demonstrate a dissenting tradition passed down, as it were genetically, through certain bloodlines. These are possibilities, but no more than that, and they are not the subject of this essay.[23]

My subject is both the cultural continuities illustrated by my opening snapshots, and a discontinuity within the continuities which was the Protestant Reformation, as it impacted on the consciousnesses of the kinds of people named in Turton's letter, or in the annals of the Marian persecution, or in the trials of Lollards in Coventry or Buckinghamshire. The essence of that discontinuity was the conviction, which may have been wholly or relatively absent before the Reformation, that these loosely associated cells, or networks, of 'brethren' and 'known men', were churches, indeed constituted the only true church, confronting the false anti-church of their persecutors – and neighbours.

This is the story, hard to piece together, of how 'schools of heresy', or 'conventicles' – both pejorative terms used to criminalise what may have been relatively innocuous household gatherings for a religious and sociable purpose – became Protestant congregations, underground or 'privy' churches. As such they, or much of their human material, were eventually incorporated into the reformed establishment of Elizabeth I and her successors; or so we may suppose. Through this largely unrecorded but critical process, a sect-type ecclesiology (to speak in Troeltschian terms) was abandoned for a church-type.[24]

But some recalcitrant elements may never have been absorbed into mainstream Protestantism, while tensions and conflicts within the Church created conditions in which the pre-Reformation practice of

---

[22] Christopher Hill, 'From Lollards to Levellers', *Rebels and their Causes: Essays in Honour of A. L. Morton*, ed. Maurice Cornforth (1978), 49–67, reprinted in Hill's *Collected Essays*, ii (Brighton, 1986), 89–116. But in a later essay, 'A Bourgeois Revolution?', Hill was a little more cautious: 'Whether or not there was a continuing underground from Lollards via Anabaptists and Familists to the sectaries of the 1640s...'. See *Three British Revolutions, 1641, 1688, 1776*, ed. J. G. A. Pocock (Princeton, 1980), 114.

[23] *The World of Rural Dissenters 1520–1725*, ed. Margaret Spufford (Cambridge, 1995). For some reservations about the Spufford thesis, see my 'Critical Conclusion', 388–96.

[24] Ernst Troeltsch, *The Social Teaching of the Christian Churches*, trans. Olive Wyon (2 vols., 1931); Betty R. Scharf, 'Church, Sect and Denomination', in her *The Sociological Study of Religion* (1970), 93–119; Michael Hill, 'Church and Sect', in his *A Sociology of Religion* (1973), 47–70.

gathering in conventicles repeated itself. As Peter Lake has argued in mapping what he calls 'the London puritan underground', the dynamic of godly Protestant 'insiderhood' was always capable of generating its own instabilities and divisions, especially in the religious melting pot of the metropolis.[25]

Some of these groups were separatist, deliberately detaching themselves from fellowship with the established Church and claiming the status of uniquely true churches. But the membership of these gathered churches was never stable, some prominent members, and no doubt many less prominent, separating against separatism and coming back out of the cold into the parish church system.[26] Individuals, such as Lake's friend, the boxmaker John Etherington, shopped around through a long lifetime of eclectic investigation of the religious options on offer. But Etherington's final destination, if he had one, was not separatist, or so he affirmed: 'I never was in any private assembly in my life where I have either received the sacrament myself nor seen it done by others, so that for mine own part I am neither schismatic nor separatist.'[27] Many, and probably most, conventicles, to call them that, were never separatist, or only had a separatist potential, replicating or perpetuating a relationship to the majority Church better termed semi-separatist. This was another of our continuities, running from the early fifteenth century to the late seventeenth. But it lies beyond the chronology of this collection of essays and I have investigated it elsewhere.[28]

II

What students of religious forms and practices would call the phenomenology of the Lollard movement, between the early fifteenth and early sixteenth centuries, has not received as much attention from historians as the beliefs of the Lollards. This is the approach of traditional ecclesiastical history, rooted in doctrine.[29] Moreover, the beliefs in question have often been identified and classified in negative terms, denials

---

[25] Peter Lake, *The Boxmaker's Revenge: 'Orthodoxy', 'heterodoxy' and the politics of the parish in early Stuart London* (Manchester, 2001), 170–83, 406–9.

[26] Patrick Collinson, 'Separation In and Out of the Church', and Collinson, 'Sects and the evolution of Puritanism', *Puritanism: trans-Atlantic perspectives on a seventeenth-century Anglo-American faith*, ed. Francis Bremer (Boston, MA, 1993), 147–66.

[27] Lake, *The Boxmaker's Revenge*, 95.

[28] Patrick Collinson, 'The English Conventicle', *Voluntary Religion*, ed. W. J. Sheils and Diana Wood, *SCH* 23 (1986), 223–59.

[29] Thomson, *Later Lollards*.

of orthodox belief rather than affirmations of those positive convictions which may have nourished the piety of those often obscure and poorly documented groups. This is a reflection of the interest of inquisitors, who both perceived and convicted those brought before them as negators of Catholic doctrine. Sniffers-out of heresy, it has been said, were not capable of identifying their quarry in any other terms than that of an anti-church. But this does not necessarily mean that that was what it was.[30]

On these foundations, historians have been ready, perhaps too ready, to identify the gatherings of Lollards as in some sense churches, 'congregations'. This bears the mark of denominational history, writers such as W. H. Summers (and no one knew more about the environment of Lollardy in the Chiltern Hills) looking for evidence of 'Our Lollard Ancestors'; 'our' relating to Summers's own Congregationalist denomination.[31] And from there it is but a short step to speculation about the kinds of 'services' the Lollards may have conducted, which and what sacraments they may have celebrated, and how, and whether women were allowed to celebrate.[32] It is the beginning of wisdom to approach the phenomenology of this subject on the basis of what we know, which is not enough to justify all these assumptions.

Norman Tanner, in his edition of the 1428–31 Norwich heresy trials, suggests that the Lollard sectarian vocabulary was employed 'in the context of worship', whereas the trial records contain no evidence of any activity which could properly be called 'worship'.[33] Indeed, to my knowledge, after the early years of the movement there is no record whatsoever of Lollards meeting for a liturgical purpose, or even to pray. We

---

[30] Euan Cameron, *The Reformation of the Heretics: the Waldenses of the Alps 1480–1580* (Oxford, 1984), 261. The line I take in this essay is supported by Richard G. Davies in 'Lollardy and Locality', *Transactions of the Royal Historical Society* 6th series 1 (1991), 191–212 and especially 192 and 212: 'If Wycliffitism was what you knew, Lollardy was whom you knew.' See also McSheffrey, *Gender and Heresy*, especially 10, 45–6, 139–40: 'Certainly adherence to Lollardy was partly about religiosity, about a search for a more meaningful approach to religious life and expression. It was also about belonging.' See also an influential essay by Natalie Zemon Davis, 'Some Tasks and Themes in the Study of Popular Religion', *The Pursuit of Holiness in Late Medieval and Renaissance Religion*, ed. Charles Trinkhaus and Heiko A. Oberman (Leiden, 1974), 307–36.

[31] W. H. Summers, *Our Lollard Ancestors* (1904); W. H. Summers, *The Lollards of the Chiltern Hills: Glimpses of English Dissent in the Middle Ages* (1906).

[32] Margaret Aston, 'Lollard Women Priests?', in her *Lollards and Reformers: Images and Literacy in Late Medieval Religion* (1984), 49–70. Aston begins her discussion with the sensible comment: 'We know, indeed, very little about Lollard rites of any kind.' But even this suggests that there were such things as Lollard 'rites'. But for evidence of Lollard masses in the early years, particularly relating to the Lollard 'priest' William Ramsbury, see Hudson, 'A Lollard Mass', *Lollards And Their Books*, 111–23.

[33] *Heresy Trials* ed. Tanner, 28.

know that, unlike the Bohemian Hussites, they had no hymns or songs, and Anne Hudson has suggested that this was one of the reasons why their premature 'reformation' proved abortive.[34] Susan Brigden, noting that Lollardy was 'a faith practised in homes, not churches', tells us that her London heretics did not meet to pray. 'Vocal prayer was but "lip labour".'[35] We have no evidence that Lollards practised their own initiation rites, though it must surely have survived if they did, since these would have been of great interest to the inquisitors. (Some Lollards denied the efficacy of or need for baptism or confirmation, evidence which Foxe scouted, but that was another matter.[36])

What is fully and repeatedly documented is the Lollard practice of imparting lessons, either in the form of passages of scripture, read or recited from memory, or aphoristic statements, close in form to proverbs, containing denials of orthodox Catholic doctrine or, more rarely, positive affirmations of their own faith. Where conditions made this possible, these heretical lessons were taught and learnt in conventicles attended by members of more than one household. These gatherings were sometimes called, presumably by hostile and suspicious authorities and other outsiders, 'schools of heresy'. So it was that Mrs Hawisia Moone of Loddon in Norfolk confessed, in words put into her mouth in 1430, to have 'oft times kept, held and continued schools of heresy in privy chambers and privy places of ours, in the which schools I have heard, conceived, learned and reported the errors and heresies which be written and contained in these indentures'.[37] A century later Thomas More would complain of 'night schools'.[38] And as late as December 1557, at the height of the Marian persecution in Essex, a correspondent of Bishop Bonner reported on the 'rank heretics' of Great Bentley, who met sometimes in one house, sometimes in another, 'and there keep their privy conventicles and schools of heresy'.[39]

---

[34] Anne Hudson, *The Premature Reformation: Wycliffite Texts and Lollard History* (Oxford, 1988), 512. Hudson speaks helpfully (513) of 'an unpalatable restriction of the holy to the intellect'. Shannon McSheffrey, whose *Gender and Heresy* argues, contrary to a common assumption, that Lollardy was not especially attractive to women, suggests (138) that Lollardy attacked those aspects of late medieval Catholicism 'that most reflected popular creativity, and thus women's devotion'.

[35] Susan Brigden, *London and the Reformation* (Oxford, 1989), 87–8.

[36] *Heresy Trials*, ed. Tanner, 52, 60, 66, 81, 86, 94–5, 107, 111, 115, 121, 131, 134, 140, 146, 153, 159–60, 165, 169, 176, 182, 185, 196; *AM*, 661; John A. F. Thomson, 'John Foxe and some Sources for Lollard History: Notes for a Critical Appraisal', *SCH* 2 (1965), 253–4.

[37] *Heresy Trials*, ed. Tanner, 140.

[38] Gordon Rupp, *Six Makers of English Religion 1500–1700* (1957), 16; Thomas More, *Dialogue concerning Heresies*, ed. Thomas Lawler et al. (New Haven and London, 1981), 328; Brigden, *London and the Reformation*, 87.

[39] *AM*, 2006.

One condition for such gatherings must have been the availability
of a house large enough to accommodate such a gathering in reasonable safety, and to provide ample food and drink. The Moones of
Loddon were yeomen farmers of some substance. They employed servants and were, in Hawisia Moone's statement, 'right homely and privy
with many heretics', who included four priests, fifteen other named persons, 'and many others'.[40] A hundred years later the investigation by
Bishop Longland of Lincoln into the activities of the Lollards of the
Chiltern Hills, who according to Derek Plumb 'had a very high profile
in their communities', uncovered the same sorts of safe houses at Iver
Court, Staines, the household of the affluent patriarch 'Old Durdant',
and at Amersham, where Robert Bartlett was a seriously rich man and a
leading figure.[41] The adherents of that shadowy sect, the Family of Love
in late sixteenth-century Cambridgeshire, investigated by Christopher
Marsh, benefited in similar ways from the substance and the leading
role in village society enjoyed by their leaders. These Familists appear
to have perpetuated an old Lollard tradition in moving from one safe
location to another, networking with the aid of their own 'vocabulum
secretum' and finding wives for themselves.[42]

However, heretical lessons seem to have been communicated by means
of one-to-one tutorials as much as in well-attended schools of heresy.
Bishop Longland's thought police were told about Agnes Ashford of
Chesham, who had taught the fifth chapter of St Matthew's Gospel to
James Morden, 'and five times went he to the foresaid Agnes to learn
this lesson'.[43]

In 1511–12 a major drive against heresy was mounted in Kent under
the auspices of Archbishop Warham of Canterbury, and by a high-
powered team of investigators who included Bishops Fisher of Rochester
and Nykke of Norwich, together with the future bishop of Durham and
London, Cuthbert Tunstall. The copious record of these trials contains
only one reference to a conventicle (significantly, perhaps, in and around
Maidstone), and none to 'schools of heresy'. Either the inquisitors were
not interested in illegal and suspicious gatherings of this nature, but only

---

[40] *Heresy Trials*, ed. Tanner, 140.
[41] *AM*, 818–36; Derek Plumb, 'The social and economic status of the later Lollards', and 'A gathered
church? Lollards and their society', *World of Rural Dissenters*, ed. Spufford, 103–63.
[42] Christopher Marsh, *The Family of Love in English Society, 1550–1630* (Cambridge, 1994); Christopher
Marsh, 'The gravestone of Thomas Lawrence revisited (or the Family of Love and the local
community in Balsham, 1560–1630)', *World of Rural Dissenters*, ed. Spufford, 208–34.
[43] *AM*, 823. James Morden was a relative. For the interrelationships of the Ashfords and Mordens,
see McSheffrey, *Gender and Heresy*, 104–5.

in establishing a chain of heretical contamination from one person to another; or, more probably, these Kentish Lollards, whose heretical opinions in some cases went back for decades, held no such meetings. For the majority were artisans from the industrial villages of the Weald (a cutler, a glover, two tailors, several weavers), whose modest domestic circumstances would have ruled out being as 'homely' as the Moones of Loddon or Old Durdant at Iver Court. They learnt their lessons and shared their opinions one to one, at the loom, by the fireside, in the local pub, in the garden, in walking along the road, and even in church. These heretics were insistent, as the twenty-two-year-old tailor Christopher Grebill of Cranbrook attested, that there were 'none other person or persons that heard the said communication but only they two'; while his father, John Grebill of Benenden, when asked who else had been present at his dealings with the veteran heresiarch William Carder, 'he saith none'. William Ryche of Benenden, a glover by trade, was another disciple of Carder who testified that when they communed of such things there was present 'no person at no time, for they would never make anybody privy nor of counsel when they went about such matters'.[44]

It may beggar belief that the essential substance of early sixteenth-century Kentish Lollardy should have consisted of a traffic in Chinese whispers. What did it do for the heretical convert to be persuaded, sworn to secrecy, that the sacrament of the altar was not transubstantiated but remained bread, if he or she were quite bereft of the 'Protestant' experience of meeting with likeminded believers in appropriate acts of communal and sectarian devotion? We cannot say.

The Warham trials contain only a fragment of evidence which may point to the existential experience of being a Lollard. Christopher Grebill of Cranbrook told his judges that he had been taught his heretical beliefs by his parents. 'But he saith that he hath no feeling in that matters of errors till he heard John Ive teach him and till he saw in John Ive's books', when he was already nineteen years of age.[45] But if we want to know what Christopher Grebill meant by 'feeling', we find ourselves in a foreign country where people spoke a different language. One could write a whole book about 'feeling', across the centuries. Although Grebill had imbibed these heresies with his mother's milk, did he need to have

---

[44] *Kent Heresy Proceedings 1511–12*, ed. Norman Tanner, Kent Records (Maidstone, 1997), 4–5, 11–12, 45–6, 54–5.

[45] Ibid., 20. Christopher's brother John deposed that although his parents had taught him heretical opinions 'many times' when he was fourteen or fifteen years of age, 'he never could perceive their teachings nor give any heart thereunto till this year last past'. See ibid., 21.

them confirmed by someone outside his own family? So some of the history of modern sects and cults may suggest. But in the early sixteenth century? Facing evidence filtered through the formularies and expectations of tribunals and the long-lost mentalities and languages of Wealden peasants and craftsmen, we may have to say 'pass'.[46]

Perhaps what Christopher Grebill testified suggests what the religious experience of being a Lollard may have been really about: not only or principally the negative and intrinsically barren denial of orthodox Catholic belief and structures, which was what interested their interrogators, but a newly discovered New Testament 'feeling' of what it was to be a Christian, even the experience of being born again. Of this there is some suggestive evidence in the Buckinghamshire trials, albeit subject, as always, to interpretation. When Thomas Hardyng's wife saw the wealthy Richard Bartlett coming into her house, she said that here was a good man, 'and I hope he will be a good man', but that his wheelings and dealings in property had distracted his mind from 'all goodness'. A later generation would have called Bartlett a 'backslider'. Thomas Rowland of Amersham was quoted as saying: 'Ah good Lord, where is all our good communication which was wont to be among us when your master was alive?'[47] It seems unlikely that this 'communication' consisted only of sterile denials of the efficacy of baptism, or of the eucharist, or of going on pilgrimage. More likely it meant a reappropriation of the religious world of the New Testament.

Pious verbal capsules, apparently current among the Lollards, resemble the slogans of perfectly orthodox guilds and fraternities. Among three Lollards, herding cattle in the fields, one would say, 'Now the son of the living God help us', to which another would reply, 'Now Almighty God so do.'[48] The heretical character of the curriculum aside, the methods of instruction employed in Lollard conventicles were not different from the household readings and catechisings advocated by the entirely orthodox monk of Syon Abbey, Richard Whitford. Whitford wrote, 'A very good sure pastime upon the holy day is to read or to hear this book or such other good English books as you can. For I tell you there should be no time lost nor misspent upon the

---

[46] But see Shannon McSheffrey's discussion of 'Lollards and the Family', and, specifically, 'Parents and Children', in her *Gender and Heresy*, 80–107.

[47] *AM*, 821, 826.

[48] Ibid., 819. The 'secretum vocabulum' of the Coventry Lollards included the saying: 'May we all drink of a cup, and at the departing God keep you and God bless you.' See Staffordshire Archives, Lichfield Episcopal Archives BC 13.

holy day.'[49] Another close parallel is provided by the household meetings held for the purpose of sermon repetition in the Elizabethan
and Jacobean church.[50] Eamon Duffy's justly celebrated *The Stripping
of the Altars* restores the vital juice of a living faith to our late medieval Catholic ancestors.[51] But we need to acknowledge, as Duffy
does not, the religious vitality of those subjects of Henry VII and
Henry VIII who stood somewhat apart from the Church of the social
majority.

III

Still eluding us is the sociological and ecclesiological substance of the
shared experience of being a Lollard. Let us first deal with the distract-
ing presence of the word 'sect' in both primary and secondary sources.
Foxe's account of the Norwich trials of 1428–31 both draws upon some
depositions which apparently no longer exist in manuscript, and distorts,
at least in the language he employs, the records which do survive, and
which have been edited by Dr Tanner.[52] So we are entitled to treat with
some caution the evidence supposedly given by a certain William Wright
that William Taylor of Ludney was 'one of the sect', the Moones were
'of the same sect', that John Perker of a village near Ipswich was 'a famous doctor of that sect', and that a certain Tuck 'knoweth all of that
sect in Suffolk, Norfolk, and Essex'.[53] However, it is more certain that
a hundred years later the Lollard teacher John Hacker spoke of various
individuals as 'of his learning and sect', 'of his sect and learning', 'of
his learning and opinions', 'of the same sect', and 'one of this respon-
dent's disciples'; while the paintmaker Thomas Philip admitted to being

---

49 Richard Whitford, *A werke for housholders, or for them that haue the gydynge or of ony company* (1530 and
many subsequent editions), D2v.
50 Collinson, 'English Conventicle', 240–4. Another activity in the Elizabethan/Jacobean conventicle or household and a reinforcement of an at least invented continuity was the reading of
Foxe's *Actes and Monuments*. The relapsed Separatist Peter Fairlambe testified that he had read
'the first column' (volume?) of Foxe 'four times over in one winter distinctly'. See *The recantation
of a Brownist. Or, a reformed puritan* (1606), C3.
51 Eamon Duffy, *The Stripping of the Altars: Traditional Religion in England 1400–1580* (New Haven and
London, 1992).
52 *Heresy Trials*, ed. Tanner, 8; Thomson, 'John Foxe', 252–4; Patrick Collinson, 'Truth and Legend:
The Veracity of John Foxe's Book of Martyrs', in Collinson, *Elizabethan Essays* (London and
Rio Grande, OH, 1994), 151–77. A good example of Foxe's doctoring of the record through
language is his rendering of a description of the Lollard martyr William White current in Norfolk,
'sanctissimus et doctissimus doctor legis divinae' and 'magnus sanctus in celo' (*Heresy Trials*,
ed. Tanner, 45, 47) as 'a true preacher of the law of God' and 'a good and godly man'. See
Collinson, 'Truth and Legend', 173.
53 *AM*, 665.

'of Hacker's sect', and John Pykas of Colchester named various persons as being 'of the same sect and learning' as himself.[54]

But the construction 'sect and learning' is formulaic and was not unprompted, while the formula may be suggestive of shared heretical opinions rather than 'sect' as understood by Troeltsch or Bryan Wilson and other modern sociologists of religion.[55] The Chilterns evangelist Thomas Man, who was burned in 1518, was credited with having converted no less than 700 people not to his 'sect' but 'to his religion and doctrine', although elsewhere the Buckinghamshire trials (if Foxe is quoting accurately) do contain a reference to 'the sect of the heretics', which may indicate something of social substance.[56] However, it is not clear that Derek Plumb, who credits his Chilterns Lollards with belonging to 'a gathered church', is entitled to refer to 'members of the sect'. 'Membership' of an affinity, or tendency, without regularised leadership, rites of initiation, discipline or common funds, may not be the right concept. And when John Thomson asserts that some Berkshire Lollards 'definitely described themselves as a sect', and that Lollards in general 'are entitled to be considered as a sect', it appears that he has not given sufficient thought to what one of the Berkshire men may have meant when he spoke (and once again, the words may not have been his) of those 'of our sect and opinions'.[57]

Sects in socio-religious taxonomy are radically separatist, distinguished from churches by inversion. The only thing they have in common with churches (on the model, especially, of the Roman Catholic Church) is that they make equally exclusive and intolerant demands and claims. Their own small world is as exalted and totalitarian in belief and organisation as the 'urbe et orbe' world of Catholicism. The Lollards do not seem to have inhabited such a world. There is evidence from more than one place that they went to mass along with their neighbours, and did not hold meetings which clashed with parish church services. At Amersham, where they ran the town, they were sufficiently self-confident to behave with ostentatious contempt when the sacrament was elevated, behaviour which would have been fatal in the reign of Mary. But they had to be in

---

[54] BL Harleian MS 421, 11v–14v, 21v, 22r, 26v.

[55] Troeltsch, *Social Teaching*; B. R. Wilson, *Sects and Society: A Sociological Study of Three Religious Groups in Britain* (1961); B. R. Wilson, *Patterns of Sectarianism* (1967); B. R. Wilson, *Religious Sects: A Sociological Study* (1970). 'Sect' was clearly employed in a non-Troeltschian sense indicative of no more than shared opinion when Stephen Kempe deposed (in the 1530s) that the Augustinian canon and academic Robert Barnes was 'likewise of the same sect'. See BL Cotton MS Cleopatra E.v, 398.

[56] *AM*, 818, 821.

[57] Plumb, 'A gathered church?'; Thomson, *Later Lollards*, 81, 239. Shannon McSheffrey prefers to speak of Lollard 'communities'. See *Gender and Heresy*, 15–20 and *passim*.

church to do that. Some Amersham women who met in an all-female conventicle in the house of Joan Collingworth went there 'when they go and come from the church'.[58] The act books of the archdeaconry of Buckingham record only seven cases of failure to attend mass between 1483 and 1523.[59] Evidently, whatever brought the Chilterns Lollards to the attention of the authorities, it was not absence from church. In Coventry, where the Lollards were a small and exposed minority, they behaved in church with exceptional devotion – Foxe suspected 'to colour the matter'.[60]

The outward conformity of many Lollards was more than a deceitful subterfuge. In the face of great legal, moral and social pressures, it is not surprising that they should have chosen to toe a line, the line taken by many post-Reformation Catholics, which provided the maximum of self-determining capacity and the minimum of destructive isolation.[61] A similar strategy of endogamous and exogamous integration characterised Christopher Marsh's Elizabethan Familists, and the Baptists and Quakers of late seventeenth-century Cambridgeshire and Huntingdonshire studied by Bill Stevenson.[62] Abandoning sociological jargon, this may be called having your cake and eating it. Respectable householders who witnessed the wills of their nonsectarian neighbours and even bore office in the parish church benefited simultaneously from the tight network of the semi-sectarian brotherhood, and preferred, if possible, to marry within it.

But this may have been a matter not only of pragmatism but of principle. Although we have no means of knowing how representative it may

---

[58] *AM*, 823.

[59] *The Court of the Archdeaconry of Buckingham 1483–1523*, ed. E. M. Elvey, Buckinghamshire Record Society 19 (1975), 128, 161, 163, 175, 288, 289, 292. For the diocesan background, see Margaret Bowker, *The Henrician Reformation: The Diocese of Lincoln under John Longland, 1521–1547* (Cambridge, 1981).

[60] *AM*, 973. Of course, many Lollards probably attended mass insincerely and merely to avoid danger. At Reading in 1499 a Lollard group confessed that they attended church 'only for dread of the people and to eschew the jeopardy and danger that we dread to fall in if we had not done as other Christian people did'. See Thomson, *Later Lollards*, 80.

[61] John Bossy, *The English Catholic Community*, 1570–1850 (1975); Alexandra Walsham, *Church Papists: Catholicism, Conformity and Confessional Polemic in Early Modern England* (2nd edition, Woodbridge, 1999).

[62] Marsh, *Family of Love*, and Marsh, 'Gravestone of Thomas Lawrence'; Bill Stevenson, 'The social and economic status of post-Restoration dissenters, 1660–1725', and 'The social integration of post-Restoration dissenters, 1660–1725', *World of Rural Dissenters*, ed. Spufford, 332–87. Andrzej Bida found very similar patterns of conduct among the Catholics of Linton, a Cambridgeshire village only a few miles from the Familist stronghold of Balsham: 'Papists in an Elizabethan parish: Linton, Cambridgeshire, 1560–1600' (unpublished Diploma in Historical Studies thesis, Cambridge, 1992).

have been, the Wycliffite treatise called *The lanterne of light* (no later than 1415) offered a threefold definition of 'holy church'. The first meaning of 'church' was the little flock spoken of by Christ in Luke 12, 'the chosen number of them that shall be saved'. But the second church, 'diverse from this', was the 'coming together of good and evil in a place that is hallowed, far from worldly occupation, for there sacraments shall be treated and God's law both read and preached'. This was a material place, built by man's handicraft. *The lanterne of light* denounced 'our new feigned sects', but these were the religious orders and their great monastic and collegiate churches, 'for people should draw to parish churches and hear her service there'.[63]

This was strikingly consistent with both the ecclesiology and the practice of so many sixteenth- and seventeenth-century dissenters: a practice of occasional conformity and occasional nonconformity. The theological basis for this behaviour was the dualistic doctrine of the visible and invisible church, and also the Parable of the Tares. And yet the invisible church, the congregation of the elect, was at least semivisible, and itself given material presence in the conventicle, understood to be a private form of religion. In the mid-seventeenth century Roger Quatermayne would tell Archbishop Laud, 'I did always think that public duties did not make void private, but that both might stand with a Christian.'[64]

No one, even out and out separatists, ever claimed that their godly conventicles were exactly coterminous with the *congregatio predestinatorum*. But as one Wycliffite text put it, 'We may not [know] for certain which person is of Christ's spouse of all the men that wandren here, but we may guess and that is enough.'[65] The intelligent guess was likely to identify the true, hidden, little flock of Christ with the 'known men', 'good people', 'God's people'. But it was no more than a guess.

The first two churches identified in *The lanterne of light* were both, in their different senses, 'Christ's church'. But there was a third church, 'the Fiend's church', whose priests jangled their lessons like 'jays chattering in a cage', and whose rich temples were Satan's seat.[66] Nothing so far said should disguise the vicious strength of the Lollard polemic mounted even in as moderate a tract as this against the corrupt priesthood, false sacraments and religious rackets of the established Church of the day. Norfolk Lollards of the 1420s denounced baptism and confirmation; Christian matrimony; virtually all functions of priesthood, including the power of

---

[63] *Selections from English Wycliffite Writings*, ed. Anne Hudson (Cambridge, 1978), 115–9, 195–6.
[64] Collinson, 'English Conventicle', 223–4.   [65] Hudson, *Premature Reformation*, 315.
[66] *Selections from English Wycliffite Writings*, ed. Hudson, 118–9.

consecration and the role of confessor, for 'every true man and woman being in charity is a priest'; tithes; the papacy; and all pilgrimage 'in adoration of stocks and stones and dead men's bones'.[67] Martin Luther in his *Prelude on the Babylonish Captivity of the Church* (1521) merely moderated what had been said long before, by these English Lollards.

This was a radically reduced ecclesiology. Some Lollards entertained the fantasy of a total dissolution of the visible, institutional Church, leaving nothing but belief, Bible-based, religious and moral lessons, a Christianity stripped more bare than even the Quakers would strip it in the seventeenth century, the total dechurching of society. A Norfolk miller of the 1420s affirmed that 'material churches be but of little avail and [ought] to be of little reputation, for every man's prayer said in the field is as good as the prayer said in the church'.[68]

By that very token, the Lollards had little interest in conjuring into existence a visible, true Church, at total odds with the visibly false Roman Church. Their ecclesiology was more radical than that. But that was precisely the mentality and the programme of the first generation or two of English Protestants. Can we identify some of the flashpoints of this critical discontinuity, some of the moments when scattered groups in a dissenting minority realised among themselves the conviction that they were indeed the Church?

IV

The argument of what follows will rest only partly on the risky assumption that the first English Protestants were recruited from the last generation of Lollards. Protestant polemicists and historians, Foxe above all, had an obvious interest in eliding late Lollardy and early Protestantism, making the point that their religion was no 'new broached matter', but that fifty or a hundred years earlier there had been 'plenty of the same profession and like doctrine which we now profess' – the knockdown answer to the question, 'Where was this church and religion forty years ago, before Luther's time?'[69] If the Lollards had not existed, it would have been necessary to invent them.

And they were, in a sense, invented. The almost too perfect Foxeian paradigm was the story of John Browne, a cutler of Ashford, who had

---

[67] *Heresy Trials*, ed. Tanner, 42, 57–8.   [68] Ibid., 58.
[69] *AM*, 661, 819. See Margaret Aston, 'Lollardy and the Reformation: Survival or Revival?', and 'John Wycliffe's Reformation Reputation', both in *Lollards and Reformers*, 219–71. See also Anne Hudson, ' "No Newe Thyng": The Printing of Medieval Texts in the Reformation Period', *Lollards And Their Books*, 227–48.

been convicted of heresy in the reign of Henry VII and burned as a relapsed heretic in 1511, one of his judges being John Colet.[70] Someone had said that Browne's children might as well be thrown into the same fire, 'for they would spring (said he) of his ashes'. Browne's son Richard was in prison in Canterbury and due to be burned the day before Mary I died.[71] The story was 'often' told by John Browne's wife Elizabeth to her daughter Alice, who told it to Foxe. Here was ample opportunity for manipulation, if not falsification, of the evidence.[72]

By no means all the first generation of Protestants, even at a 'popular' level, were last-generation Lollards. The English Reformation was in part a youthful protest against parental error.[73] When the father of young William Maldon found his son reading the New Testament and trying to correct his mother's pious habits, he beat him within an inch of his life.[74] John Christopherson, the Marian bishop of Chichester, put these words into the mouth of a young 'gospeller': 'My father is an old doting fool . . . and my mother goeth always mumbling on her beads.' He would not 'walk in the papistical paths' of his parents.[75] The Essex gentry martyrs Thomas Causton and Thomas Higbed, formally charged by Bishop Bonner with 'swerving' from the faith of their parents and ancestors, said that they had 'a just and lawful cause and ground to swerve and go from the said faith and religion, because they have now read more Scripture than either themselves or their parents and kinsfolk, godfathers or godmothers have read or seen heretofore in that behalf'.[76] These were true converts, not reconstructed Lollards.

It is equally the case that not all old Lollards necessarily embraced what was emergent as orthodox Protestantism. We have already noted that as late as Mary's reign, heretics were burned for old-fashioned reasons. The stories told by Foxe or preserved in his papers about Thomas Bilney, and about the encounter between the rustic Lollards of Steeple Bumpstead in Essex and the Protestant intellectual Robert Barnes, suggest that the two currents were interactive; that if the new heresy recruited from the old, the old was capable of rubbing off on the new.[77]

---

[70] *Kent Heresy Proceedings*, ed. Tanner, 43–9.   [71] *AM*, 805, 1292–3.

[72] Patrick Collinson, 'Truth, lies, and fiction in Protestant historiography', *The Historical Imagination in Early Modern Britain: History, Rhetoric, and Fiction, 1500–1800*, ed. Donald R. Kelley and David Harris Sacks (Cambridge, 1997), 37–68; Collinson, 'Truth and Legend'.

[73] Susan Brigden, 'Youth and the English Reformation', *Past & Present*, 95 (1982), 37–67; A. G. Dickens, *The English Reformation* (1964; 2nd edition 1989), 334–8.

[74] *Reformation Narratives*, 348–51.

[75] John Christopherson, *An exhortation to all menne to take hede and beware of rebellion* (1554), T2v.

[76] *AM*, 1540.

[77] Ibid., 999–1013; BL Harleian MS 421, 35.

It has been suggested that Bilney's fierce invectives against images may have owed something to the Lollard circles in which he appears to have moved. When the Colchester Lollard John Pykas heard Bilney preach at Ipswich that it was but folly to go on pilgrimage to saints, 'for they be but stocks and stones', he found the sermon 'most ghostly made and best for his purpose and opinions as any that ever he heard in his life'.[78] It sounds as if Pykas learnt nothing new from Bilney, but was glad to have his own opinions confirmed by a learned man speaking from a pulpit. Similarly, when Miles Coverdale preached in Steeple Bumpstead against the veneration of images, the local heretics, who had already converted their curate Richard Foxe to their opinions, would merely have nodded in approval.[79]

But not all old heretics deferred to the standing of the new preachers, or willingly succumbed to their instruction. The old heretical teacher Henry Hart was given to pronouncing, in conventicles held in Bocking in Essex and at Faversham in Kent, in about 1550, that 'his faith was not grounded upon learned men, for all errors were brought in by learned men'.[80] This provocative opinion Hart had already consigned to print in a little book called *A godly newe short treatyse instructyng every parson howe they shuld trade theyr lyves* (1548). 'Knowledge is dangerous', where love and obedience are lacking.[81] A kindred spirit, John Champneys, a Somerset man, added his pennyworth in a radical tract called *The harvest is at hand* (1548), 'grossly compiled without any clerkly eloquence', and critical of 'long clerkly protestation and circumstances'.[82]

John Strype called the likes of Hart and Champneys 'the first that made separation from the reformed Church of England', and it is true that Hart's followers were absentees from the services of the Protestant,

[78] Ibid., 17v. This is the argument of John F. Davis in his *Heresy and the Reformation in the South-East of England, 1520–1559* (1983), especially 46–53, and in his article 'Lollardy and the Reformation in England', *Archiv für Reformationsgeschichte* 73 (1982), 227–32.

[79] *AM*, 1047.

[80] BL Harleian MS 421, 133–4v, printed in Burrage, *Early English Dissenters*, i. 1–6.

[81] Hart, *A godly newe short treatyse*, A8r. That Hart came from Pluckley on the rim of the Kentish Weald is established in a list of 'persons indicted within the county of Kent', c. 1538, PRO, SP 1/131, 241. That he was elderly by 1550 is a supposition based on evidence that he died (of natural causes?) in 1557, and that he was the same Henry Hart who had lent a book to a Colchester carpenter, James Brewster, who was burned in Smithfield in 1511. See Trinity College Dublin, MS 775, 123v. John Bradford addressed Hart in a letter as 'Father Hart'. See ECL MS 260, 175v; I owe this reference to Thomas Freeman. Hart's Lollard roots are suggested by the godly aphorisms with which his book ends: 'The grace of God be with your spirit'; 'Yours as charity bindeth me'; 'Give all praise to God, and be always thankful unto him.' See *A godly newe short treatyse*, B8v. Much about Hart will be found in D. Andrew Penny, *Freewill or Predestination: The Battle over Saving Grace in Mid-Tudor England* (Woodbridge, 1990).

[82] John Champneys, *The harvest is at hand* (1548), preface, D3v.

Edwardine Church.[83] But from the perspective of Hart, far from causing
a schism, he and his followers were themselves victims of a sheep-stealing
operation. It was their long-established beliefs and traditions which had
been disturbed by intrusive new doctrines, their leadership which had
been hijacked by 'learned men'. Thanks to an inquiry mounted by
Archbishop Cranmer in 1543, we can be present at a moment when this
happened in Hart's native Kentish Weald, as a preacher called Hugh
Cooper mounted the pulpit of Tenterden church. Tenterden was an old
Lollard centre, the place of origin of William White, who had sowed the
seeds of heresy in Norfolk in the 1420s, and the home of two of the victims of Warham's anti-heresy drive in 1511.[84] Any surviving Tenterden
Lollards would have been no more surprised than Pykas at Ipswich or
the men of Steeple Bumpstead to hear an attack on prayers to saints. But
then came something new and different. Cooper taught that alms deeds,
fasting and prayers to saints could not help the soul, but 'faith allonly'.[85]

Historians of the English Reformation are agreed that what was
exotic, that is to say Lutheran, and what distinguished the new
Protestantism from the old Lollardy, was justification by faith.[86] And from
Lutheran solifidianism followed, logically, a reinvigorated Augustinian
doctrine of predestination. This was the shibboleth which divided
'orthodox' Protestants from the Freewillers who in their sternly moral-
istic, antidogmatic Pelagianism, merely perpetuated the no-nonsense
old-time religion of the Lollards, which had been reinforced by the 'faith
without works is dead' theology of the Epistle of James.[87] Their views
were articulated with particular pungency by Hart: 'Saint Paul might
have damned himself if he listed.' John Plume of Lenham said that 'it is

---

[83] J. W. Martin, ' "The First that Made Separation from the Reformed Church of England" ', in
his *Religious Radicals in Tudor England* (London and Ronceverte, WV, 1989), 41–70.

[84] *Heresy Trials*, ed. Tanner, 29–30; Thomson, *Later Lollards*, 120, 122–3, 173–5, 187–90; *Kent Heresy
Proceedings*, ed. Tanner, 10–11, 12, 21, 26, 38, 41–2, 52.

[85] *LP* XVIII (ii) 546, p. 310 (CCCC MS 128, 63).

[86] Dickens, *English Reformation*, 82–7; Dickens, 'Heresy and the Origins of English Protestantism',
363–82. See also Peter Marshall's essay in this volume.

[87] Burrage, *Early English Dissenters*, i. 1–4. John Pykas of Colchester confessed to having twice
communicated with Robert Best in his house about the epistles (*sic*) of James, and that Best
could say 'them' by heart, and that he had 'communicated' a chapter of James to John Gyrlyng.
References to the epistles of Paul mingle with mentions of James in these trials in the diocese of
London in 1528–9, Gyrlyng having 'rehearsed' one of the Pauline epistles. See BL Harleian MS
421, 13r, 17r, 21, 24v, 34. The problem for those hovering between the doctrines of free will and
predestination was how to reconcile Paul with James. John Philpot of the Kentish Weald in his
Marian trial confessed that 'faith doth not justify without works, neither do works without faith'.
See ibid., 93. The writer of one of the prison letters preserved by Foxe confesses, 'I myself could
not understand St Paul and St James to make them agree together till our good preachers which
were my prison fellows did open them unto me.' See BL Harleian MS 416, 160r.

a general affirmation among them that the preaching of predestination is a damnable doctrine'; 'Cole of Faversham' that it was a doctrine 'meeter for devils than for Christian men'. His namesake, Thomas Cole, the first master of Maidstone grammar school, a convert from freewill views, taught in a sermon which Cranmer ordered him to preach that the error of separation was directly linked to the doctrine of those who denied predestination.[88]

Freewillers and predestinarians were to share the same Marian prisons and even the same fires. In July 1555, when the first four of the forty-one martyrs incinerated at Canterbury went to their deaths, there was an element of black humour, which their executioners may or may not have appreciated. Tied to the same stake were two 'orthodox' clerics, including John Bland, the most commanding of the early Protestant preachers of East Kent, and two leading Freewillers, Nicholas Sheterden, a native of Henry Hart's village of Pluckley, and Humphrey Middleton, who had taught in the Faversham conventicle that 'all men being in Adam's loins were predestinate to be saved, and that there were no reprobates'.[89]

This essay will not delve deeper into this chapter of religious history, which has its own historians,[90] other than to raise, though not pursue, the question of what happened to the Freewillers. Were they all, or all their leaders, burned at the stake – in which case the Marians did English Protestantism a great favour? Or were they in the process of time absorbed into mainstream Elizabethan Protestantism? This would have been an active, violently polemical absorption, not a quiet one. The battle was all but over in the third year of Elizabeth, when the leading Protestant preacher in London, the Frenchman Jean Veron, wrote *A most necessary treatise of free wil* (1561), denouncing 'the viperous brood of the free will men'.[91] Or (the Hill-Spufford theory) did the deviant sectarianism of the Freewillers and other so-called 'Anabaptists' persist, like underground watercourses in limestone country, to reemerge a century later in the newly propitious circumstances of the English revolution? We know that one secondary strand did persist, for at least two or three generations: the Family of Love, which in its advanced and cryptic Nicodemism (Familism had no martyrs) seems to have been in conscious

---

[88] Thomas Cole, *A godly and frutefull sermon, made at Maydstone* (1553).
[89] *AM*, 1665–6; Burrage, *Early English Dissenters*, i. 3.
[90] See Thomas Freeman's essay in this volume.
[91] Jean Veron, *A most necessary treatise of free wil* (1561), Epistle (dedicated to Lord Robert Dudley). These were dialogic lectures, delivered in St Paul's Cathedral. Veron published two or three other works on the same theme, all in 1561: *STC* 24680, 24681, 24684. See Penny, *Freewill or Predestination*, 194–8.

reaction against the willingness of some of the first generation of Protestants (and last of Lollards?) to stand up and be counted, and burned. Familists were perhaps reverting to the pragmatism under pressure of the Lollards, most of whom had always preferred abjuration to a very unpleasant death.[92]

V

And so we come, late in the day, to the point of this essay. What happened in the so to say chemical interaction of old and new heresy, and as Protestant evangelists either moved out into the old Lollard underworld or created their own (one must allow for both scenarios), was, at a superficial level, a change of identifying labels. We begin to hear less about 'known men' and more about 'Christian brethren', which as a more or less organised movement of London merchants concerned itself particularly with the importation and dispersal of Tyndale's New Testament and other unauthorised books, a kind of 'forbidden book of the month club'.[93]

But more was going on than a mere change of badges. These groups were now being told, and were coming to believe, that they were the true Church, a new and dynamic conviction; and linked to this was another new label, Protestant, which for the first time drew a clear and confessional divide between two different versions of the Christian religion. Diarmaid MacCulloch has warned us that we must not be too hasty in using this defining word. The hazier 'evangelical', suggestive of transition, eclecticism, or simple fudge, may be safer for the 1530s and 1540s.[94] But when Thomas Hancock arrived to preach in Poole in Dorset in the first year of Edward VI, he found that leading elements in the town already embraced 'God's word': 'They were the first that in that part of England were called Protestants.'[95] With the adoption of 'Protestant', the religious map of England was redrawn for ever.

What the source of this conviction may have been is a matter for speculation. But a likely candidate is the distinctively Protestant doctrine of justification by faith, mediated especially through the print of Tyndale's New Testament and its critical and polemical apparatus, the principal vehicle by which Lutheranism entered England. For it was the sharp

---

[92] Marsh, *Family of Love*; Alastair Hamilton, *The Family of Love* (Cambridge, 1981).
[93] Rupp, *Six Makers of English Religion*, 365; Gordon Rupp, *Studies in the Making of the English Protestant Tradition* (Cambridge, 1947), 6–14; Brigden, *London and the Reformation*, 106–18.
[94] Diarmaid MacCulloch, *Tudor Church Militant: Edward VI and the Protestant Reformation* (1999), 2–4.
[95] *Reformation Narratives*, 77.

sword of Luther's 'by faith alone' which made a more definitive schism in western Christendom than any of the would-be reformers or heretics who had preceded him, the Englishman John Wyclif and his Lollard disciples not excepted – an awkward fact which Catholic and Protestant ecumenists are trying hard to write out of the record, but on which historians have to insist. But the conviction can only have been reinforced by the apocalyptic scenarios of the last book of the Bible, wherever these were read and applied to the contemporary scene.[96]

Now for some illustrative snapshots of the conviction that evangelical conventicles constituted the true Church. When the formidable lawyer and pastor, the rector of Hadleigh, Rowland Taylor, prepared to make his last journey to his old parish, where he would be burned, he wrote to his wife, 'We have undoubtedly seen the true trace of the prophetical, apostolical, primitive Catholic church.'[97] When Matthew Plaise, a Kentish weaver, was asked by the bishop of Dover whether any part of Christ's church was to be found in England, he replied: 'I will tell you where. Christ sayeth whereas two or three be gathered together in his name, there he is in the midst of them.'[98] At the opposite end of the country, a poor Cornish woman said to her judges, 'God give me grace to go to the true church.' The bishop retorted, 'The true church: what doest thou mean?' She answered, 'Not your popish church, full of idols and abominations, but where three or four are gathered together in the name of God, to that church I will go as long as I live.'[99]

Had these illiterates taught themselves the radically reduced and yet confident ecclesiology of Matthew 18: 20, or did they owe it to 'learned men'? In 1536 William Barlow, one of the first Protestant bishops and a doctor of theology who had taught in both universities, was quoted as affirming in a public sermon that 'wheresoever two or three simple persons as two cobblers or weavers were in company and elected in the name of God, that there was the true church of God'.[100] Perhaps that was a lesson which Barlow had learnt from simple men. Yet it was this bishop who, having identified the true Church with two or three cobblers or weavers, was to preserve the episcopal succession in the English Church by consecrating Archbishop Matthew Parker, and who fathered five daughters who all married bishops! Nothing more vividly illustrates the strange anomaly which was the reformed Church

---

[96] BL Harleian MS 421, 12v, 14v.   [97] *AM*, 1528.   [98] Ibid., 1982.
[97] Ibid., 2050.   [100] BL Cotton MS Cleopatra E.v, 415.

of England.[101] Among 69 errors exhibited to Convocation in about 1541 as commonly preached and taught, all aphoristic and easily memorable statements, was the claim that 'the church that is commonly taken for the church is the Synagogue. And that the church is the congregation of good men only.'[102]

It was the Marian persecution which, in the perception of those not prepared to compromise, underlined and underwrote the drastic distinction between the true and false churches which would permeate the thousands of pages and columns in Foxe's *Actes and Monuments*, as well as providing the programme for Foxe's dramatic engraved title-page, with the true Church of faithful martyrs on Christ's right hand, the popish Church going down into confusion and Hell on his left. This dichotomy owed much to John Bale's *The image of both churches* (1545?).

But since the martyrs had read neither Foxe nor Bale, we must suppose that they came to the same radical conclusions from within their own resources, with the help of their preachers and teachers. To the text 'where two or three are gathered together' they added that other scripture: 'Come ye out from among them, and be ye separate' (2 Corinthians 6: 17), which was apparently unknown to the Lollards. For these were some of the first separatists, and but for the accident of Mary's death and the accession of Elizabeth, the long-term future of English Protestantism would have been as separatist as that of the French Huguenots. In a prison letter exhorting 'all God's faithful servants' to eschew the society of idolaters and God's enemies, the Essex minister William Tyms wrote, 'Wherefore come out from among them, and separate yourselves, saith the Lord, and touch no unclean thing.'[103] The Cambridge scholar John Hullier wrote letters to 'the Christian Congregation' and 'the Congregation of Christ's faithful Followers', in which he reminded them of the wide gate leading to destruction and the narrow way leading to life, admonishing them 'as ye tender the salvation of your soul, by all manner of means to separate yourselves from the company of the pope's hirelings'.[104]

There is much evidence in Foxe that these lessons had been learnt and were rigorously applied, at least by that minority which went all

---

[101] Patrick Collinson, *The Religion of Protestants: the Church in English Society 1559–1625* (Oxford, 1982), 45–6.
[102] BL Harleian MS 419, 118. In 1555 John Scory, formerly bishop of Chichester and the future Elizabethan bishop of Hereford, wrote of 'the little flock of Christ . . . spoiled and robbed of their own tutors'. See *An epistle wrytten by John Scory the late bishop of Chichester unto all the faythfull that be in pryson in Englande* (Emden, 1555), A2.
[103] *AM*, 1900–2.   [104] Ibid., 1900–8.

the way, rejecting all compromise. In many recorded instances – and, it seems, unlike the Lollards – the martyrs who refused to darken the doors of what they believed to be false synagogues met in conventicles at the same time as the celebration of mass, and used the services of the Edwardine Prayer Book. This was what happened in the butcher Dirick Carver's house in Sussex. In London we hear of a secret christening 'in a house, after the order of the service book in King Edward's time'.[105]

We know most about this London congregation: that it was a single congregation of variable membership, drawing on many parts of the city, the names of members recorded in a book, presumably for the purpose of keeping track of their contributions, and that it exercised discipline; that it met in safe houses, pubs, the woods, or even boats on the Thames; that it used the Prayer Book; and that while some of its ministers were duly ordained clergy, and even future bishops, on at least one occasion the congregation called to the ministry one of their own, a pointer to what might have been the future of this 'privy' church in a Catholic England.[106]

What many martyrs in their interrogations testified about the Church, often called 'the holy Catholic church', makes it clear that this was one of those proverbial but also credal lessons which had been systematically taught and absorbed. John Denley of Uxbridge testified that he believed in 'the holy Catholic church which is builded upon the foundation of the Prophets and Apostles, Christ being the head, which holy church is the congregation of the faithful people dispersed through the whole world'. John Newman, a pewterer of Maidstone, used the selfsame formula: 'I believe that there is an holy church, which is the company of the faithful and elect people of God, dispersed abroad throughout all the world.'[107]

The Catholic Church so defined was contrasted with its opposite. Richard Woodman, the Sussex ironmaster, affirmed before the bishop of Chichester his belief in the true Catholic Church. But when Bishop Christopherson, who was sympathetic, asked why in that case he was absent from his parish church, Woodman replied, 'I trust I am in the true church every day. But to tell you truth, I come not at the church where the most do resort.' Seven martyrs who died in one fire in Smithfield in

---

[105] Ibid., 1680, 2082. On the use of the Edwardine liturgy by the Marian secret congregations, see David Loades, 'Protestant sectarianism in England in the mid-sixteenth century', *The Church in a Changing Society: Conflict – Reconciliation or Adjustment?* (CIHEC Conference in Uppsala, 17–21 August, 1977), 76–81.
[106] *AM*, 2074–5, 2028–34, 2145–6; Usher, ' "In a Time of Persecution" '.
[107] *AM*, 1684, 1688.

January 1556 testified that there is a Catholic Church, but 'that the Church of England as it was at that present was no part of the true Catholic church'. Thomas Spurge declared, 'As for your church of Rome, I do utterly deny it. But to the true Catholic church I am content to return and continue in the same, whereof I believe the church of Rome to be no part or member.' Five martyrs who suffered in Smithfield in April 1556 confessed, 'there was one true and Catholic church whereof they steadfastly believe, and thought the church of Rome to be no part or member'.[108]

Foxe recorded what is perhaps the most extreme separatist statement ever made in the entire course of English religious history when he told the story of Gertrude Crockhey (or Crokehay), a wealthy merchant woman with interests across the North Sea, who at one stage was imprisoned in Antwerp and accused of being an Anabaptist. Back in London, Gertrude fell ill and was warned by a ranking London clergyman that if she refused the last rites, she would be denied Christian burial. 'Oh (said she) how happy am I, that I shall not rise with them but against them.'[109]

In the event, Mary was a transient episode. If the immediate consequences of the new Protestant ecclesiology were separatist, its longer-term implications were antiseparatist. With the Elizabethan restoration of Protestantism and the Prayer Book to the parish churches, the centrifugal forces which had expelled uncompromising Protestants into separation, and the pyres of Smithfield or foreign exile, became strongly centripetal. But this was not, of course, the end of schismatic separation, certainly not for England's continuing Catholics. Soon Gregory Martin would be calling on his co-religionists 'to abstain altogether from heretical conventicles', deploying the very same texts which Marian Protestants had so often spouted: 'Depart from the tabernacles of these wicked men ... touch nothing that appertaineth unto them.'[110] And London's hottest Protestants, survivors of the Marian holocaust and dissatisfied with the compromises enforced by the Elizabethan settlement, soon began to revive meetings of their secret congregation, where they now worshipped not according to the Prayer Book but with the aid of the

---

[108] Ibid., 1988, 1844, 1898, 1874.

[109] Ibid., 2082, 2145–6. The account as printed in 1563 (1740–1) has further circumstantial detail. Gertrude was denied burial in the churchyard and there was talk of burying her by the highway, but her husband persuaded the authorities to allow him to inter her in his garden.

[110] Gregory Martin, *A treatise of schisme. Shewing, that al Catholikes ought in any wise to abstaine altogether from heretical Conventicles* (Douai, 1578), Preface. Martin's stark rejectionism (replicated in Robert Persons's *A brief discours contayning certayne reasons why Catholiques refuse to goe to Church* (London secret press, 1580)), is placed in its complex casuistical context by Walsham, *Church Papists*.

purer liturgy of Geneva: the beginnings of separatist Protestant dissent. We have a list of the names and addresses of those involved: seventy-two persons, thirty-nine of them women, from forty-two streets or localities, stretched out from Islington to Southwark, Fleet Street to the Tower.[111] This was the world of Thomas Turton and Humphrey Newman.

---

[111] 'An examination of certayne Londonners before the Commissioners. June 20th, 1567', reprinted from *A parte of a register* (Edinburgh, 1593) in *Remains of Edmund Grindal*, ed. W. Nicholson (PS, 1843); Burrage, *Early English Dissenters*, i. 9–11.

Index

Alsop, J. D., 86
Ambrose, George, 140
Anabaptism, 68, 69–70, 73, 76, 79–81, 130, 133, 146, 191, 213
anticlericalism, 63, 82, 84, 95, 224–5
Antwerp, 168–9, 171, 174
Armstrong, Clement, 7, 11, 60–83 *passim*
Arthur, John, 55
Ashford, Agnes, 218
Askew, Anne, 33, 92, 122–4, 192–4
Augustine, saint, 29, 37, 77n
Austen, William, 132
Avington, Thomas, 136, 141, 146, 153

Bacon, Sir Nicholas, 195
Baldwin, William, 195, 204
Bale, John, 25, 26, 30, 33, 34, 35, 39, 42, 51, 92, 97, 122–4, 171, 186, 189, 196, 198, 199, 232
Barclay, Alexander, 56
Barlow, William, bishop, 34, 41–2, 92, 231
Barnes, Robert, 21, 35, 39, 40, 42, 44, 226
Barrett, John, 45
Barrow, Thomas, 210
Barry, John, 130, 143, 146, 148, 152, 154
Bartlett, Richard, 220
Bartlett, Robert, 218
Baskerville, Dr Edward, 53
Baskerville, Geoffrey, 40
Bassett, Gregory, 53
Bayfield, Richard, 26, 34
Baynton, Sir Edward, 31
Beaufort, Lady Margaret, 29
Becke, Edmund, 184, 189, 190–1, 195, 200
Becon, Thomas, 30, 88, 91, 93, 96–7, 101, 173, 174, 184, 190, 193, 197, 205
Bentham, Thomas, 143, 144

Berkeley, Gilbert, bishop, 50
Bernher, Augustine, 127, 135, 136, 143–4, 147, 151, 205–6
Bernher, Elizabeth, 127
bible (*see* scripture)
Bigod, Francis, 27
Bilney, Thomas, 16, 17, 26, 27, 35, 53, 226–7
Bird, John, bishop, 50, 53, 96
Bland, John, 229
Blickle, Peter, 36
Boccacio, Giovanni, 202
Bocking, Essex, 130–32, 138, 153, 227
Bodmin, Cornwall, 109
Bonner, Edmund, bishop, 132, 154, 198, 199
Boughton, Joan, 212
Bowes, Elizabeth, 124
Bradford, John, 134–5, 136–7, 141, 148–9, 151, 152, 153, 199, 206
Bradshaw, Christopher, 173
Brandon, Catherine, duchess of Suffolk, 186–8, 189, 193, 206
Brenz, Johannes, 172
Brewster, James, 131
Brigden, Susan, 217
Brighton, Sussex, 95
Brinkley, Peter, 56
Brinklow, Henry, 24, 25, 103
Bristol, 46, 54, 91, 94
Broadridge, George, 130, 131, 153
Browne, Anthony, 43, 57
Browne, George, archbishop, 49, 53
Browne, John, 225–6
Browne, Richard, 226
Brownists, 210–11
Bruisyard, John, 53
Brunfels, Otto, 41
Brygett, Edmund, 56

Brynstan, John, 58
Bucer, Martin, 172, 183
Bucher, Joan, 191
Buckenham, Dr Robert, 55
Bull, Henry, 137, 155, 206
Bullinger, Heinrich, 30, 121–2, 172

Call, William, 53
Calvin, Jean, 51, 172, 175, 190
Cambridge, 6, 26, 36, 38, 40, 53, 95, 107
Cambridge, Thomas, 40, 44
Carder, William, 219
Cardmaker, John, 35, 48
Careless, John, 127, 135, 136, 137, 138–9, 140, 141, 149, 151, 152, 154
Carew, Sir Nicholas, 27
Carthusianus, Dyonisius, 29
Carver, Dirick, 210n, 233
Causton, Thomas, 226
Cavell, John, 140
Caxton, William, 157, 163
Cecil, William, 174, 175, 184, 188, 195, 204
Champneys, John, 145, 227
Charnock, Dr Thomas, 54
Chedsay, William, 90
Chelmsford, Essex, 27
Christopherson, John, bishop, 226, 233
churching, 113
Clay, Richard, 49
Clement, John, 138, 141, 152
clerical marriage, 48–9, 102
Clerkson, Simon, 54
Clitherow, Margaret, 125n
Colchester, Essex, 34
Cole, Robert, 130, 131, 134, 137, 142, 143, 144, 146, 149
Cole, Thomas, 131, 133, 146, 147, 229
Colet, John, 226
Collingworth, Joan, 223
Collinson, Patrick, 4, 84, 104, 127
Cologne, 168
Coloribus, John de, 53
confession, auricular, 35, 40, 58–9, 64
Constantine, George, 87
conversion, 9, 14–37 *passim*, 84–110 *passim*, 123, 136–7, 140, 146, 222
Cook, Margery, 134, 135
Cooke, Anne, 195

Cooke, Sir Anthony, 195
Cooke, Laurence, 57
Cooke, Sir William, 198–9
Cooper, Hugh, 228
Cope, Anthony, 185
Cosyn, James, 45
Coventry, Giles, 56
Coverdale, Miles, bishop, 26, 40, 50, 51, 121, 169, 186, 206, 227
Covert, Friar, 56
Cowbridge, William, 54
Cox, Richard, 96, 145
Cranmer, Thomas, archbishop, 24, 25, 30, 55, 118, 131, 133, 134, 135, 152, 170, 173, 182, 190, 206
Crayford, John, 53
Cressy, David, 113
Crockhey, Gertrude, 234
Crom, Mattheus, 169, 171
Cromwell, Thomas, 39, 46, 55, 56, 63, 81, 82–3, 170, 186
Crowley, Robert, 145, 173, 175, 190, 192, 193
Cuningham, William, 204
Curl, cutler, 139–40
Curson, Friar, 56

Darcy, Thomas Lord, 39
Day, John, 174, 175, 179, 180–208 *passim*
Denley, John, 233
Dering, Edward, 127
de Worde, Wynkyn, 164
Dickens, A. G., 18, 98, 105, 129, 213
dissolution of religious houses, 43, 121
Drake, Robert, 140
Dryver, John, 57
Dudley, John, duke of Northumberland, 182, 186, 196
Dudley, Robert, 204
Duffield, William, 42
Duffy, Eamon, 26, 113, 221
Dusgate, alias Bennett, Thomas, 53

Edgeworth, Roger, 91, 100, 102, 104, 118n
Edward VI, 181–2
Eliot, Francis, 44
Elstow, Henry, 56
Elton, G. R., 85, 87
enclosure, 75
Erasmus, Desiderius, 64, 71, 118, 119

Erikson, Erik, 18
Erley, John, 46
Etherington, John, 215
Eton, Guy, 48
eucharist, 66, 68, 69, 124–5, 190, 191, 192, 219
excommunication, 68

Family of Love, 130, 146–7, 213, 218, 223, 229–30
Fane, Lady Elizabeth, 193n
fasting, 102–3, 114, 192
Feckenham, John, 102
Ferrar, Robert, bishop, 136
Fines, John, 85
Fish, Simon, 184
Fisher, John, bishop, 112, 116, 218
Fitzroy, Mary, duchess of Richmond, 196
Ford, William, 32
Forest, John, 56, 57
Foxe, John, 25, 26, 34, 35, 45, 108, 124, 137, 143, 153, 154–5, 180, 193, 198, 199, 200, 201, 206–8, 212, 217, 221, 222, 223, 225, 232–3, 234
Foxe, Richard, 227
Franke, Peter, 34
Frankfurt, 165
free will, 64, 68, 72–3, 129–56 *passim*
Freeman, Thomas, 122
Freewillers, 129–56 *passim*
friars, 31, 38–59 *passim*
Frith, John, 27, 34, 35, 190
Froben, Johannes, 165
Fyloll, Jasper, 82

Gardiner, Stephen, bishop, 41, 53, 59, 61, 81, 95–6, 99, 100, 103, 182n, 192–3, 198, 199, 204
Gemini, Thomas, 200
Geneva, 142–3, 165
Gibson, Richard, 137, 140, 141, 142, 146, 149
Gibson, Thomas, 181
Gilby, Anthony, 190, 197
Glasier, Hugh, 46
Gloucester, 94
Golden Legend, The, 20, 29
Goodman, Christopher 124
Goodwin, John, 44
Gough, John, 29, 88
Gratwick, Stephen, 141, 146, 151
Gray, William, 51

Grebill, Christopher, 219–20
Grebill, John, 219
Gresham, Sir John, 191
Grey, Lady Jane, 197–8
Griffith, Maurice, bishop, 50

Hacker, John, 221
Hadleigh, Suffolk, 44, 57, 231
Haigh, Christopher, 4, 85, 150
Hales, Joyce, 134, 135, 139, 151
Hancock, Thomas, 230
Harcock, Edmund, 54
Hardyman, Dr John, 48
Hargrave, Richard, 55
Harland, Thomas, 154
Harmon, Richard, 156
Harpsfield, Nicholas, 154
Hart, Henry, 130, 131–2, 133, 134–5, 136, 139, 140–41, 146, 152, 154, 191, 227–8
Hawes, Stephen, 20
Henry VIII, 6, 53, 80, 109
Higbed, Thomas, 226
Hill, Christopher, 213
Hill, Nicholas, 175
Hilsey, John, bishop, 46, 49, 51, 54
Hodgkins, John, bishop, 50, 53
Hoffman, Melchior, 72
Honeywood, Mrs, 127
Hooper, John, 30, 47, 124–6, 150, 152, 173, 175, 184, 190, 198, 208
Hopkins, John, 205
Hopton, John, bishop, 53
hours, books of (*see* primers)
Howard, Thomas, duke of Norfolk, 57
Hubbardine, William, 91
Hubmaier, Balthasar, 71
Hudson, Anne, 217
Huggarde, Miles, 91, 92, 99, 100, 102, 126, 192, 212
Hullier, John, 212, 232
humanism, 39, 71, 116
Huntingdon, John, 90
Hurleston, Dr John, 49
Hussites, 217
Hut, Hans, 61, 70
Hutchinson, Roger, 200
Hyrde, Richard, 116

iconoclasm, 99, 181, 182
images, 40, 42, 131, 196, 227

Ingworth, Richard, bishop, 50
Ive, John, 219

Jackson, John, 140, 152, 153, 154–5
Jeffrey, John, 132, 152
Jewel, John, 145
Johnson, Francis, 210
Johnson, Thomas, 57
Jones, Gavin, 56
Joseph, John, 46
Joye, George, 21, 23, 25, 26, 27, 32, 33,
    34, 91, 97, 171, 173
Julles, Geoffrey, 53
justification by faith, 17, 22–3, 32, 37, 64,
    100, 184, 188, 228, 230–1

Kelly, Joan, 112, 115
Kemp, John, 139–40, 146, 147, 152, 154
Kempe, Margery, 20
Kempis, Thomas á, 19
Kent, 94–5, 96
King, John, 173
King's Bench prison, 135–42, 147
King's Book (1543), 96, 109
Kington, John, 53
Kirkham, Dr Thomas, 42, 49, 54
Knevet, Lady Anne, 135
Knollys, Dr Robert, 47
Knox, John, 124, 142, 146, 152

Lake, Peter, 215
Lambert, John, 25, 26, 34
Large, Edward, 47
Latimer, Hugh, bishop, 26, 30–1, 35,
    46–8, 60, 91, 92, 111–12, 121, 127,
    134, 135, 152, 173, 175, 185, 188,
    190, 198, 205
Laud, William, archbishop, 224
Laurence, John, 45–6, 132, 143, 146, 148,
    149, 152, 154
Law, John, 49
Lawrence, alias Shefforde, Peter, 56
Lawson, Elizabeth, 124
Ledley, John, 130, 137, 142, 144, 146, 154
Lee, Edward, archbishop, 42
Leland, John, 39
Leo X, pope, 38
Lever, Thomas, 190, 197
Lewes, Joyce, 124
Locke, Anne, 124

Lollards, Lollardy, 8–9, 32, 58–9, 65, 69–70,
    72–3, 131, 211–28, 232–3
London, 53, 93–4, 157, 162, 209
Longland, John, bishop, 44, 218
Lord's Supper (*see* eucharist)
Luther, Martin, 16–19, 38, 53, 72, 165–6,
    172, 225
Luther, Paul, 43
Lynne, William, 172, 175

MacCulloch, Diarmaid, 3, 10, 104, 173, 230
McGrath, Alister, 18
Machyn, Henry, 199
Madowell, John, 44, 55
Maldon, William, 26–7, 226
Man, Thomas, 222
Mandeville, Sir John, 20
Marcourt, Antoine, 172, 181
Marguerite of Navarre, 29
Markham, Sir John, 39
marriage, 114–28
Marsh, Christopher, 86, 218, 223
Marshall, John, 92
Marshall, Dr Richard, 55
Martin, Gregory, 234
Martin, J. W., 131
martyrs, martyrdom, 34–5, 36, 92, 140, 152–5,
    211–12, 229
Marius, Richard, 18
Mary I, 176, 199
mass (*see* eucharist)
Melanchthon, Philip, 23n, 31, 172, 183
mendicant orders (*see* friars)
Middleton, Humphrey, 130, 131, 133, 141,
    153, 229
Mierdman, Steven, 171, 175, 184
Milton, Anthony, 19
monks, 52
Moone, Hawisia, 217, 218
Morant, William, 153
Morden, James, 218
More, Sir Thomas, 6, 17, 91, 169, 217
Morice, Ralph, 24
Morison, Richard, 91, 92, 96
Morwyng, Peter, 205
Müntzer, Thomas, 73
Musculus, Andreas, 172

Neswyk, Friar, 56
Newman, Humphrey, 209, 235

Newman, John, 233
Newman, Roger, 141, 146
Nock, A. D., 36–7
Norfolk, duke of (*see* Howard, Thomas)
Northumberland, duke of (*see* Dudley, John)
Nykke, Richard, bishop, 218

Ochino, Bernardino, 172, 195, 197
O'Day, Rosemary, 85, 106
Olde, John, 25, 35
Oliver, William, 54, 55
Osward, John, 155
Overton, John, 186
Oxford, 6, 38, 53, 95

papacy, 64, 81, 96, 199
Parker, Matthew, 21, 231
Parr, Katherine, 25, 27, 29, 30, 33, 185,
    188, 193
Parr, Maude, 39
patriarchy, 112–13, 120
Payne, Hugh, 57
Peak District, 93
Pecock, Gabriel, 57
Pecocke, Reginald, bishop, 211
Peryn, William, 55, 90, 97
Peto, William, 56
Pettegree, Andrew, 10
Petyt, John, 27
Petyt, Thomas, 200
Philip, Thomas, 221–2
Phillips, Rowland, 94
Philpot, John, 136, 139, 141, 149, 151
Pickering, Anthony, 95
Pico Della Mirandola, Giovanni, 71
plays, 51
Plumb, Derek, 218, 222
Plume, John, 228
Pickering, Dr John, 55
Pilgrimage of Grace, 55, 57, 92
Plaise, Matthew, 231
Plumpton, Robert, 24
Ponet, John, 174, 175, 196, 197
post–revisionism, 3–4
Powell, Kenneth, 213
Poyntz, Sir Nicholas, 46
preaching, 39–40, 42–3, 58, 98–9
predestination, 73, 129–56 *passim*, 228–9
priesthood of all believers, 65

primers, 51, 70, 96, 116, 163, 164, 177–8, 200
printing, 12, 70, 157–79 *passim*, 180–208 *passim*
Proude, Richard, 146
purgatory, 64, 72, 103–5, 114, 121
Pykas, John, 222, 227
Pynson, Richard, 163, 164–5

Quartermayne, Roger, 224

radical Reformation (*see* Anabaptism)
Rastell, John, 34, 60
Ratcliffe, Jane, 115
Read, Thomas, 153
Redman, Richard, 165
Regnault, François, 170
relics, 40, 212, 225
repentence, 21–2, 28
revisionism, 2–4, 85, 98, 180–1
Reynolds, John, 47
Rich, Hugh, 56
Richmond, duchess of (*see* Fitzroy, Mary)
Ridley, Nicholas, bishop, 133, 134, 135, 136,
    141, 149, 152, 173, 206
Risby, Richard, 56
Rix, alias Ryckes, John, 41
Robynson, Friar William, 56, 57
Rolle, Richard, 19
Roper, William, 17, 34
Rogers, John, martyr, 199
Rogers, John, anti-familist writer, 146
Rough, John, 144
Rowland, Thomas, 220
Rowley, Alice, 211
Roy, William, 41
royal supremacy, 61, 63, 68, 74–9, 81–3
Ryche, William, 219

sacraments (*see also* eucharist, marriage), 65–6,
    69–70
Sadler, Ralph, 60
saints, cult of (*see also* images, relics), 43, 58,
    96, 113
Salisbury, 45, 94
sanctification, 22–3
Sandys, Edwin, 145
Savonarola, Girolamo, 38, 212
Scarisbrick, J. J., 3, 85
Schwenckfeld, Caspar, 61, 69
Scoloker, Anthony, 185–6

Scory, John, bishop, 45, 50
Scott, Cuthbert, 90
scripture, 16–17, 26–7, 29, 33–4, 70–1, 88, 123, 148, 160, 167–8, 169, 189–90
Seaver, Paul, 150
Sebastian, Friar, 56
Seres, William, 175, 185–6, 193
Seymour, Edward, duke of Somerset, 172, 173, 182, 184, 196, 204
Shaxton, Nicholas, bishop, 34, 45, 192
Shepherd, Luke, 175, 191
Sheterden, Nicholas, 130, 134, 141, 153, 229
Simpson, John, 130
Simpson, Thomas, 138, 143
Six Articles, Act of, 48, 96, 170, 182, 186
Skelthorpe, Robert, 137, 146
Skevington, Thomas, 52
Smith, Richard, 98, 100
Smith, Thomas, 90
solifidianism (*see* justification by faith)
Some, Thomas, 188
Somerset, duke of (*see* Seymour, Edward)
Spagnuoli, Baptista Mantuanus, 197
Speyer, Diet of, 5
Spufford, Margaret, 213
Spurge, Richard, 140
Spurge, Thomas, 140, 234
Standish, John, 100
Stanhope, Anne, 193
Stationers' Company, 179, 181
Sternhold, Thomas, 205
Stevenson, Bill, 223
Stevenson, Cornelius, 140, 146
Stokes, Dr John, 53, 56
Stokesley, John, bishop, 31
Stow, John, 196
Stretham, Edmund, 57
Strype, John, 129, 132, 192, 227
Suffolk, duchess of (*see* Brandon, Catherine)
Summers, W. H., 216

Tanner, Norman, 216
Tauler, Johannes, 71
Taylor, Rowland, 25, 34, 136, 231
Taylor, William, 221
Tewkesbury, John, 34
Thomson, John, 222
Thorold, Lawrence, 47
Thredar, Clement, 49

Thyxtyll, Dr Robert, 55
Todd, Margo, 127
Topley, Thomas, 30n
Tracy, Richard, 32
translation of foreign texts, 41, 51, 121, 166, 172, 173, 181, 184, 188, 195, 205
Trent, Council of, 7
Trew, John, 136, 137–9, 141, 146, 148, 151, 152–3, 154, 156
Troeltsch, Ernst, 222
Tunstall, Cuthbert, bishop, 16, 53, 167, 218
Turner, William, 25, 35–6, 95–6, 110, 171, 175, 185, 190
Turton, Thomas, 209, 235
Tyacke, Nicholas, 107
Tyball, John, 33
Tyms, William, 140–1, 154, 199, 232
Tyndale, William, 21–2, 23–4, 27, 34, 35, 70, 167–9, 172, 181, 184, 188, 190, 192, 230
Tyrel, John, 35

Underhill, Edward, 191
universities (*see* Cambridge, Oxford)
Upcher, Thomas, 130n, 138
Usher, Brett, 144

van der Delft, Francis, 89–90
van der Erve, Gilles, 175
van der Straten, Derick, 186
Veale, Abraham, 200
Vermigli, Peter Martyr, 172
Veron, Jean, 145, 172, 229
Viret, Pierre, 188
Vives, Juan Luis, 115–21
von Wied, Hermann, archbishop, 173, 183
Vyall, Dr John, 44

Wager, Lewis, 51
Walbott, Thomas, 145–6
Wallington, Nehemiah, 150
Walsh, Sir John, 46
Walsham, Alexandra, 126
Walton, William, 47
Ward, Robert, 43
Warham, William, archbishop, 218
Watts, William, 55
Wayland, John, 202, 204
Wentworth, Thomas Lord, 35
Whitchurch, Edward, 188, 195, 204

Whitford, Richard, 116, 220–1
Whittle, Thomas, 140, 153
Wilkins, John, 209
Wilkinson, William, 147
Williams, George, 62
Williams, John, 47
wills, 86–7
Wilson, Bryan, 222
Wilson, Stephen, 44
Wisdom, Robert, 93
Wittenberg, 165
Wolfe, Raynold, 197
Wolsey, Thomas Cardinal, 41, 53

women (*see also* churching, patriarchy), 111–28
   passim, 134, 149, 151, 188, 195, 217n, 235
Wood, Michael (pseudonym of John Day),
   198–9, 208
Woodman, Richard, 138, 139, 142, 152,
   233
Wright, William, 221
Wyche, Rychard, 211–12
Wyclif, John, 69, 71, 72–3, 77n, 231
Wyse, Nicholas, 25, 27

Zouche, George, 25
Zwingli, Huldrich, 172